EUROPEAN REVIEW OF SOCIAL PSYCHOLOGY

EUROPEAN REVIEW OF SOCIAL PSYCHOLOGY

Wolfgang Stroebe has published widely on the topics of attitudes, psychology and economics, group processes, intergroup relations and bereavement. He has been President of the European Association of Experimental Social Psychology and is currently Professor of Social, Organizational and Health Psychology at Utrecht University.

Miles Hewstone has published widely on the topics of attribution theory and intergroup relations. He was awarded the British Psychology Society's Spearman Medal in 1987 and was a Fellow at the Center for Advanced Study in the Behavioral Sciences, Stanford, California. He is Professor of Psychology at the University of Wales, Cardiff.

EUROPEAN REVIEW OF SOCIAL PSYCHOLOGY

VOLUME 6

Edited by

WOLFGANG STROEBE
Utrecht University, The Netherlands
and
MILES HEWSTONE
University of Wales, Cardiff, UK

JOHN WILEY & SONS
Chichester · New York · Brisbane · Toronto · Singapore

European Review of Social Psychology
ISSN 1046–3283
Published annually by John Wiley & Sons

For information on other volumes
in this series please complete the reply card
at the back of this volume

British Library Cataloguing in Publication Data:

European review of social psychology. Vol 6. 1995.
 – (European review of social psychology)
   I. Stroebe, Wolfgang   II. Hewstone Miles
   III. Series
   302.094

ISBN 0-471-95707-0

Typeset in 10/12pt Times by Dorwyn Ltd, Rowlands Castle, Hants
Printed and bound in Great Britain by Bookcraft (Bath) Ltd

Contents

Contributors

GERD BOHNER, *Lehrstuhl Sozialpsychologie, Universität Mannheim, 68131 Mannheim, Germany*

ROGER BUEHLER, *Simon Fraser University, Burnaby, British Columbia, Canada*

PETER J. D. CARNEVALE, *Department of Psychology, University of Illinois at Urbana-Champaign, 603 E. Daniel Street, Champaign, IL 61820, USA*

SHELLY CHAIKEN, *Department of Psychology, New York University, 6 Washington Place, 4th Floor, New York, NY 10003, USA*

N. K. CLARK, *Institute of Social and Applied Psychology, University of Kent at Canterbury, Kent CT2 7LZ, UK*

CARSTEN K. W. DE DREU, *Sectie Sociale en Organisatie Psychologie, University of Groningen, Grote Kruisstraat 2/1, NL-9712 TS Groningen, The Netherlands*

BEN J. M. EMANS, *Sectie Sociale en Organisatie Psychologie, University of Groningen, Grote Kruisstraat 2/1, NL-97112 TS Groningen, The Netherlands*

DALE GRIFFIN, *University of Waterloo, Waterloo, Ontario, Canada*

LOUK HAGENDOORN, *Utrecht University, PO Box 80140, 3508TC Utrecht, The Netherlands* viii

ANTHONY S. R. MANSTEAD, *Vakgroep Sociale Psychologie, Universiteit van Amsterdam, Roetersstraat 15, NL-1018 WB Amsterdam, The Netherlands*

GORDON B. MOSKOWITZ, *Department of Psychology, Princeton University, Green Hall, Princeton, NJ 08544, USA*

DIANNE PARKER, *Department of Psychology, University of Manchester, Manchester M13 9PL, UK*

T. POSTMES, *Vakgroep Sociale Psychologie, Universiteit van Amsterdam, Roetersstraat 15, NL-1018 WB Amsterdam, The Netherlands*

S. D. REICHER, *Department of Psychology, University of Exeter, Exeter EX4 4QG, UK*

MICHAEL ROSS, *University of Waterloo, Waterloo, Ontario, Canada*

R. SPEARS, *Vakgroep Sociale Psychologie, Universiteit van Amsterdam, Roetersstraat 15, NL-1018 WB Amsterdam, The Netherlands*

G. M. STEPHENSON, *Institute of Social and Applied Psychology, University of Kent at Canterbury, Kent CT2 7LZ, UK*

EVERT VAN DE VLIERT, *Sectie Sociale en Organisatie Psychologie, University of Groningen, Grote Kruisstraat 2/1, NL-97112 TS Groningen, The Netherlands*

Preface

Social psychology is an international endeavour. This fact, which underlies our decision to make the *European Review of Social Psychology* an international review that publishes outstanding work of authors from *all* nations rather than restricting it to Europeans, is again reflected by the scholars who contributed to this volume. However, even though the *European Review of Social Psychology* is worldwide in terms of the nationality of the authors, it is European in terms of the nationality of the editors who select the contributions and shape the editorial policies. Our goal in publishing the *European Review* is to further the international exchange of ideas by providing an English-language source for important theoretical and empirical work that has not been previously published in English. With the help of an editorial board consisting of senior scholars drawn from across the globe, we invite outstanding researchers to contribute to the series. The emphasis of these contributions is on critical assessment of major areas of research and of substantial individual programmes of research, as well as on topics and initiatives of contemporary interest and originality. Volumes contain three types of contribution:

(1) Reviews of the field in some specific area of social psychology, typically one in which European researchers have made some special contribution.
(2) Reports of extended research programmes which contribute to knowledge of a particular phenomenon or process.
(3) Contributions to a contemporary theoretical issue or debate.

Although this is only the sixth volume, the *European Review of Social Psychology* has already been widely accepted as one of the major international series in social psychology. Not only have reviews been very complimentary, but many of the chapters published in previous volumes have already been widely cited in the international literature.

ACKNOWLEDGEMENTS

We would like to thank the following reviewers, who helped us and the authors to shape these chapters into their final versions: Michael Diehl, Carsten de Dreu, Alice Eagley, Klaus Fiedler, Samuel Gaertner, Kenneth Gergen, Charles Judd, Ad van Knippenberg, Arie Kruglanski, David Messick, Gerold Mikula, Dean Pruitt, Norbert Schwarz, Bernd Simon, Charles Stangor, Bas Verplanken, and Nanne de Vries.

Introduction to Volume 6

This volume of the *European Review of Social Psychology* brings together contributions on two main areas of social psychology, at least as they are classified by one of the leading journals in the field. The first three chapters all deal with the area of 'attitudes and social cognition', and the final four chapters all bear on 'groups'.

The lead-off chapter in this volume, by Buehler, Griffin, and Ross, deals with people's estimates of how long they will take to complete various tasks and with their forecasts concerning the future course of their romantic associations. Social psychologists have, surprisingly, paid little attention to people's predictions of task completion times. Yet, as these authors point out, the ability to estimate completion times accurately is important for both applied and theoretical reasons. In their first set of studies, Buehler and colleagues examined people's predictions of how long it would take them to complete various tasks and activities. They found evidence of an optimistic bias whereby people under-estimate their completion times. The authors present a sophisticated theoretical account of this phenomenon, based on attributional mechanisms that seem to help perceivers to deny the relevance of their past failures. However, this optimistic bias disappears when observers make forecasts concerning the completion times of other people. Indeed these observers' estimates show a pessimistic bias, whereby observers over-estimate the time taken for completion by others. Although these findings may seem rather critical of human perceivers' abilities for time estimation, the authors point out that individuals' predictions were actually strongly correlated with their actual completion times, and may sometimes even be causally related to actual completion times. In the second part of their chapter, Buehler and colleagues looked at forecasts concerning the future course of romantic relationships. There they found basically the same pattern of results, actors were too optimistic and observers too pessimistic. The authors are aware that this relatively new area requires further research before we can make conclusive statements about underlying mechanisms, but on the basis of the research reported here the domains of love and work certainly provide a rich context for the study of intuitive prediction for the very reason that they occupy a central place in almost everyone's life.

Chapter 2 by Bohner, Chaiken, and Moskowitz presents the most recent version of the heuristic-systematic model and explores its potential as a general model of information processing. The heuristic-systematic model assumes two modes of information processing, an effortful systematic mode and a relatively effortless heuristic model. When systematically processing a persuasive message, individuals engage in message-relevant thinking and attempt to evaluate the arguments and issues raised in the communication. Under heuristic processing individuals rely on a relatively superficial assessment of the available information, using rules of thumb, schemas, and other theories about the world. The model also assumes that individuals processing information strike a balance between the goal of exerting least effort and the goal of having sufficient confidence in their judgments. Which processing strategy predominates depends on how high the sufficiency threshold is set and how much effort is deemed necessary for a judgment to be confidently held. In its original conception, the model assumed that information processing was driven by accuracy motivation (reflecting the desire to hold accurate views of the world). In a recent extension of the model, two further processing motivations were assumed to operate, namely defence motivation (reflecting the desire to form and defend a conclusion), and impression motivation (reflecting the desire to maintain attitudes, beliefs, and actions that serve one's interpersonal needs). To illustrate the usefulness of the model as a general theory of information processing, the chapter presents research based on the model in the area of mood and persuasion as well as minority influence.

Chapter 3, by Manstead and Parker, concerns the most popular social-psychological framework for analysing the relationship between attitudes and behaviour, namely the theory of planned behaviour. These authors consider recent theoretical and empirical developments to the theory, drawing in particular on their own continuing research programme in the domain of driver behaviour. On the basis of their research, and their review of the literature, they reach a number of important conclusions. First, while the addition of the perceived control construct to the original theory of reasoned action is certainly a valuable one, they believe that the optimal manner in which to measure this construct remains unclear. Second, they argue that the modest correlations typically observed between direct and belief-based measures of the moral constructs may reflect theoretical problems rather than simply methodological shortcomings. Third, they argue that the model should be significantly extended by adding measures of moral norm and anticipated regret, and they show from their own research that these changes result in worthwhile increments in predictive utility, at least in behavioural domains when moral issues are at stake. Finally, they conclude that further attention needs to be given to the role played by affective behavioural beliefs in shaping behavioural intentions and behaviours themselves. Thus this chapter concurs that the theory of planned behaviour is certainly a useful model for predicting and understanding social behaviour, but that there is plenty of scope for future developments of the model.

The chapters dealing with social groups fall themselves into two subsections dealing with 'small groups' and 'intergroup relations' respectively. The first of these chapters, Chapter 4 by De Dreu, Carnevale, Emans, and van de Vliert, brings together research on decision making and social judgment with research on the classic area of negotiation. De Dreu and colleagues review research and theory concerning outcome frames in negotiation, specifically whether the negotiator views the dispute as involving gains or losses. This detailed review allows the authors to draw five general conclusions. First, negotiator frames affect the negotiator's resistance to concession making (negotiators with a gain frame demand less, concede more, and settle more easily than do negotiators with a loss frame). Second, negotiator frames affect the choice of linguistic labels to describe and evaluate overtly the anticipated or obtained outcomes (negotiators with a gain frame communicate more about gains and profits than about costs and losses, whereas the opposite is true for negotiators who have a loss frame). Third, negotiators are influenced by their opponent's communicated gain or loss frame, in that they tend to adopt the frame communicated by the other person, especially when they themselves have a gain rather than a loss frame. Fourth, prior knowledge about the frame held by the other person seems to evoke two processes. First, foreknowledge seems to affect helping motives, with a stronger inclination to help in the case of the other person having a loss rather than a gain frame. Second, foreknowledge about the other person's frame appears to bias the perception of the other's concessionary behaviour (the other party looks more co-operative when he or she has a loss rather than a gain frame). Fifth, and finally, gain and loss frames assume their importance in conjunction with other characteristics. For example, when the loss frame is paired with high concern for the other person, there may be even more constructive problem solving and integrative negotiation than there is in the case of the gain frame alone. Thus as a whole this chapter successfully indicates how the opponent's communications affect the individual's *representation* of outcomes which (in interaction with the disputants' concern for the other person) determines whether conflict management will be constructive or destructive.

Chapter 5, by Clark and Stephenson, presents another fascinating example of how links can and should be made between social cognition and the area of group processes. They provide a systematic analysis of social aspects of remembering, drawing on their own programme of research, as well as a review of related studies in the literature. They point out that relatively few studies have examined remembering as both an individual and a group phenomenon, and when the stimulus material to be recalled is a purposive social interaction. Their review of their own research programme looks at the theoretical implications of a series of studies which compared individual with social (or collaborative) remembering. A great strength of this research programme is the richness and variety of the measures of memory, including the quantity (accuracy and error) and the quality of what was recalled, and an underlying concern of these researchers is the central relationship between accuracy and confidence, and the implications thereof. These implications are seen primarily in the area of social psychology and law, to which these researchers address themselves. Despite the strides forward that their research programme has made, the authors acknowledge that our knowledge of the effects of group discussion on what is remembered (and how this may influence subsequent individual remembering) still requires greater clarification. Theoretically, future research should investigate the nature and products of social remembering when each group member possesses both shared and unique information about an event, rather than cases where all subjects have been exposed to the same stimulus information. Further detailed study will also be required to identify the relationships between the nature and content of group discussion and a group's memorial product. The authors are at pains to emphasize the important applied psychological consequences of past and present research, particularly in the area of legal testimony. Should, for example, police officers be permitted to compile joint accounts of their arrest notes? Should they be permitted to 'confer', but prepare individual notes of the incident? With their continuing programme of research Clark and Stephenson will provide answers to these important social, as well as many other psychological, questions.

Chapter 6 by Reicher, Spears, and Postmes, provides a new theoretical analysis of a classic term in social psychology. The term 'deindividuation' has originally been suggested to account for the fact that under the protection of their groups, members often appear to behave in anti-normative ways. This was attributed to the fact that individual identity can be lost in groups and that this results in a loss of behavioural control. This chapter questions both the empirical evidence as well as the traditional explanations of deindividuation. Results of a meta-analysis are presented which indicate that, in contrast to predictions from traditional theories, deindividuation manipulations (e.g., group immersion, anonymity, lack of self-awareness) are associated with increases in normative rather than anti-normative behaviour. The chapter argues that traditional models depend on an individualistic conception of the self. It develops a social identity model of deindividuation which consists of two elements. On the one hand, deindividuation manipulations are assumed to affect the cognitive salience of social identity. In particular immersion in the social group and lack of personalization can enhance social identity and thus adherence to standards associated with the social category. On the other hand, deindividuation manipulations are assumed to have strategic effects on the ability of the group members to express their social identity in the face of outgroup opposition. The chapter reviews a number of studies conducted to test this social identity model against traditional theories of deindividuation.

Finally, the chapter by Hagendoorn, is an important reminder that the social-psychological study of intergroup relations is and should be more than the study of intergroup social cognitions. Hagendoorn's research on social distance suggests the existence of consensual ethnic hierarchies in social distance in Western societies. Thus, outgroups are ranked as more or less attractive social partners and there is widespread social consensus about the assigned rank. This chapter argues that the phenomenon of an ethnic hierarchy in its various aspects, such as intergroup preference, ingroup consensus, and intergroup consensus, cannot be explained by just one social-psychological theory. Realistic conflict theory and social identity theory can explain certain aspects, such as ingroup bias and the ethnic hierarchies of subordinate groups. However, ethnic hierarchies of dominant ethnic groups and the consensus among different ethnic groups escape a simple explanation by either realistic conflict theory or social identity theory. The chapter develops an explanation in terms of the different functionality of stereotypes for dominant and subordinate groups. It suggests that these hierarchies result from different motives for different groups. To test these explanations, the chapter reviews results of a number of surveys performed in The Netherlands and the former Soviet Union on the generality of ingroup bias, the cumulative structure of intergroup bias, and the existence of intergroup consensus on the ethnic hierarchy.

Chapter 1

It's About Time: Optimistic Predictions in Work and Love

Roger Buehler
Simon Fraser University
Dale Griffin and Michael Ross
University of Waterloo

ABSTRACT

We review our research on predictions in two different domains: (a) people's estimates of how long they will take to complete various academic and everyday tasks and (b) forecasts by individuals in dating relationships of the future course of their romantic association. Our research indicates that people underestimate their completion times. Further, people appear to base their estimates on plan-based, future scenarios and they use attributional mechanisms to deny the relevance of their past failures to complete tasks on time. The optimistic bias disappears when observers forecast the completion times of other individuals (actors). Observers' estimates are no more accurate, however; instead observers exhibit a pessimistic bias, overestimating actors' task completion times. Compared to actors, observers make greater use of relevant previous experiences in generating their predictions; also while proposing future scenarios, observers are more likely to mention circumstances that might impede the actor's progress on the task. Our findings in the domain of love were generally consistent with those in the domain of work.

INTRODUCTION

People's forecasts shape the way they plan and lead their lives. Before deciding whether to turn off the alarm clock for a few minutes of extra sleep,

European Review of Social Psychology, Volume 6. Edited by Wolfgang Stroebe and Miles Hewstone.
© 1995 John Wiley & Sons Ltd.

commuters may estimate how much traffic they will encounter on their way to work. Prior to asking a woman for a date or his boss for a raise, a man may attempt to divine the chances of rejection. Individuals select professions, spouses, and vacation destinations, in part, by trying to foresee the consequences of their choices.

In the present chapter, we review our research on the accuracy and determinants of predictions in two quite different social domains. In one series of studies, we examined people's predictions of how long it would take them to complete various tasks and activities. In a second line of research, we obtained people's assessments of the future course of their romantic relationships. We tested a number of parallel hypotheses in the two sets of studies.

First, in both contexts we anticipated that people would generate forecasts that are too optimistic. Ambrose Bierce (1914) described the future as 'that period of time in which our affairs prosper, our friends are true and our happiness is assured' (p. 12). Our work on prediction has been guided by the assumption, shared by psychologists and lay people alike, that people's expectations often exceed their actual attainments. We are especially intrigued by people's tendency to generate optimistic forecasts in the face of contradictory experience. People know that they and others frequently underestimate task completion times and that relationships are prone to failure. For example, in a classroom survey that we conducted, students reported finishing about two-thirds of their previous projects later than they had expected. Thus people possess self-knowledge, at a general level, implying that a cautious or even pessimistic prediction is warranted. When people make specific predictions about their future, however, they seem to throw caution to the wind.

Second, we expected to find discrepancies between self and social predictions in both task completion estimates and relationship forecasts. Individuals' own time predictions tend, we suspect, to be optimistic relative to predictions made by disinterested others. Similarly, romantic partners may anticipate a brighter (and longer-lasting) future for their own relationships than observers would predict for them.

Third, we examined the bases of people's forecasts, and especially the processes by which people achieve some degree of accuracy in their predictions. People's forecasts can be overly optimistic and yet at the same time have considerable validity. For example, a student may always expect higher grades on tests than she achieves; nonetheless, she may perform better when she expects an A than when she expects a C.

There are reasons for supposing that people may generate moderately accurate forecasts in the present research. First, the forecasters have the power to influence their own destinies. To some extent, people can decide when to complete a task or to end a relationship. The forecasters' control is limited, however. Unanticipated circumstances arise and other people can influence when the forecasters complete their tasks or end their relationships.

Second, forecasters can base their predictions on a history of personal experiences. Past experiences can be valuable guides but they can also be imperfect foundations for predictions: people and circumstances can change; the future is not merely a repetition of the past. In our research on task completion times, we examined whether people ignore, use, or reject the past as a basis for prediction. We also assessed whether attentiveness to the past increases the accuracy of prediction.

PREDICTING TASK COMPLETION TIMES

The Importance of Time Predictions

Psychologists have extensively studied a variety of time-related topics, including the perception and cognitive representation of time (Fraisse, 1963, 1984; Levin & Zakay, 1989; Macar, Pouthas, & Friedman, 1992). The present research extends this list to include people's predictions of the time they will take to complete tasks and activities. Despite an enduring interest in people's ability to foresee their own future actions and outcomes (for reviews, see Johnson & Sherman, 1990; Rehm & Gadenne, 1990), social psychologists have paid little attention to people's predictions of task completion times. This neglect is surprising. The ability to estimate task completion times accurately is important for both applied and theoretical reasons. From a practical perspective, the problem of forecasting completion times is one of the major challenges decision makers face in organizational contexts, including business, government, and academia. Similarly, accurate planning helps people to regulate their behavior and achieve desired outcomes in their everyday lives. Moreover, people's task completion estimates have implications for other individuals. A man may plan leisure activities in accordance with his spouse's estimates of when she will finish her work. In collaborative work settings, task completion estimates are of utmost importance. Individuals may schedule their own contribution on the basis of the forecasts that their co-workers' offer of their completion times. Inaccurate completion estimates can have economic, personal, and social costs.

From a theoretical perspective, people's everyday tasks provide a particularly rich context for the study of self-prediction processes because individuals possess vast reservoirs of relevant personal experience to draw upon. Also, unlike many other prediction domains, the criteria for evaluating the accuracy of people's predictions are relatively unambiguous. It is thus possible to examine the factors that influence how people make use of their personal experiences as well as the determinants of accurate prediction. In sum, we suggest that people's completion estimates for everyday tasks provide an intriguing context in which to study self-prediction, particularly from a social psychological perspective.

Our research on the prediction of task completion times was guided by two questions that have surely puzzled many people: Why do individuals frequently seem to underestimate how long their tasks will take to complete? Why don't people learn from past experience and adjust their predictions accordingly? To address these questions, we examined the relations among people's predictions of when they will finish tasks, their actual completion times, and their reports of relevant past experience.

Assessing the Accuracy of Time Predictions

Our first step was to assess the accuracy of people's completion estimates and, in particular, to determine whether people tend to be overly optimistic. There is considerable anecdotal support for an optimistic bias. The history of grand construction projects, for example, contains striking evidence of unrealistically rosy predictions (Hall, 1980). Many consider the Sydney Opera House to be the champion of all planning disasters. According to original estimates in 1957, the Opera House would be completed early in 1964 for $7 million. A reduced version of the Opera House finally opened in 1973 at a cost of $102 million (Hall, 1980). Despite numerous examples of this sort, current planners remain overly optimistic about their own projects: for example, the builders of the Channel tunnel connecting Britain and France predicted that passenger trains would run between London and Paris in June, 1993, after an expenditure of 4.9 billion pounds. The real cost will apparently be at least 10 billion pounds and, despite official opening ceremonies held in May 1994, the tunnel is not due to open for passenger traffic until November 1994. The tendency to hold a confident belief that one's own project will proceed as planned, even while knowing that the vast majority of similar projects have run late, has been termed the 'planning fallacy' (Kahneman & Tversky, 1979).

The planning fallacy is not limited to commercial mega-projects. From a psychological perspective, it can perhaps be studied most profitably at the level of daily activities. Consider one familiar example described by Taylor (1989):

> Each day, the well-organized person makes a list of the tasks to be accomplished and then sets out to get them done. Then the exigencies of the day begin to intrude: phone calls, minor setbacks, a miscalculation of how long a task will take, or a small emergency. The list that began the day crisp and white is now in tatters, with additions, cross-outs and, most significantly, half its items left undone. Yet at the end of the day, the list maker cheerfully makes up another overly optimistic list for the next day, or if much was left undone, simply crosses out the day at the top of the list and writes in the next day. This all-too-familiar pattern is remarkable not only because a to-do list typically includes far more than any person could reasonably expect to accomplish in a given time period, but also because the pattern persists, day after day, completely unresponsive to the repeated feedback that it is unrealistic (Taylor, 1989, p. 34).

Along these same lines, we have observed that many academics who carry home a stuffed briefcase on Fridays, fully intending to complete every task, are often aware that they have never gone beyond the first one or two jobs on any previous weekend. The intriguing aspect of this phenomenon is the ability of people to hold two seemingly contradictory beliefs: although aware that most of their previous predictions were overly optimistic, they believe that their current forecasts are realistic. Apparently, people can know the past and still be doomed to repeat it.

Of course, we should not presume on the basis of such anecdotal evidence that people habitually underestimate their own completion times. Conceivably, with a lifetime of experience people become quite adept at estimating the length of time required to complete various projects. Moreover, people's retrospective reports of excessive optimism may be of little help in establishing the existence of a prediction bias because the memories themselves may be biased. Perhaps the negative consequences of completing tasks later than expected render memories of these instances more salient and accessible than memories of tasks completed on time. There is a need for prospective studies to assess the validity of people's predictions.

We were able to locate a few studies in the psychological literature that examined the accuracy of people's task completion estimates. In one relevant investigation, professional engineers consistently underestimated how long they would take to finish equipment overhauls in electricity generating stations (Kidd, 1970). An important feature of the study distinguishes it from our research, however: the repair projects involved teams of technicians and the engineers' predictions reflected group judgments, which are often more extreme than those made by individuals (Janis, 1982; Myers & Lamm, 1976). Previous researchers have also found that individuals assigned hypothetical tasks in the laboratory seem to overestimate how much they can accomplish in a given time period and continue to do so in the face of repeated negative feedback (Hayes-Roth, 1981; Hayes-Roth & Hayes-Roth, 1979). In contrast to this research, our own studies involve people's task completion estimates for their own, real-life activities.

Several areas of research provide indirect support for our hypothesis that people tend towards optimistic completion estimates. In general, with the exception of depressed individuals, people report unrealistically positive evaluations of their own skills (Alicke, 1985; Dunning, Meyerowitz, & Holzberg, 1989) and of their chances of attaining beneficial future outcomes while avoiding negative ones (Perloff & Fetzer, 1986; Weinstein, 1980; Weinstein & Lachendro, 1982). Also, people believe that desirable events are more likely to occur than undesirable incidents (Cantril, 1938; Pruitt & Hoge, 1965; Sherman, 1980; Zakay, 1983). There is no reason to suppose that people's task completion estimates will be impervious to the optimism that apparently pervades individuals' thinking about future events.

In a recent series of studies (Buehler, Griffin, & Ross, 1994), we provided a direct assessment of the hypothesis that people tend to predict they will finish tasks earlier than they actually do. In an initial study (Buehler *et al.*, Study 1), we assessed the accuracy of university students' time estimates for an important academic project, their psychology honors thesis. The honors thesis was a year-long project completed by senior psychology undergraduates which required them to conduct an independent research study, to analyze the results, and to submit a written report to their faculty advisor. We waited until most students were approaching the end of the project, and then asked them to predict when they realistically expected to submit their thesis. The students' predictions were optimistic: only 30% of the students finished their thesis by the predicted time. On average, the students took 55 days to complete their thesis, 22 days longer than they had anticipated.

Despite this optimistic bias, the respondents' forecasts were by no means devoid of information: the predicted completion times were highly correlated with actual completion times ($r = 0.77$). Compared to others in the sample, then, respondents who predicted that they would take more time to finish actually did take more time. Predictions can be informative even in the presence of a marked prediction bias.

In the remaining studies (Buehler, Griffin, & Ross, 1994), we examined students' ability to predict when they would finish a variety of different school assignments, as well as everyday tasks around their homes. The optimistic bias was robust. On average, respondents took almost twice as long as they had predicted. As in the initial study, however, students' forecasts were strongly correlated with their actual completion times.

Confidence in Completion Time Estimates

We obtained further evidence of the participants' unwarranted optimism by assessing their subjective confidence in the forecasts. Conceivably, people could offer optimistic completion estimates, but have little confidence in those forecasts. We included two measures of participants' confidence in their predictions (Buehler, Griffin, & Ross, 1994, Studies 2 and 3). First, participants reported how certain they were that they would finish by the time that they predicted, on a scale ranging from 0% (not at all certain) to 100% (completely certain). The 50% or half-way mark on this scale indicated that respondents were as likely to not finish as to finish by the time that they predicted. For the most part, subjects were quite confident that they would meet their predictions. The average certainty was 74% for school assignments in Study 2 and 70% for household tasks in that same study. In Study 3, which included only academic tasks, subjects were, on average, 84% certain that they would finish their projects in the predicted time. The confidence data are important: by expressing such high levels of confidence, subjects indicated that they saw their predictions as realistic, and not merely as wishful thinking.

As an alternative measure of confidence, we employed a 'fractile procedure' (Lichtenstein, Fischhoff, & Phillips, 1982; Yates, 1990) in the second study.[1] Participants were provided with a series of specific confidence levels and were asked to indicate the completion time corresponding to each confidence level. In this manner, the participants indicated times by which they were 50% certain they would finish their projects (and 50% certain they would not), 75% certain they would finish, and 99% certain they would finish. When we examined the proportion of subjects who finished by each of these forecasted times, we found evidence of overconfidence. Consider the academic projects: only 12.8% of the subjects finished their academic projects by the time they reported as their 50% probability level, only 19.2% finished by the time of their 75% probability level, and only 44.7% finished by the time of their 99% probability level. The results for the 99% probability level are especially striking: even when they make a highly conservative forecast, a prediction that they feel virtually certain that they will fulfill, people's confidence far exceeds their accomplishments.

Why Do People Underestimate their Completion Times?

What psychological mechanisms underlie people's optimistic forecasts? We suspect that, as with most robust psychological phenomena, this prediction bias is multiply determined. We began by adopting a cognitive or informational approach to the problem faced by individuals as they formulate task completion estimates. The cognitive processes by which people generate their predictions may be an important determinant of the degree of accuracy or bias (e.g., Griffin, Dunning, & Ross, 1990; Kahneman & Tversky, 1979; Osberg & Shrauger, 1986). We focused, in particular, on the mechanisms by which people segregate their general theories about their predictions (i.e., that they are usually unrealistic) from their specific expectations for an upcoming task.

In their theoretical analysis of the planning fallacy, Kahneman and Tversky (1979) suggested that people can use *singular* and *distributional* information when predicting task completion. Singular information relates to aspects of the specific target task that might lead to longer or shorter completion times. Distributional information concerns how long it took to complete other, similar tasks. In the present research, where individuals make predictions about everyday activities, the distributional information could either be their own past experiences (personal base rates) or the experiences of others (population base rates). Kahneman and Tversky suggest that people who focus on

---

[1] Note that these data are not reported in the published article, falling victim to an editor's request for condensation.

case-based or singular information adopt an *internal* perspective: they concentrate on working out how they will complete the target task. In contrast, people who primarily consider distributional information embrace an *external* perspective: they compare the present task to past projects. Thus, the two general approaches to prediction differ primarily in whether individuals treat the target task as a unique case or as an instance of an ensemble of similar problems.

Kahneman and his colleagues suggested that for many prediction problems, particularly in contexts where planning is involved, people seem to favor the internal approach (Kahneman & Lovallo, 1991; Kahneman & Tversky, 1979). People tend to generate their predictions by considering the unique features of the task at hand, and constructing a scenario of their future progress on that task. For instance, in deciding how much work to take home for the weekend, individuals may try to imagine when they will start a particular project and how many hours of actual working time they will require. They may also consider the other activities they have planned for the weekend and try to determine precisely when, where, and how they will find time to work on the project. They may even try to envision potential obstacles to completing the project, and how these obstacles could be overcome. Essentially this internal approach to prediction involves sketching out a scenario that captures how the future project is likely to unfold. It involves a mental simulation of the future. Several theorists have offered related views of the prediction process, emphasizing people's tendency to construct scenarios, narratives, or mental simulations as they generate inferences and forecasts (Dawes, 1988; Griffin, Dunning, & Ross, 1990; Johnson & Sherman, 1990; Kahneman & Lovallo, 1991; Kahneman & Tversky, 1982; Klayman & Schoemaker, 1993; Read, 1987; Zukier, 1986).

People's completion estimates are likely to be overly optimistic, however, if their forecasts are based exclusively on plan-based, future scenarios. A problem with the scenario thinking approach is that people may fail to appreciate the vast number of ways in which the future may unfold (Arkes *et al.*, 1988; Fischhoff, Slovic, & Lichtenstein, 1978; Hoch, 1985; Shaklee & Fischhoff, 1982). For instance, expert auto mechanics typically consider only a small subset of the possible ways that things can go wrong, and hence underestimate the probability of a breakdown (Fischhoff, Slovic, & Lichtenstein, 1978). Similarly, when individuals imagine how people will act in the future, they often fail to entertain the possibility of alternative scenarios or to make adequate allowance for the uncertainty of scenarios they construct (Griffin, Dunning, & Ross, 1990; Hoch, 1985). Indeed, developing a scenario for one outcome appears to interfere with people's ability to generate scenarios that would yield alternative outcomes (Hoch, 1984).

In addition, the act of scenario construction may lead people to exaggerate the likelihood of the scenario taking place. Individuals who are led to imagine a given event come to perceive the event as more likely to occur (Anderson,

1983; Anderson & Godfrey, 1987; Carroll, 1978; Gregory, Cialdini, & Carpenter, 1982; Levi & Pryor, 1987; Sherman *et al.*, 1981; Sherman *et al.*, 1983; for reviews see Johnson & Sherman, 1990; Koehler, 1991). In one study, for example, individuals who explained why they might succeed on an upcoming anagram task predicted that they would perform better than those who described hypothetical failure (Sherman *et al.*, 1981). The implication of this research is clear: if people focus on their plans for successful task completion while generating a prediction, they may become overly optimistic about when the tasks will be finished.

The scenario thinking approach threatens the accurate estimation of completion times because there are many ways for the future to unfold that are *not* as planned. Even when a particular scenario is relatively probable, the likelihood that a somewhat different sequence of events will occur is often greater (Dawes, 1988; Kahneman & Lovallo, 1991). Consider a woman who plans to finish many complex projects on the weekend. That person's carefully detailed scenario for completing the projects may be more probable—in advance—than any other single scenario. Nevertheless, the chances of some event occurring that would prevent her from completing all of the projects may be greater, simply because of the vast number of potential impediments (power failures, automobile problems, illness, an unexpected visit from a friend, computer crashes, writing block, and so forth). Although each of these impediments may have a relatively low likelihood of occurrence, the probabilities are additive. The likelihood that *some* unexpected event will arise is often quite high.

The Potential Value of Distributional Information

Given these potential problems with the scenario thinking approach, people might improve their predictions by adopting an external approach to prediction and consulting relevant distributional information (Kahneman & Tversky, 1979). The value of attending to *population base rates* has been demonstrated in several studies examining the accuracy and confidence of people's predictions about their own future behavior (Hoch, 1985; Shrauger & Osberg, 1982; Vallone *et al.*, 1990). There is also empirical evidence that people are able to improve the accuracy of self-prediction by attending to *personal base rates* (Osberg & Shrauger, 1986; Shrauger & Osberg, 1982). Participants in the Osberg and Shrauger experiment rated their likelihood of experiencing each of a series of life events in the next two months. Individuals who were instructed to focus on their own previous experiences when generating the likelihood estimates forecast their future behavior more accurately than control subjects. In the present context personal base rates would seem to be a particularly useful type of information to consider, given the recurrent nature of prediction and performance.

We suspect, however, that people do not spontaneously use their personal base rates to generate self-predictions. As noted previously, individuals frequently appear to recognize, at a general level, that their previous completion times have usually exceeded expectations. If individuals incorporated such information about their past experiences into their predictions, then they would not *repeatedly* underestimate their completion times. On the basis of this reasoning, we suggest that respondents in our previous prediction studies were overly optimistic, in part, because they failed to take into account their own personal histories.

Obstacles to Using Past Experiences

Why might people tend to neglect their past experiences while forming predictions? Prediction, by its very nature, elicits a focus on the future rather than the past; a future orientation may prevent individuals from looking backwards in time. However, a failure to use personal base rates need not always result from neglect of the past. People may sometimes attend to their past experiences, but nevertheless fail to incorporate this information into their predictions. The connection between past experiences and a specific prediction task is not straightforward. The person may first select an appropriate standard for comparison, a past experience or class of experiences similar in important ways to the one under consideration. People may have difficulty detecting an apppropriate set of past experiences; the various instances seem so different from each other that individuals cannot compare them meaningfully (Kahneman & Tversky, 1979).

Furthermore, people might actively process information about the past in a manner that reduces its pertinence to the current prediction. The meaning and relevance of any past behavior depends largely on an individual's explanation of why it occurred (Jones & Davies, 1965; Kelley, 1967; Weiner, 1985). Certain types of attributions link a past event to the present and future whereas other attributions isolate the past. To the extent that people perceive a previous episode to be caused by external, unstable, and specific factors, they need not connect its outcome to future occasions. For example, a woman may attribute her inability to complete a past weekend task to an unexpected visit by her in-laws. Thus she may generalize the previous failure only to weekends when that external and specific factor is present. Knowing that her in-laws are away this weekend, she may suppose that she can readily attain her objectives.

We suggest that people often make attributions that diminish the relevance of past experiences to their current task. People are probably most inclined to deny the significance of their personal history when they dislike its apparent implications (for instance that a project will take longer than they hope). If they are reminded of a past episode that could challenge their optimistic plans, they may invoke attributions that render the experience uninformative for the present forecast. This analysis is consistent with evidence that individuals are inclined to explain away negative personal outcomes (for reviews see Snyder & Higgins, 1988; Taylor & Brown, 1988).

Research Examining Cognitive Processes

We conducted two studies to examine the bases of overly optimistic task completion estimates. (Buehler, Griffin, & Ross, 1994, Studies 3 and 4). In Study 3, we included a 'think-aloud' procedure to record the 'on-line' narratives of participants as they estimated their completion times for various academic tasks, most of which had specific deadlines. We instructed respondents to say aloud every thought or idea that came into their minds while they predicted when they would finish an upcoming school project. We later analyzed the verbal protocols for evidence that people focus on plan-based scenarios for the task at hand, rather than distributional information such as their previous experiences. Consistent with our hypothesis, the majority of respondents' thoughts were directed toward the future ($M = 74\%$). The participants focused overwhelmingly on their plans for the current project, for the most part describing scenarios in which they finished the task without impediments (only 3% of respondents' thoughts included potential impediments); their verbal protocols indicated a neglect of other kinds of information, including their own past experiences with similar projects. Only 7% of the thoughts revealed a consideration of the past.

At the end of this study, we conducted a preliminary test of our attributional hypothesis. We asked these same participants to recall an occasion when they had failed to complete a task by the time they originally anticipated, and then to recall a similar prediction failure experienced by a close acquaintance. Next, we asked them to explain why each of the two tasks was not finished by the expected time. As hypothesized, the reasons participants reported for their own lateness were more external, transitory, and specific than the reasons they provided for similar tardiness by close acquaintances. Participants attributed their own lateness to such rare events as their computer 'blowing up' while they were typing their last English essay. Apparently, people interpret their own tardiness in a manner that makes it seem relatively unique and unlikely to recur. Such attributions may serve to diminish the relevance of previous experience for prediction.

In our next experiment (Study 4), we examined the impact on prediction of asking people to focus on memories of relevant past experiences. Participants predicted when they would finish a standard, one-hour computer assignment. To manipulate the focus of participants' thoughts as they formulated their predictions, we varied the the questions participants answered immediately prior to their predictions. Participants in the Recall condition reported on their previous experiences with similar assignments just before making their predictions. They indicated how far before the deadlines they had typically finished school assignments similar to the present one. Participants in the Recall-Relevant condition answered two additional questions that explicitly required them to forge a connection between the reported past experiences and the present computer assignment. First, they indicated the date and time they would finish the computer assignment if they finished it as far before its deadline as they typically completed assignments. Second, they described a plausible scenario—based on their past experiences—that would result in their completing the computer assignment at their typical time. After writing the hypothetical scenario, they made their predictions for the computer assignment. In the Control condition, we made no attempt to direct the focus of participants' thoughts. Control participants were not asked any questions concerning their past experiences until after they had reported their predictions.

In all three conditions, participants remembered finishing the majority of their previous projects very close to deadlines. Thus, if simply remembering past episodes leads people to make use of the experiences, predictions in both the Recall and the Recall-Relevant condition would be closer to the deadline than predictions in the Control condition. We have argued, however, that individuals may consider past episodes but judge them to be irrelevant. Unless people forget a direct connection between past episodes and the task at hand, they will not use their experiences to guide their predictions. Participants in the Recall-Relevant condition were required to construct a hypothetical scenario that would illuminate the relevance of their previous experiences to the current prediction. We expected that these participants would be most likely to use their previous experiences while generating their forecasts; hence, their predicted completion times would be more realistic than those of participants in the other two conditions.

As depicted in Figure 1.1, the results were consistent with our hypothesis. Participants in the Recall-Relevant condition predicted they would finish the assignment significantly later than participants in either the Recall condition or the Control condition. The actual completion times recorded by the computer did not differ among the three conditions. Participants underestimated their actual completion times significantly in the Control and Recall conditions, but not in the Recall-Relevant condition. Moreover, a higher percentage of participants finished assignment in the predicted time in the Recall-Relevant condition (60%) than in either the Recall condition (38%) or the Control condition (29%).

Although the completion estimates were *less biased* in the Recall-Relevant condition than in the other conditions, we found no evidence that the predictions were *more accurate*. The predictions were not more strongly correlated with actual completion times; nor was the absolute difference between predicted and actual completion times smaller in the Recall-Relevant condition.

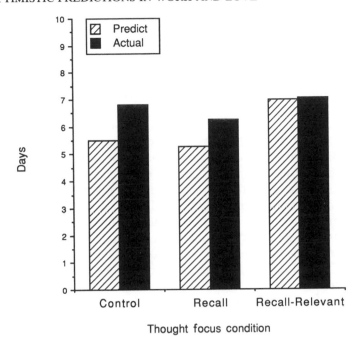

Figure 1.1 Predicted and actual completion times by thought focus condition (Buehler, Griffin, & Ross, 1994, Study 4)

The optimistic bias was eliminated in the Recall-Relevant condition because participants' predictions were as likely to be too pessimistic as too optimistic.

In sum, the thought focus manipulation achieved its primary purpose of demonstrating that, at least under some circumstances, leading people to consider their pasts can result in more conservative, unbiased predictions. Further research is required to identify the conditions that make people more attentive to the implications of their previous performance.

Actor/Observer Differences in Prediction

We have explored one context in which people may spontaneously use distributional information for prediction. Individuals may rely on distributional information when they make predictions for others, rather than themselves. Anecdotally, it seems that the planning fallacy vanishes when individuals forecast other people's task completions. We are not surprised when our colleagues' journal reviews are late or when their house renovations take twice the time that they predicted. Even without the benefit of hindsight, we would have anticipated these outcomes.

An actor/observer difference in prediction may be partly due to differing attributions for past behaviors. Because they are not explaining their own inability to meet predictions, observers may be less inclined than actors to discount previous prediction failures by attributing them to external, transitory, or unstable causes. Also, observers tend to ascribe actors' behaviors to characteristics of those individuals; conversely, the actors, themselves, are disposed to attribute their behaviors to external circumstances (Jones & Nisbett, 1972). When explaining failures to meet previous predictions, observers may see actors as procrastinators, but actors see themselves as the victims of circumstances. Indeed, this very pattern of attributions was obtained in Study 3. There is another possible basis for actor/observer differences in predictions. In comparison to actors, observers may be relatively unaware of the actors' future activities and commitments. Consequently, it may be difficult for observers to imagine the details of how and when another individual will complete a task. If observers cannot readily construct a future scenario, they may rely on available sources of distributional information, including the other individual's previous performance.

Our last study in this series was conducted to explore the possibility of actor/observer differences in task completion predictions (Buehler, Griffin, & Ross, 1994, Study 5). We asked observers to predict when another individual—a participant in Study 4—would finish the computer assignment. Observers were each yoked to a participant (actor) from the *control condition* of Study 4. Observers received the following items of information concerning their target actor: demographic information provided by the actor (sex, age, academic major), the instructions the actor received for completing the computer assignment, the actor's deadline for the assignment (one or two weeks), and the actor's self-predicted completion time. Two additional sources of information that had been potentially available to the actors at the time of prediction were (a) their thoughts about completing the assignment and (b) their memories of relevant previous expriences. The control actors had written their thoughts while generating their predictions and they reported their previous completion times for similar projects immediately after making their predictions. To explore the impact of these different types of information on prediction, we varied which of the two sources of actor-generated information observers received. In one condition (Thoughts), observers received the thoughts reported by the actor as he or she generated a completion estimate. In a second condition (Memories), observers received the actor's reports of previous completion times. In a third condition (Thoughts and Memories Combined) observers received both sources of information in counterbalanced order. After reviewing the information, observers tried to estimate as accurately as possible when the target actor would finish the assignment and also wrote their thoughts as they arrived at their predictions.

The results shown in Figure 1.2 reveal dramatic actor/observer differences in prediction. As hypothesized, the observers offered more conservative predictions than the individuals performing the project. Although the observers' conservatism could reflect a variety of processes, there was support for the hypothesis that people make greater use of previous experience for social than for self-predictions. While generating their forecasts, observers in the Memories and Combined conditions were more likely than actors to refer to the target actor's past experiences. Similarly, observers' predictions were significantly correlated with the actors' typical completion times in both the Memories and Combined conditions; in contrast actors' predictions were not significantly related to their typical completion times. Thus, even when observers obtained both past completion times and future scenarios they seemed to make use of the distributional information. On the other hand, actors involved in the project—who had access to the same two sources of information—appeared to rely more exclusively on their own future plans as a basis for self-prediction.

Results were also consistent with our hypotheses about the effects of information on prediction, as revealed by comparisons among the observer conditions. Observers who were offered only the actors' future scenarios generated more optimistic predictions than observers who were provided with the actors' reports of their typical past performances. Note, however, that participants in

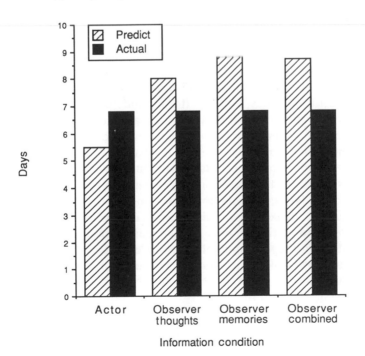

Figure 1.2 Predicted and actual completion times by actor/observer status and observer information condition (Buehler, Griffin, & Ross, 1994, Study 5)

all three observer conditions made more conservative predictions than the actors. Thus, the conservatism displayed by observers was not due entirely to their greater use of the actors' past experience.

Improving Prediction: Accuracy versus Bias

Importantly, the observers' predictions were no more or less accurate than the actors' predictions, as assessed by absolute difference scores or correlations between predicted and actual completion times. Instead, the two groups of subjects tended to err in opposite directions. The actors' optimistic bias was matched by an equally strong pessimistic bias in observers. This finding is consistent with the results of the thought focus manipulation in Study 4; subjects in the Recall-Relevant condition were not optimistically biased, but their predictions were no more accurate than those of subjects in the other conditions. It remains for future research to identify those factors that lead people to make more *accurate* as well as *unbiased* predictions.

This pattern of results prompts us to consider whether (or when) we should advise people to base their predictions on their previous experiences. In the real world, absolute accuracy is sometimes not as important as (a) whether tasks are completed by the 'best guess date' and (b) whether we dramatically underestimate completion times. By both of these criteria, factors that serve to decrease the optimistic bias also serve to 'improve' the quality of intuitive prediction. In many contexts, however, absolute levels of accuracy do matter. There can be costs for finishing either earlier or later than one expected. In the world of business, for example, individuals may be paid for services on the basis of the estimates they provide. If they underestimate their completion times they will be underpaid; if they overestimate their completion times they may be undercut by competitors and lose potential clients.

If using memories of past experiences as a basis for prediction increases the conservativeness of people's estimates without improving accuracy, then the value of this approach to prediction may depend on the relative costs associated with the two types of prediction errors, underestimation and overestimation. For example, those ever-optimistic academics who routinely carry home too much weekend work may have more to gain than lose from an optimistic outlook. Although they are unlikely to complete all of their work, it may be impossible to do so unless they have it with them. By comparison the costs may seem minimal. At worst, they may suffer a sprained wrist or sore back from carrying home all of that work.

Relations Among Goals, Plans, Prediction, and Behavior

In keeping with a cost–benefit analysis, we are currently extending our research on time predictions to explore two central issues: (a) the role of goals and motives in the prediction process and (b) the functions and consequences of making optimistic time predictions.

Although we have focused to this point on the cognitive processes underlying task completion estimates, it is also important to consider motivational determinants. In recent years, researchers in most areas of social psychology are, once again, recognizing the importance of considering the impact of goals and motives on information processing and judgment (e.g., Fiske, 1993; Gollwitzer, 1990; Gollwitzer, Heckhausen, & Steller, 1990; Pervin, 1989; Srull & Wyer, 1986). Several theorists have emphasized a distinction between accuracy-oriented or open-minded motivation and directional or closure seeking motivation (Fiske, 1993; Kruglanski, 1989, 1990; Kunda, 1990). These two types of motives or goals differ in their effects on information processing and judgment. Accuracy goals may lead people to entertain a greater number of alternative hypotheses, to consider more evidence, and to use more complex inferential procedures. Directional goals may enhance the use of beliefs and cognitive strategies that are most likely to yield the desired conclusion.

To explore further the motivational determinants of time predictions, we are currently conducting experiments that vary independently people's goals at the time of prediction. The relative strength of accuracy goals versus directional goals may affect people's time predictions by influencing the cognitive strategies that they adopt. Specifically, individuals with a strong desire to make accurate forecasts may be more likely to adopt an external approach to prediction, incorporating relevant distributional information. In contrast, people with a strong desire to finish tasks promptly may maintain an internal approach, focusing exclusively on optimistic future scenarios. Preliminary support for this hypothesis may be found in the actor/observer differences in prediction and information usage described above: presumably the actors had a goal of completing their task promptly that was not shared by the observers. Although the actor/observer differences might be accounted for without assuming a motivational mechanism, we suspect that people's motives interact with cognitive processes to produce the optimistic predictions we have observed.

In one recent study we have examined the impact of directional goals on people's predictions of when they would complete an important, albeit onerous, task. The study took advantage of a naturally occurring variation in people's desire to finish a task promptly. Each year, Canadian residents are required to complete income tax forms; they report on their sources of income, their deductible expenses, and the amount of taxes they have already paid (e.g., via paycheque deductions). At year end, some individuals owe the government money whereas others receive a refund. Those individuals expecting a refund should have a relatively strong motive to submit the forms early (and thus receive an early refund). Approximately two months before the deadline for submitting the tax forms, we contacted a sample of Canadian taxpayers randomly selected from telephone listings and asked them (a) to predict when they would complete and mail in their tax forms, (b) to recall when they had typically completed the forms in previous years, and (c) to indicate how important they felt it was to finish the forms as soon as possible. Shortly after the deadline for submitting the forms we contacted these individuals again to ask when they had actually submitted their forms. If people's directional goals contribute to the optimistic bias in their predictions, then the bias should be exaggerated in people expecting a refund. Results supported this hypothesis. In comparison to people who owed taxes, those expecting a refund felt it was more important to finish the task promptly and also predicted that they would finish the task more than 10 days earlier on average. There were not significant differences in when they actually completed the forms or in their typical completion time in previous years. Apparently, the directional motive had a stronger impact on people's predictions than on their behavior and hence exacerbated the optimistic prediction bias.

As a second approach to exploring the role of goals and motives, we consider the consequences of people's optimistic time estimates. Accurate time estimates are vital to the efficient scheduling and planning of our time, but time predictions may serve other functions for which accuracy is less crucial. One intriguing possibility is that optimistic forecasts may result in enhanced motivation and performance (for reviews see Taylor, 1989; Taylor & Brown, 1988). Previous research in other domains has found that predictions can be self-fulfilling: asking people to predict their future actions increases the likelihood of the predicted action taking place (Johnson & Sherman, 1990; Sherman, 1980; Sherman et al., 1981; Shrauger, 1990). Similarly, optimistic time estimates may lead individuals to finish tasks, if not by the predicted time, sooner than they would have otherwise. Note that we failed to obtain such an effect in a previous study (Buehler, Griffin, & Ross, 1994, Study 4). When we manipulated the focus of subjects' thoughts before they offered their predictions, participants in the Recall-Relevant condition generated more conservative predictions than those in the remaining conditions; in contrast, subjects' actual completion times were not affected significantly by the focus manipulation. Note, however, that the mean difference in predictions between conditions in this study, although significant, was rather small (see Figure 1.1). A stronger manipulation which yielded a larger difference in predictions might also produce effects on completion times.

Buehler, MacDonald, & Griffin (1994) employed an 'anchoring' procedure in an attempt to assign people randomly to relatively optimistic or pessimistic predictions. Participants were informed that the researchers were trying out a new response-eliciting procedure that involved providing participants with an initial 'starting point' and asking them to adjust from this starting pont to give their final responses. Participants were further informed that their initial estimate would be randomly determined by a card which they would draw from the experimenter. Participants were then assigned a standard, hour-long computer assignment to complete within the next three weeks, drew an initial value between 1 and 21, and were asked to adjust from this value to predict the number of days until they completed the task. The card draw was rigged so that all participants received a starting point of either 4 days (Low Anchor) or 17 days (High Anchor). Participants first were asked whether they would finish the assignment either in 4 days or 17 days and then asked to predict their completion time as accurately as possible. Finally, the experimenter told participants that they were not required to complete the assignment at the time of their prediction, but were free to finish it at any time within the next 3 weeks. To reduce experimental demands to finish at the predicted time, the experimenter took the slip of paper on which the prediction had been recorded and, in full view of the subject, crumpled it and tossed it into the waste bucket.

Buehler *et al.* expected that the initial starting point, although ostensibly randomly determined, would serve as an anchor for the prediction and that participants would fail to adjust fully from this anchor (Tversky & Kahneman, 1974). This expectation was confirmed. Participants assigned to the low anchor expected to finish the task in less than half the time (M = 4.2 days) than participants in the high anchor condition (M = 9.2 days). Thus, the procedure exerted a powerful effect on participants' predictions and permitted an examination of whether these forecasts would influence actual completion times. Consistent with the hypothesis, the anchoring manipulation (and hence the predictions) had a significant impact on participants' actual completion times. Those participants who were induced to predict relatively early completion times also finished the assignment *relatively* early (Ms = 6.7 versus 12.0 days). Apparently, people's optimistic predictions can sometimes influence their behaviour, leading them to complete tasks earlier than they would have if their predictions were more conservative. Note, as well, that participants in both conditions revealed a substantial optimistic bias in predictions: participants in the two anchor conditions underestimated their actual completion times by an equivalent amount (see Figures 1.3).

We do not suggest that people's predictions will always exert a causal impact on actual completion times. In the anchoring study, the target task was straightforward, highly circumscribed, and brief in duration. Tasks requiring greater persistence may be more vulnerable to unexpected delays. In addition, subjects expressed their forecasts publicly to the experimenter and may have felt a sense of commitment to her (although evidently not a sufficient sense of commitment to finish the task by the predicted time); conceivably, private self-predictions would not have affected behavior. It remains for future research to identify the factors that determine precisely when and how people succeed in turning their forecasts into reality.

Literature in related areas offers clues as to how people's predictions might produce effects on behavior. A particularly intriguing possibility is that

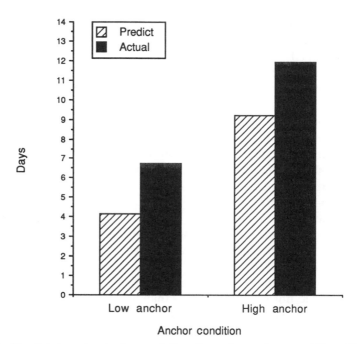

Figure 1.3 Predicted and actual completion times by anchor condition (Buehler, MacDonald, & Griffin, 1994)

behavioral effects occur as the result of people constructing mental simulations or future scenarios. Until now we have focused on the effects of such cognitive processes (mental simulation or scenario thinking) on prediction. It is important to note, however, that the same cognitive activity may also produce behavioral effects. A considerable amount of recent theorizing and research suggests that the construction of detailed, concrete, mental simulations may have facilitating effects on behavior (Johnson & Sherman, 1990; Roese, 1994; Taylor & Schneider, 1989). Taylor and Schneider (1989) have postulated that mental simulations of future events can provide crucial links between thought and action in the following ways: by increasing the expectancy that the imagined event will occur, by providing concrete plans, and by increasing levels of motivation. Empirical support for this viewpoint is seen in such diverse areas as the effects of mental practice effects on athletic performance (Feltz & Landers, 1983; Hall & Erffmeyer, 1983) and the effectiveness of cognitive rehearsal and mental planning as tools in cognitive behavior therapies (Marlatt, 1978; Meichenbaum & Goodman, 1971). By mentally rehearsing likely future circumstances and their own effective actions in them, people can help to bring those effective actions about.

A recent program of research by Gollwitzer and his colleagues (Gollwitzer, 1993; Gollwitzer, Heckhausen, & Ratajczak, 1990) is also relevant to the present concerns, because it explored the relations among people's goals, plans, and achievement. Gollwitzer has focused on the psychological processes by which goals may have an impact on relevant behavior, how people turn their wishes and desires into action. Gollwitzer suggests that people's *intentions* provide a crucial link between their goals and their actions. Although different types of intentions occur during different phases of the goal attainment processes, the *implementation intention* is particularly relevant because it involves a process akin to planning. Forming an implementation intention involves committing oneself to when, where, and how, the implementation of a goal is to be started and what course the subsequent goal pursuit will take. The implementation intention connects an anticipated situational context (opportunity) with a specific goal-directed behavior (action), for example: 'As soon as my child falls asleep, I will go to my office, turn on the computer, and begin revising the manuscript'. Such intentions are similar in nature to the plan-based, future scenarios that appear to guide people's time predictions.

Importantly, implementation intentions promote goal achievement. In general, evidence of this effect comes from studies in which people share a similar goal, but only a subset of these individuals has formed supplementary implementation intentions (i.e., planned when, where, and how they would implement their goals). In one pertinent study (Gollwitzer & Brandstätter, 1990, reported in Gollwitzer, 1993), subjects were given an essay assignment to complete during the Christmas break. They were asked to report on their experience of Christmas Eve, and to complete the assignment no later than two days after Christmas Eve. Half of the subjects then completed a questionnaire that instructed them to specify when and where during these two holiday days they intended to write their report. These subjects were more than twice as likely as control subjects (who were not requested to form implementation intentions) to complete the assignment in the allotted time. Apparently, people's chances of accomplishing goals increase when they explicitly state how they will achieve the goal.

The act of planning, or forming implementation intentions, appears to have a number of consequences that promote the pursuit of goals (Gollwitzer, 1990, 1993). It sets in motion various psychological processes that help individuals to overcome problems with initiating and successfully executing goal-directed behaviors. For example, implementation intentions may make people more likely to detect the situational opportunities for achieving their goals and to seize those opportunities when they arise.

The above accounts, which suggest that processes of mental simulation and planning are effective strategies for achieving desired outcomes, might seem to challenge our hypotheses. We have contended that people generate overly optimistic predictions, in part, because they construct detailed, plan-based, future scenarios for the upcoming task. On the other hand, research on mental simulation reveals the efficacy of plan-based scenarios. We suggest, however, that the two views are not contradictory. Mental simulation and planning may increase the degree of optimism in people's predictions and may also have a directive impact on behavior. Whether these processes contribute to an optimistic bias in prediction (i.e., the tendency to underestimate actual completion times) depends on their relative impact on prediction versus behavior. If mental simulation exerts a stronger impact on people's predictions than on their behavior, the magnitude of the optimistic bias will increase. This may often be the case, we believe, because of the relatively great opportunity for unexpected factors to intervene between planning and the execution of those plans; in comparison, the connection between planning and stating a prediction is relatively immediate and direct. Therefore, plan-based, scenario thinking may facilitate task completion but also contribute to the degree of optimistic bias in people's task completion predictions.

In summary, our program of research on the prediction of task completion times provided considerable evidence for the main guiding hypotheses. First, people tended to underestimate their own, but not others', task completion times. Second, when predicting their own task completion times, individuals adopted an internal approach, focusing on plan-based scenarios rather than distributional information such as previous experiences. Third, individuals appeared to use attributional mechanisms to deny the relevance of past experiences to their current self-predictions. Fourth, despite the optimistic bias, individuals' predictions were strongly correlated with their actual completion times, and may sometimes be causally related to actual completiom times.

In the next section we review research that we have recently conducted to examine people's forecasts concerning the future course of their romantic relationships. Intuitively, it would seem that romantic forecasts are very different from time completion estimates. Our theoretical analysis of underlying process suggests, however, that we should expect to find parallels and indeed we do.

PREDICTING THE OUTCOMES OF ROMANTIC RELATIONSHIPS

According to the cultural stereotype, romantic love is a state in which human rationality and logic hold no sway. For example, Nietzsche characterized love as the condition in which the 'force of illusion reaches its zenith'. The misery that can result from the irrational nature of love is a great source of wit and mockery in our culture, as illustrated by Congreve's famous couplet, 'Married in haste, we may repent at leisure'. According to this view of unredeemed optimism, predictions made about romantic relationships—by the starry-eyed participants in those relationships—should be both markedly overconfident and almost entirely unpredictive of success.

In contrast, uninvolved onlookers seem to look beyond the rosy reports of the actors and be more realistic about the chances of any given relationship succeeding. There are several reasons to believe that this actor/observer difference in relationship predictions may exist. First, as discussed earlier, there is considerable evidence that the likelihood of desirable events is exaggerated by all except the most dysphoric predictors. Second, again paralleling the logic developed in the task prediction studies, lovers may be more likely to plan the future in terms of their unique abilities to *overcome* obstacles such as time apart, whereas observers may focus on the bleaker implications of situational obstacles faced by the romantic partners. Furthermore, observers may be more likely than lovers to incorporate their generally pessimistic theories— reflecting the low base rate likelihood of relationship success—into their specific predictions. Love-struck actors, caught up in their unique plans, may be both less likely to consider base rates and more motivated to explain away their relevance.

It may be, of course, that observers' general theories are overly pessimistic. Perhaps, as Romeo argued, 'Thou canst not speak of that thou dost not feel', and observers' predictions are not better but more poorly calibrated than the lovers' themselves. Therefore, a second purpose of this investigation is to contrast the calibration of relationship predictions made by lovers with those made by neutral observers.

In our study, we examined the informational basis of the relationship predictions made by actors and observers to test two questions. Do observers focus on available distributional evidence whereas lovers dwell on the unique characteristics of their current relationship, such as their feelings for each other? Second, do lovers—as Romeo's words imply—have special insight into the future of their relationships?

These questions were tested in a longitudinal study that included judgments from lovers in a relationship (actors) and from neutral observers (Filyer, Griffin, & Ross, 1994). The actors were eighty-one university students who had been dating at least one month, but no longer than six months. We obtained three types of information from these students. (a) First they offered their predictions about the future of their own relationships. Actors reported the expected length of their relationship and their certainty (in percent) that their own relationship would last for specified time periods: 2 months, 6 months, 1 year, 2 years, 5 years, until marriage, and for a lifetime. (b) They reported their general theories concerning the outcomes of the relationships of similar others. Actors considered other university couples who had been involved as long as the actor's own relationship and predicted the proportion of such couples that would be together at each of the specified time periods. (c) Finally, they described their feelings of love for their partner and their satisfaction with their current relationship on a series of scales commonly used in research on relationships. To this point, we have telephoned actor participants at the intervals specified in the prediction questionnaire for the first 2 years (2 months, 6 months, 1 year, and 2 years) to determine whether they were still dating their same partner.

A same-sex observer was matched to each actor. Observers were 'experts' in the domain in the sense that they were all involved in an ongoing romantic relationship. Observers were presented with parts (b) and (c) of the target actor's original questionnaire (everything except the actors' predictions about the future course of their relationship) and were asked to make parallel predictions about the future of the dating relationship of their target actor.

Recall that we expected that actors would be overconfident in their relationship time predictions. One indication of overconfidence is that of these 81 university students (mean age of 21) who had all been involved for less than *six months*, fully one-third expected to remain together for a lifetime. A more direct measure of optimistic bias comes from the comparison of actors' certainty with the actual proportion of relationships that survived a specified interval. For example, on average, our actor subjects were 77% certain that their relationships would survive six months and 56% certain that their relationships would survive two years. In reality, 65% of the couples remained together after six months and 43% remained together after two years. Although both of these comparisons are in the direction of overconfidence, the discrepancies are relatively modest and thus do not support the notion of mindless optimism on the part of our 'romantic' participants. Furthermore, actors' certainty ratings showed considerable predictive validity: correlations between confidence and outcome exceeded 0.4 for both time periods.

Given the evidence for an optimistic bias in actors' specific beliefs, it is instructive to examine their general theories about other couples like them. Paralleling the task prediction data, general theories about other couples were overly pessimistic: actors predicted that, of other couples who had been involved with dating partners as long as they had, 56% would survive six months and 34% would survive two years. Both of these figures are about 10% below the actual rates of survivals, as given above. Would actors have been well advised to ignore the unique qualities of their own relationships and simply use their general theories to generate their certainty ratings? The answer is clearly no. At the mean level actors' theories were too pessimistic; moreover their estimates of how many similar couples would remain together at each time point were uncorrelated with actors' actual outcomes. This is in sharp contrast to the actors' certainty ratings of the continuance of their own relationships, which were strongly related to the actual outcomes.

We next turn to the certainty judgments of our observer subjects. Recall that each observer rated the likelihood that a given relationship would last each of several time points. Consistent with our expectations, observers' judgments were considerably more pessimistic than the actors' at each time point (22% lower at six months and 29% lower at two years). But were these dispassionate observers more accurate than the love-struck actors? In fact, observers' pessimistic bias (10% at six months and 16% at two years) was as great as actors' optimistic bias, paralleling the results of our task prediction studies.

Observers' certainty judgments were very similar to actors' general beliefs about similar others, deviating by only 1% at six months and 6% at two years. This finding might seem to imply that observers rejected the case-specific information (actors' reported feelings of love and satisfaction) in favor of more general (and more pessimistic) theories about relationships in general. However, this implication is inconsistent with the observed pattern of correlations. For example, observers' certainty ratings were just as predictive of a successful outcome as were actors' ratings of certainty in their own relationships, indicating that observers were able to discriminate among relatively more versus less successful relationships. Thus, the observers could not have ignored the case-specific information and relied on their own pessimistic theories. Furthermore, the partial correlation between actors' ratings of love and satisfaction (summed into a simple summary measure) and observers' certainty (holding actors' general theories constant) was just as large as the partial correlation between actors' ratings of love and satisfaction and their own certainty ratings at each point. Together, these results portray observers who are just as sensitive to the *relative* implications of the actors' level of love and satisfaction as the actors' are themselves. The observers simply have a lower expectation of success given a particular level of relationship satisfaction.

Overall, then, the actors are just as accurate as the observers (although the two groups have opposite directional biases at the mean level) and the observers are just as sensitive to the case-specific information as are the actors. These two factors can be seen simultaneously on a calibration curve as plotted in Figure 1.4. For this curve, certainty judgments have been divided into quartiles and each point on a line represents a quarter of the sample, or about 20 people. Each point represents the average certainty for those 20 people on the X axis and the proportion of relationships still together on the Y axis. The diagonal line represents the points of perfect calibration, where the certainty rating equals the proportion together. Points above the identity line (where the observer judgments are found for the six-month predictions in Figure 1.4a, and for the two-year predictions in Figure 1.4b) represent aggregate judgments were certainty is less than the proportion together (underconfidence or pessimism) and points below the identity line (where the actor judgments are found for both time periods) represent aggregate judgments where certainty is greater than the proportion together (overconfidence or optimism). Aside from the general tendency for observers to be overly pessimistic and actors to be overly optimistic, the graphs also reveal the impressive predictive validity of both sets of judgments: there is a strong, positive relation between certainty

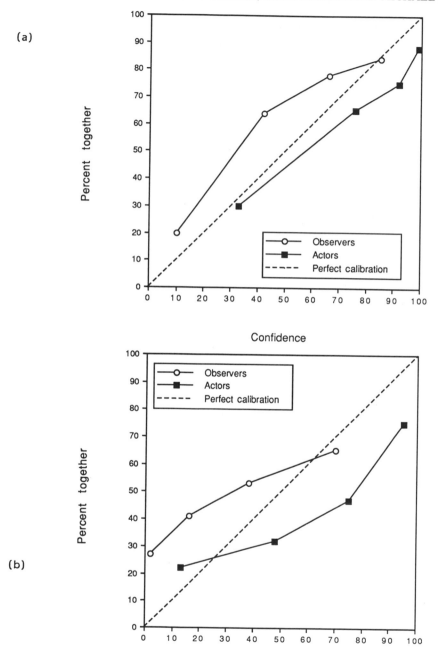

Figure 1.4   The calibration of confidence for actors' and observers' predictions (a) for the six-month and (b) for the two-year time intervals.

and outcome. Again, this is not consistent with illusory thinking by the actors or with the mindless application of general theories by the observers.

Actors' certainty was highly predictive of the outcome of their relationships. Is certainty merely *diagnostic* of good relationships or does it exert a *causal* impact on the success of relationships? A diagnostic relation between certainty and outcome implies that although relatively high certainty in future success may be a marker of a good relationship, the certainty-outcome relation is actually a spurious result of the fact that good relationships last longer. In contrast, a causal relation implies that people with higher certainty in the success of their relationship translate that certainty into action in such a way as to increase the likelihood of their relationship lasting. Obviously, the domain of love—unlike the domain of task predictions—is not amenable to experimental manipulations of certainty and so we cannot demonstrate a causal link between certainty and relationship success. We can, however, test the relation between certainty and relationship outcome when actors' rated love and satisfaction is held constant. If the certainty-outcome relation is then reduced to zero, we can infer a spurious link that reflected the tendency for happier couples to be more confident *and* to be more likely to stay together. In fact, that is just what we found. Given several actors with the same level of relationship satisfaction, variations in certainty held no predictive validity. Apparently, lovers' optimistic forecasts did not contribute to the success of their relationships.

CONCLUSION

In general, the overall pattern of results in the domain of love was consistent with those that we found in the domain of work. Actors are too optimistic and observers are too pessimistic; at a correlational level, actors' forecasts have about the same (quite high) predictive validity as observers'. We had hypothesized that observers' forecasts would possibly be more accurate than actors', because observers might be more inclined than actors to take distributional information into account. Although observers did appear to make more use of distributional information, their forecasts were no more accurate. Nonetheless, it is perhaps also worth emphasizing that strangers who simply read a few questionnaries that actors had completed generated forecasts that were just as accurate as, albeit more pessimistic than, those produced by the actors. Apparently, the actors did not possess any additional privileged information that improved the accuracy of their predictions in either context.

It is premature at this point to conclude that the same underlying mechanisms give rise to the similar pattern of results in task and romantic predictions. Instead, we need to investigate the process underlying optimistic relationship predictions to discover the generality of the mechanisms that we identified in our task prediction studies. For example, do romantic partners use attributional mechanisms to deny the pessimistic implications of their past failures or the failures of similar others? Do memory biases contribute to the belief that each relationship is uniquely promising? Can we identify, through narrative analysis and similar techniques, a tendency for those making relationship predictions to focus on future plans and avoid a consideration of future impediments?

According to Freud, the measure of mental health is the ability 'to love and to work'. The domains of love and work also provide a rich context for the study of intuitive prediction because of their central place in almost everyone's lives. These kinds of real-life social predictions are a testing ground for social cognitive theories developed in the more rarefied atmosphere of the laboratory. The studies presented in this chapter provide strong support for the proposal that explorations of meaningful, everyday phenomena can yield clear insights into basic psychological processes.

ACKNOWLEDGEMENT

The research described in this chapter was supported by grants to the authors from the Social Sciences and Humanities Research Council of Canada.

REFERENCES

Alicke, M. D. (1985). Global self-evaluation as determined by the desirability and controllability of trait adjectives. *Journal of Personality and Social Psychology*, **49**, 1621–30.

Anderson, C. A. (1983). Imagination and expectation: The effect of imagining behavioral scripts on personal intentions. *Journal of Personality and Social Psychology*, **45**, 293–305.

Anderson, C. A., & Godfrey, S. S. (1987). Thought about actions: The effects of specificity and availability of imagined behavioral scripts on expectations about oneself and others. *Social Cognition*, **5**, 238–58.

Arkes, H. R., Faust, D., Guilmette, T. J., & Hart, K. (1988). Eliminating the hindsight bias. *Journal of Applied Psychology*, **73**, 305–7.

Bierce, A. (1914). *The Devil's Dictionary*. New York: World Publishing Company.

Buehler, R., Griffin, D., & Ross, M. (1994). Exploring the 'planning fallacy': Why people underestimate their task completion times. *Journal of Personality and Social Psychology*, **67**, 366–81.

Buehler, R., MacDonald, H., & Griffin, D. (1994). *The impact of optimistic predictions on task completion times*. Paper presented at the annual meeting of the Canadian Psychological Association, Penticton, British Columbia, Canada.

Cantril, H. (1938). The prediction of social events. *Journal of Abnormal and Social Psychology*, **38**, 6–47.

Carroll, J. S. (1978). The effect of imaging an event on expectations for the event: An interpretation in terms of the availability heuristic. *Journal of Experimental Social Psychology*, **14**, 88–96.

Dawes, R. M. (1988). *Rational Choice in an Uncertain World*. Orlando, FL: Harcourt Brace Jovanovich.

Dunning, D., Meyerowitz, J.A., & Holzberg, A. (1989). Ambiguity and self-evaluation: The role of idiosyncratic trait definitions in self-serving assessments of ability. *Journal of Personality and Social Psychology*, **57**, 1082–90.

Feltz, D. L., & Landers, D. M. (1983). The effects of mental practice on motor learning and performance: A meta-analysis. *Journal of Sports Psychology*, **5**, 25–57.

Filyer, R., Griffin, D., & Ross., M. (1994). Unpublished manuscript.

Fischhoff, B., Slovic, P., & Lichtenstein, S. (1978). Fault trees: Sensitivity of estimated failure probabilities to problem representation. *Journal of Experimental Psychology: Human Perception and Performance*, **4**, 330–4.

Fiske, S. T. (1993). Social cognition and social perceptions. In L. W. Porter & M. R. Rosenberg (Eds), *Annual Review of Psychology* (Vol. 44, pp. 155–94). Palo Alto: Annual Reviews Inc.

Fraisse, P. (1963). *Psychology of Time*, New York: Harper & Row.

Fraisse, P. (1984). Perception and estimation of time. *Annual Review of Psychology*, **35**, 1–36.

Gollwitzer, P. M. (1990). Action phases and mind sets. In E. T. Higgins & R. M. Sorrentino (Eds), *Handbook of Motivation and Cognition: Foundations of social behavior* (Vol. 2, pp. 53–92). New York: Guilford Press.

Gollwitzer, P. M. (1993). Goal achievement: The role of intentions. In W. Stroebe & M. Hewstone (Eds), *European Review of Social Psychology* (Vol. 4, pp. 141–185). Chichester: John Wiley.

Gollwitzer, P. M., & Brandstätter, V. (1990). *Do initiation intentions prevent procrastination?* Paper presented at the 8th General Meeting of the European Association of Experimental Social Psychology, Budapest.

Gollwitzer, P. M., Heckhausen, H., & Ratajczak, H. (1990). From weighing to willing: Approaching a change decision through pre- or postdecisional mentation. *Organizational Behavior and Human Decision Processes*, **45**, 41–65.

Gollwitzer, P. M., Heckhausen, H., & Steller, B. (1990). Deliberative and implemental mind-sets: Cognitive turning toward congruous thoughts and information. *Journal of Personality and Social Psychology*, **59**, 1119–27.

Gregory, W. L., Cialdini, R. B., & Carpenter, K. M. (1982). Self-relevant scenarios as mediators of likelihood estimates and compliance: Does imagining make it so? *Journal of Personality and Social Psychology*, **43**, 89–99.

Griffin, D. W., Dunning, D., & Ross, L. (1990). The role of construal processes in overconfident predictions about the self and others. *Journal of Personality and Social Psychology*, **59**, 1128–39.

Hall, E. G., & Erffmeyer, E. S. (1983). The effect of visuo-motor behavior rehearsal with videotaped modelling of free throw accuracy of intercollegiate female basketball players. *Journal of Sport Psychology*, **5**, 343–6.

Hall, P. (1980). *Great planning disasters*. London: Weidenfeld & Nicholson.

Hayes-Roth, B. (1981). *A cognitive science approach to improving planning*. Proceedings of the Third Annual Conference of the Cognitive Science Society. Berkeley, CA: Cognitive Science Society.

Hayes-Roth, B., & Hayes-Roth, F. (1979). A cognitive model of planning. *Cognitive Science*, **3**, 275–310.

30   ROGER BUEHLER, DALE GRIFFIN AND MICHAEL ROSS

Hoch, S. J. (1984). Availability and interference in predictive judgment. *Journal of Experimental Psychology: Learning, Memory, and Cognition*, 10, 649–62.

Hoch, S. J. (1985). Counterfactual reasoning and accuracy in predicting personal events. *Journal of Experimental Psychology: Learning, Memory, and Cognition*, 11, 719–31.

Janis, I.L. (1982). *Groupthink: Psychological studies of policy decisions and fiascoes* (2nd edn). Boston, MA: Houghton Mifflin.

Johnson, M. K., & Sherman, S. J. (1990). Constructing and reconstructing the past and the future in the present. In E. T. Higgins & R. M. Sorrentino (Eds), *Handbook of Motivation and Social Cognition: Foundations of social behavior* (Vol. 2, pp. 482–526). New York: Guilford Press.

Jones, E. E., & Davis, K. E. (1965). From acts to dispositions: The attribution process in person perception. In L. Berkowitz (Ed.), *Advances in Experimental Social Psychology* (Vol. 2). New York: Academic Press.

Jones, E. E., & Nisbett, R. E. (1972). The actor and the observer: Divergent perceptions of the causes of behavior. In E. E. Jones, D. E. Kanouse, H. H. Kelley, R. E. Nisbett, S. Valins, & B. Weiner (Eds), *Attribution: Perceiving the causes of behavior*. Morristown, NJ: General Learning Press.

Kahneman, D., & Lovallo, D. (1991). Bold forecasting and timid decisions: A cognitive perspective on risk taking. In R. Rumelt, P. Schendel, & D. Teece (Eds), *Fundamental Issues in Strategy*. Cambridge: Cambridge University Press.

Kahneman, D., & Tversky, A. (1979). Intuitive prediction: Biases and corrective procedures. *TIMS Studies in Management Science*, 12, 313–27.

Kahneman, D., & Tversky, A. (1982). The simulation heuristic. In D. Kahneman, P. Slovic, & A. Tversky (Eds), *Judgment under Uncertainty: Heuristics and biases* (pp. 201–8). Cambridge: Cambridge University Press.

Kelley, H. H. (1967). Attribution theory in social psychology. In D. L. Vine (Ed.), *Nebraska Symposium on Motivation* (Vol. 15, pp. 192–240). Lincoln, NB: University of Nebraska Press.

Kidd, J. B. (1970). The utilization of subjective probabilities in production planning. *Acta Psychologica*, 34, 338–47.

Klayman, J., & Schoemaker, P. J. H. (1993). Thinking about the future: A cognitive perspective. *Journal of Forecasting*, 12, 161–8.

Koehler, D. J. (1991). Explanation, imagination, and confidence in judgment. *Psychological Bulletin*, 110, 499–519.

Kruglanski, A. W. (1989). *Lay Epistemics and Human Knowledge*. New York: Plenum.

Kruglanski, A. W. (1990). Motivation for judging and knowing: Implications for causal attribution. In E. T. Higgins & R. M. Sorrentino (Eds), *Handbook of Motivation and Cognition: Foundations of social behavior* (Vol. 2, pp. 333–68). New York: Guilford Press.

Kunda, Z. (1990). The case for motivated reasoning. *Psychological Bulletin*, 108, 480–98.

Levi, A. S., & Pryor, J. B. (1987). Use of the availability heuristic in probability estimates of future events. The effects of imagining outcomes versus impinging reasons. *Organizational Behavior and Human Decision Processes*, 40, 219–34.

Levin, I., & Zakay, D. (1989). Time and human cognition: A life-span perspective. In G. E. Stelmach & P. A. Vroon (Eds), *Advances in Psychology* (Vol. 59). Amsterdam: North Holland.

Lichtenstein, S., Fischhoff, B., & Phillips, L. D. (1982). Calibration of probabilities: The state of the art to 1980. In D. Kahneman, P. Slovic, & A. Tversky (Eds),

Judgment under Uncertainty: Heuristics and biases (pp. 306–34). Cambridge: Cambridge University Press.

Macar, F., Pouthas, V., & Friedman, W. J. (1992). *Time, Action and Cognition: Towards bridging the gap* (Vol. 66). Dordrecht: Kluwer.

Marlatt, G. A. (1978). Craving for alcohol, loss of control, and relapse: A cognitive-behavioral analysis. In P. E. Nathan, G. A. Marlatt, & T. Loberg (Eds), *Alcoholism: New directions in behavioral research and treatment* (pp. 271–314). New York: Plenum.

Meichenbaum, D. H., & Goodman, J. (1971). Training impulsive children to talk to themselves: A means of developing self-control. *Journal of Abnormal Psychology*, **77**, 115–26.

Myers, D. G., & Lamm, H. (1976). Group-induced polarization in simulated juries. *Personality and Social Psychology Bulletin*, **2**, 63–66.

Osberg, T. M., & Shrauger, J. S. (1986). Self-prediction: Exploring the parameters of accuracy. *Journal of Personality and Social Psychology*, **51**, 1044–57.

Perloff, L. S., & Fetzer, B. K. (1986). Self–other judgments and perceived vulnerability of victimization. *Journal of Personality and Social Psychology*, **50**, 502–10.

Pervin, L. A. (1989). *Goal Concepts in Personality and Social Psychology*, Hillsdale: Erlbaum.

Pruitt, D. G., & Hoge, R. D. (1965). Strength of the relationship between the value of an event and its subjective probability as a function of method of measurement. *Journal of Experimental Psychology*, **5**, 483–9.

Read, S. J. (1987). Constructing causal scenarios: A knowledge structure approach to causal reasoning. *Journal of Personality and Social Psychology*, **52**, 288–302.

Rehm, J. T., & Gadenne, V. (1990). *Intuitive Predictions and Professional Forecasts: Cognitive processes and social consequences*. New York: Pergamon Press.

Roese, N. J. (1994). The functional basis of counterfactual thinking. *Journal of Personality and Social Psychology*, **66**, 805–18.

Shaklee, H., & Fischhoff, B. (1982). Strategies of information search in causal analysis. *Memory and Cognition*, **10**, 520–30.

Sherman, S. J. (1980). On the self-erasing nature of errors of prediction. *Journal of Personality and Social Psychology*, **39**, 211–21.

Sherman, S. J., Skov, R. B., Hervitz, E. F., & Stock, C. B. (1981). The effects of explaining hypothetical future events: From possibility to probability to actuality and beyond. *Journal of Experimental Social Psychology*, **17**, 142–58.

Sherman, S. J., Zehner, K. S., Johnson, J., & Hirt, E. R. (1983). Social explanation: The role of timing, set, and recall on subjective likelihood estimates. *Journal of Personality and Social Psychology*, **44**, 1127–43.

Shrauger, J. S. (1990). *Some virtues of self-prediction*. Paper presented at the annual meeting of the Society for Experimental Social Psychology, Buffalo, NY.

Shrauger, J. S., & Osberg, T. M. (1982). Self-awareness: The ability to predict one's future behaviour. In G. Underwood (Ed.), *Aspects of Consciousness* (Vol. 3, pp. 267–313). London: Academic Press.

Snyder, C. R., & Higgins, R. L. (1988). Excuses: Their effective role in the negotiation of reality. *Psychological Bulletin*, **104**, 23–55.

Srull, T. K., & Wyer, R. S. (1986). The role of chronic and temporary goals in social information processing. In R. M. Sorrentino & E. T. Higgins (Eds), *Handbook of Motivation and Cognition: Foundations of social behavior* (Vol. 1, pp. 503–49). New York: Guilford Press.

Taylor, S. E. (1989). *Positive Illusions: Creative self-deception and the healthy mind*. New York: Basic Books.

Taylor, S. E., & Brown, J. D. (1988). Illusion and well-being: A social psychological perspective on mental health. *Psychological Bulletin*, **103**, 193–210.

Taylor, S. E., & Schneider, S. K. (1989). Coping and the simulation of events. *Social Cognition*, **7**, 174–194.

Tversky, A., & Kahneman, D. (1974). Judgment under uncertainty: Heuristics and biases. *Science*, **185**, 1124–31.

Vallone, R. P., Griffin, D. W., Lin, S., & Ross, L. (1990). Overconfident prediction of future actions and outcomes by self and others. *Journal of Personality and Social Psychology*, **58**, 582–92.

Weiner, B. (1985). An attributional theory of achievement motivation and emotion. *Psychological Review*, **92**, 548–73.

Weinstein, N. D. (1980). Unrealistic optimism about future life events. *Journal of Personality and Social Psychology*, **39**, 806–20.

Weinstein, N. D., & Lachendro, E. (1982). Egocentrism as a source of unrealistic optimism. *Personality and Social Psychology Bulletin*, **8**, 195–200.

Yates, J. F. (1990). *Judgment and Decision Making*. Englewood Cliffs, NJ: Prentice Hall.

Zakay, D. (1983). The relationship between the probability assessor and the outcomes of an event as a determiner of subjective probability. *Acta Psychologica*, **53**, 271–80.

Zukier, H. (1986). The paradigmatic and narrative modes in goal-guided inference. In R. M. Sorrentino & E. T. Higgins (Eds), *Handbook of Motivation and Cognition: Foundations of social behavior* (Vol. 1, pp. 465–502). New York: Guilford Press.

Chapter 2

The Interplay of Heuristic and Systematic Processing of Social Information

Gerd Bohner
Universität Mannheim
Gordon B. Moskowitz
Princeton University
and
Shelly Chaiken
New York University

ABSTRACT

The heuristic-systematic model (HSM) provides a general theory of social information processing. It features two modes of social information processing, a relatively effortless, top-down *heuristic* mode and a more effortful, bottom-up *systematic* mode. The model assumes that social perceivers strike a balance between effort minimization and achieving confidence in their social judgments. The HSM emphasizes three broad motivational forces: accuracy, defence, and impression motivation. Both heuristic and systematic processing can serve either of the three motives and are capable of co-occurring in an additive or interactive fashion under specified conditions. In this chapter, we describe the HSM and present illustrative research based on the model in the areas of mood and persuasion as well as minority influence.

European Review of Social Psychology, Volume 6. Edited by Wolfgang Stroebe and Miles Hewstone.
© 1995 John Wiley & Sons Ltd.

INTRODUCTION

When observing another person, what factors determine the manner in which we form an impression? When discussing topics with others, watching a debate, or listening to a speech, what factors influence our subsequent attitudes and beliefs? Throughout the development of social psychology, one theme has remained consistent—how we think about the social world is a joint function of the 'objective' properties of the stimuli we think about and the properties that we bring into the perceptual experience. Our expectancies, stereotypes, current goals, and more longstanding motives and needs affect how we think about and judge social objects. From this perspective people are not, as the associationists insisted, as pieces of clay upon which experience rains down, but shaped by selective interest which '*makes* experience more than is made by it' (James, 1890, p. 403). Understanding the social world is thus seen as an active process, a construction, coloured by the expectancies and goals of the individual perceiver.

A separate but related theme concerns the *manner* in which we utilize our cognitive resources when seeking to understand the social world. Allport (1954) described humans as being guided by what he called 'the principle of least effort'. People were seen as avoiding effortful expenditures of energy, cognitive or behavioural, whenever possible. We seek to maximize our outcomes with the least amount of work possible. Such cognitive economy allows us the ability to manoeuvre through a complex stimulus environment. It is well known that the human capacity for attending to and processing information is limited (e.g., Broadbent, 1958; Logan, 1980; Treisman & Geffen, 1967). The principle of least effort is one functional account of how people cope with limited resources—by developing information processing strategies for saving and maximizing their limited capacity.

Any answer to the question of 'how we think about objects in our social world' must make explicit links between the properties of the data, the individual's motives, and information processing strategies. With its focus on how motives determine not only what we think about, but the manner in which we think, the heuristic-systematic model (HSM) seeks to explicate how social knowledge is built (Chaiken, 1980, 1987; Chaiken, Giner-Sorolla, & Chen, in press; Chaiken, Liberman, & Eagly, 1989; Eagly & Chaiken, 1993). The HSM suggests that the factors shaping thoughts about our world depend on both the *motives being pursued* in a given situation and the type of *information processing utilized* in pursuit of those motives. The most basic assumption follows Allport—that when not sufficiently motivated to engage in effortful processing, the default will be to use less effort, to follow an information processing strategy based on simple rules, schemas, and prior knowledge— what is known as *heuristic processing*. However, when sufficiently motivated, 'economy' in allocating mental resources will be abandoned in favour of more effortful and *systematic processing*. Motivated effort, however, does not necessitate a search for 'truth'. The direction in which effort is exerted—toward seeking the truth or toward other goals such as getting along with others; allaying doubts through adopting any sufficient belief (e.g., Festinger, 1957; see also Dewey's, 1938, discussion of warranted assertibility); or promoting self-enhancement—will depend on what motives instigated the effortful processing in the first place (see also Fiske, 1993; Kruglanski 1989; Kunda, 1990).

THE HEURISTIC-SYSTEMATIC MODEL

Two Processing Modes

According to the HSM, the manner in which people construct their social knowledge occurs through two broad information processing strategies. These strategies can be viewed as endpoints on a continuum that reflects the amount of processing effort utilized in forming social judgments (e.g., attitudes, impressions, self-beliefs). On one end are effortless, mostly top-down types of processing. This includes a reliance on schemas, stereotypes, expectancies, and other forms of prior knowledge that can be imposed on the data in order to assimilate it easily to one's existing structures. On the other end are effortful and deliberate, bottom-up types of processing. This includes an evaluation of the individuating information characterizing a stimulus, an examination of one's thoughts and prior beliefs about this stimulus information, and integrating the information to formulate a judgment. It is important to note, however, that the HSM's processing continuum is asymmetrical in the sense that the deliberate use of more effortful strategies does not preclude the possibility that less effortful processes continue to operate. They may occur either independently or in concert with more effortful processes, as we will elaborate shortly.

The processing continuum is a widely used metaphor in social psychology. Heider (1958) used it to describe the attribution process by alluding to the possibility that our impressions of others sometimes seem to happen in an automatic fashion, simply appearing wholly made in consciousness. Other times our impressions require a mental calculus of sorts where we somewhat rationally evaluate the qualities of others. The HSM was originally developed as a reaction against the predominant research trend of the 1960s and 1970s to view attitudes as resulting solely from detailed and rational examinations of persuasive messages, and one's own thoughts about an issue. Other domains of social psychology followed suit and abandoned the view of humans as purely rational creatures. Similar dual process conceptualizations in more recent years include the distinction between automatic and controlled processing of information (e.g., Bargh, 1989), category-based versus individuating processing in person perception (Brewer, 1988) and stereotyping (Fiske & Neuberg, 1990), the theory of lay epistemics (Kruglanski, 1989), and stage models of impression formation (Gilbert, 1989).

What distinguishes the HSM from other dual process models, particularly since its multiple-motive expansion beyond the persuasion context (see Chaiken, Liberman, & Eagly, 1989; Chaiken, Giner-Sorolla, & Chen, in press), is its explicit attempt to link a variety of goals to different information processing strategies. The first broad class of strategies is subsumed under the heading of *systematic processing*. When systematically processing a persuasive message individuals actively attempt to evaluate the arguments and issues raised in the message by actively thinking about this information in relation to other knowledge they possess. The HSM is similar to earlier information processing models of persuasion (McGuire, 1972) in that it emphasizes detailed processing of message content, one's prior beliefs, and source-relevant and topic-relevant cognitions. When systematically processing information about another person the individual examines the individuating qualities of that person, weighs several interpretations of the person's behaviour, and arrives at a deliberately formed impression (Thompson *et al.*, 1994).

Because systematic processing is effortful, and people prefer to minimize effort expenditure, certain preconditions must be met in order for more than minimal amounts of systematic processing to occur. First, some degree of *motivation* is required to instigate systematic processing (this precondition will be explored in greater detail later). Further, one must also have the *ability* and the *cognitive resources* available to do so (see Thompson *et al.*, 1994). Systematic processing should not be confused with objective or unbiased processing. People often exert great amounts of effort to process information in ways that serve their vested interests, to see people in prescribed ways, and to maintain certain beliefs about the self. Effort is not necessarily open-mindedness.

The HSM's second mode of processing is labelled *heuristic processing*. Heuristic processing is proposed to entail only minimal information processing, thus requiring relatively little cognitive capacity in order to be carried out. Instead of exerting effort toward thinking carefully about content (whether it be the content of one's character or the content of a message), people instead preserve their processing resources by relying on a relatively superficial assessment of available information. That is, people use *heuristics*—rules of thumb, schemas, expectancies, and other theories about the world—to interpret the currrent situation, rather than effortfully dissecting that situation to its unique and individuating components. Such heuristics are learned by individuals through their experiences in their social world and can then be readily called to action when the situation presents the individual with a *heuristic cue* that signals their relevance (see Chaiken, 1987, for a review).

For example, through past experiences one may learn that a position that achieves a wide consensus among a group of people is typically accurate. With this 'consensus implies correctness' heuristic in hand, a future situation that confronts the individual with a majority view on an issue may be reacted to in a heuristic fashion. That is, the presence of strong consensus on an issue serves as a cue, which informs the individual of the relevance of her prior theory. Once this heuristic is found to be applicable because of the presence of the heuristic cue, the individual has a fast and efficient resolution to the challenge of forming an opinion. She can superficially assess the situation by relying on her rule of thumb, forming an opinion in a top-down fashion. In this way she simply accepts the majority position without systematically scrutinizing the actual arguments used by the majority in advocating their position. Other heuristics within a persuasion context include rules of thumb such as 'expert statements can be trusted', 'length of a message implies the strength of that message', and 'people I like are usually right'.

The use of heuristics and failure to process information extensively is not confined to persuasion contexts. The person perception literature in particular has documented that when forming an impression of another person, people often fail to examine in detail that person's actions and fail to systematically evaluate the possible causes for her behaviour. Instead they rely on cognitive shortcuts and heuristics, applying the explanation that is most readily available or *primed* (e.g., Bargh & Pietromonaco, 1982; Higgins, Rholes, & Jones, 1977; Thompson *et al.*, 1994). Yet, not just any available theory will be used to guide one's judgments of a person, as not all rules of thumb are utilized in irrelevant persuasion contexts. The heuristic is only engaged when it is both primed and *applicable* to the current situation—cues in the situation must signal that a primed construct is relevant before the heuristic is utilized (see Higgins, in press, for a review).

To illustrate, if someone has a theory that women who succeed are more aggressive than men who achieve similar levels of success, then this stereotypic expectancy will serve as a theory that is available and accessible to this person. Subsequently he can use it to guide the interpretation of events in his social environment. The theory will not lead him to see all women as aggressive. But if a woman is observed either in a situation that signals her success, or in a situation that is ambiguous as to whether she is aggressive or not, the cues in this situation can prime or activate the theory, thus making the observer perceptually ready to see her in a stereotype-consistent fashion. In fact, the more ready one is to use an heuristic, the less strong the cue may need to be. Heuristics can vary in strength so that what is needed to trigger them may range from weak cues (for strong expectancies; Bruner, 1957) to highly diagnostic cues (for weak expectancies).

It is essential in this example that there has been no extensive processing of the woman's behaviour, only a superficial application of an available theory that has been activated by the presence of a triggering cue in the environment (see Fiske *et al.*, 1991; Thompson *et al.*, 1994). What is also of interest is that such heuristics, particularly in the case of stereotypic knowledge, can often be applied without the individual being aware of his current judgments having been influenced. Much like Heider's (1958) attributions that appear ready made in consciousness, our social judgments often appear to us to be free of influence even when guided by heuristic rules. Recent research on spontaneous trait inferences (e.g., Uleman & Moskowitz, 1994) might reflect a similar, nonconscious utilization of heuristics in the person perception domain. One may infer the traits of another person without intention to do so, or knowledge of having done so, by relying on a simple information processing rule such as 'one's actions reflect one's dispositions' that is triggered when behaviour is observed.

The Least Effort Principle

Which of the two processing modes is the default? Limits in cognitive resources combined with an incredibly rich stimulus environment constrain individuals to preserve their cognitive capacity for those things which are of 'interest' (Allport, 1954; James, 1890). The HSM's *least effort principle* adopts this classic logic. Importantly, it assumes that people prefer less effort to more effort, not because they are lazy, but because they are economy-minded processors who spend their cognitive resources only when they are truly needed—when one's interests are engaged. This suggests that the heuristic mode is the default processing strategy because it requires much less effort and usurps much less capacity than systematic processing. Although heuristic processing should occur widely even when there are no specific motivating circumstances that promote it, this mode is not fully ubiquitous, since it requires at least the presence of appropriate heuristic cues in the environment to serve as a triggering stimulus. The more effortful, capacity-limited systematic mode should be far less pervasive, nor likely to occur in the absence of specific motivating circumstances. Implicit in the least effort principle is the assumption that (more than minimal amounts of) systematic processing will not occur without an explicit goal that prompts it; people should avoid its effortful nature in the interest of efficiency.

Most support for this logic has been gathered in persuasion contexts (see Chaiken, 1987; Chaiken, Liberman, & Eagly, 1989; Chaiken & Stangor, 1987), but it has also been shown to be applicable in other domains (e.g., Fiske, 1989; Fiske & Von Hendy, 1992; Gilbert, 1989; Higgins, 1989). For example, Thompson et al. (1994, Experiment 1) assumed that while people are capable of making complex evaluations and deliberating on the individuating qualities of others, their initial response is typically to make fast and effortless judgments that are guided by prior expectancies, accessible constructs, and schemas. Getting past these passive influences on judgment to more controlled and deliberate ones was hypothesized to require an effort that people need to be motivated to exert. One way to do so and diminish the simple application of accessible constructs is to raise the costs of inaccurate judgments.

Thompson *et al.* (1994) tested this assumption in a priming experiment in which trait constructs were made accessible and subjects later were asked to make judgments about a target person on dimensions related to the primed traits. Following a procedure used by Chaiken (1980) and Tetlock (1985), motivation was manipulated by making some subjects highly accountable for their judgments. Accountability often motivates people to adopt a goal of being as accurate as possible in their judgments because of the fear of having their decisions revealed to be invalid when they later come under scrutiny. Therefore, people will not simply rely on explanations that await at the top of the head, but will exert greater effort to produce a defensible judgment. In line with expectations, motivated subjects did not show priming effects; they exerted effort to generate a more balanced interpretation that considered both prime-consistent and prime-inconsistent interpretations of the target's behaviour. Unacccountable subjects, in contrast, did show a priming effect, consistent with the idea that they had engaged mainly in heuristic processing.

These and other findings have shown that the impact of heuristic processing on social judgments is typically greatest when motivation to systematically process is low. However, when motivation and capacity for systematic processing exist, heuristic processing does not come to an end. In contrast, the model assumes that the two modes co-occur in such circumstances, but that systematic processing will often obscure or attenuate the judgmental impact of heuristic processing.

The Sufficiency Principle

If heuristic processing is the default strategy, but systematic processing generally the more impactful mode when it is produced, what mechanism accounts for which strategy will be utilized in any given social situation? We have already hinted at the answer. In instances of co-occurrence, systematic processing should often be more impactful because it generally provides perceivers with more judgment-relevant information and therefore yields more reliable, trustworthy judgments which a person can be confident in. Minimizing effort is not the perceivers' sole concern; they also desire a certain degree of judgmental confidence. The HSM's *sufficiency principle* embodies the idea that people seek a balance between the goal of exerting least effort and the goal of having sufficient confidence in their judgments.

More specifically, this principle asserts that for whatever task a person is confronted with—forming an impression or attitude, making a decision, etc.— there is a point at which one feels that one's task is completed and one can move on to other tasks. This point, labelled the 'sufficiency threshold', is said to be achieved when the individual feels confident the task has been suffi-ciently performed. When confidence falls short of the threshold, people are assumed to exert more effort and continue working on the task until a feeling of sufficiency is achieved and the threshold is reached or surpassed. The notion of sufficiency is necessarily broad, because the experience of sufficient confidence depends on both individual differences and motivational states.

While heuristic processing more fully satisfies the least effort principle, systematic processing generally produces greater amounts of confidence and is thus better able to satisfy the sufficiency principle. The assumption that humans process heuristically by default suggests that on balance, the trade-off between less effort and sufficient judgmental confidence is more than ad-equately met by heuristic processing. In many situations the sufficiency threshold is set low enough so that it can be reached by heuristic processing alone (or minimal amounts of systematic processing). Systematic processing occurs when heuristic processing alone yields *insufficient* judgmental confi-dence. More specifically, the sufficiency principle claims that systematic pro-cessing is dependent on the *actual* amount of confidence that exists in one's judgment falling short of the *desired* amount of confidence. The gap between actual and desired confidence is experienced as a feeling that one's judgment is insufficient. People are presumed to be motivated to reduce this gap by raising the level of actual confidence to match the desired level. This requires systematic processing (e.g., Maheswaran & Chaiken, 1991).

To alter what is experienced as 'sufficient', two things can happen. First, one's confidence can be undermined so that a judgment that was once firmly believed is called into doubt. Here, the threshold itself does not change, but the person's actual level of confidence in her previous, heuristic-based judg-ment does (e.g., Maheswaran & Chaiken, 1991). Later we will apply this principle to instances of minority influence. A second way in which one's experienced confidence can be altered is by a shift in the sufficiency threshold—raising or lowering the level of confidence that one aspires to. In both instances, a state of lacking confidence may be produced by creating a gap between actual and desired confidence. It is within this discrepancy and the induced experience of 'insufficiency' that the motivation driving systema-tic processing is produced.

Multiple Motives

The link between motives and information processing is thus developed from this interplay between the least effort and sufficiency principles. Which process-ing strategy predominates depends on where the sufficiency threshold is set and how much effort is deemed necessary for a judgment to be confidently held. There are two distinct motivational assumptions suggested by the sufficiency principle. One is that motives are capable of setting one's level of confidence and thus establishing (and shifting) the sufficiency threshold. A variety of motives can be successfully implicated in this shifting and setting function that serves to create gaps between actual and desired confidence. The second motivational assumption is more fundamental. It is that the existence of a gap between actual and desired confidence, the experience of feeling that a judgment is not sufficient, is in itself an unpleasant state that people seek to reduce.

Whereas this latter assumption may not have been 'sufficiently' addressed by empirical studies to date, the former has been explored in some detail. Given that discrepancies between actual and desired confidence are energizing, motives that are capable of producing such discrepancies by either raising/lowering the sufficiency threshold (thus changing desired confidence) or by undermining/bolstering one's experienced sense of confidence (thus changing actual confidence) are capable of determining whether processing will follow the heuristic or the heuristic-plus-systematic route. Further, once systematic processing is engaged, the manner in which it proceeds will be determined by the motive that helped to instigate it.

Chaiken and colleagues (Chaiken, Liberman, & Eagly, 1989; Chaiken, Giner-Sorolla, & Chen, in press; Eagly & Chaiken, 1993) have to date explored the impact of three broad motivations on information processing. The first of these has been labelled *defence motivation*. It reflects a desire to form and defend conclusions that are consistent with one's self-knowledge. Such knowledge includes one's social and personal identities; issues, beliefs, and people that one is committed to; and courses of action one has chosen to pursue. The goal of the defence-motivated person is to protect, verify, and enhance the self-concept and those aspects of the world in which the self has been personally vested. Thus, the desire for positive social identity, the need for specific closure (Kruglanski, 1989), self-enhancement, self-verification, and self-completion are all motives which could trigger defence-motivated systematic processing. The defensively motivated information processor is characterized by a directional, biased, or selective manner in which information is scrutinized, so as to confirm the validity and prevent the falsification of important self-relevant knowledge, beliefs, and relationships (e.g., Liberman & Chaiken, 1992).

A second class of motives has been labelled *impression motivation*. This is the desire to maintain attitudes, beliefs, and actions that serve one's interpersonal needs in a given social situation; the motive to produce certain desired consequences in one's interpersonal relationships through expressing beliefs that will be socially acceptable. Impression motivation is guided by the desire to project a certain image, and this is typically achieved by taking into account the qualities, views, and disposition of one's partners in a social situation, be their presence real or imagined. Such impression management (e.g. Schlenker, 1980) or self-presentational (e.g., Jones, 1990) goals allow one to not only anticipate the attributes that others wish to see, but to produce the desired outcomes from another person by displaying those desired attributes for them. Need for approval, fear of rejection, desire for power, interaction goals such as communication and evaluation, and social role needs are capable of prompting impression motivated processing. Such processing is often selective and strategic, aimed at assessing the social acceptability of beliefs and judgments.

Finally, the last class of motives is labelled *accuracy motivation*. In its original conception the HSM focused exclusively on this motive as it affected processing of persuasive messages (see Chaiken & Stangor, 1987). The simple assumption was that people are motivated to hold valid beliefs; to have an objective representation of their social world. In pursuit of those valid beliefs people were said to be capable of systematically processing, but this was likely to occur only when sufficiently motivated, such as when the issue was personally relevant. Such processing promotes the attainment of valid judgments by allowing one the ability to distinguish between specious and accurate information. When accuracy motivated, processing proceeds in a more objective and unbiased fashion in an attempt to seek the 'truth'. Fear of invalidity, desire for self-assessment, accountability, outcome dependency, and increased personal responsibility are all motives which lead one to seek truth. Of course seeking the truth is only possible if one has the capacity and the ability to do so to accompany the desire (see also Chaiken & Lutz, 1993; Thompson *et al.*, 1994; Wood, Kallgren, & Priesler, 1985). Thus, while accuracy motivation may promote systematic truth-seeking, this is not the only strategy for eliminating the confidence gap and allaying doubt. Dewey (1938) suggested it is a process of inquiry, best described as the transformation of an indeterminate situation into one that is determinate (similar to the gestalt principle of closure), that often alleviates doubt. Thus, people can eliminate the confidence gap by settling on *a* belief, even if it is not *the* one true belief.

Co-occurrence of Processing Modes

Unlike most other dual-process models in social cognition (e.g., Fiske & Neuberg, 1990; Petty & Cacioppo, 1986), the HSM specifies the possibility that heuristic and systematic processing may co-occur. While heuristic processing predominates where motivation or ability to scrutinize information is low, more effortful systematic processing is likely to be instigated at higher levels of motivation and ability. *But this does not preclude the possibility that heuristics continue to be utilized as well.* This co-occurrence of processing modes may happen in either an additive or an interactive fashion, depending on a number of factors.

One possibility is that heuristic processing of non-content cues and systematic processing of content information exert independent, additive effects on judgment (*additivity hypothesis*). Studies in the domains of persuasion and social influence provided support for this hypothesis and showed that attitude judgments may be a function of both content-related thinking and cue-related evaluations (Bohner, Frank, & Erb, 1995; Chaiken & Maheswaran, 1994; Maheswaran & Chaiken, 1991). However, additivity will often be difficult to detect, for two reasons. First, systematic processing frequently provides the person with more judgment-relevant information than heuristic processing does. Although, in principle, the quantitative relation between non-content and content information may vary widely, from settings that contain numerous heuristic cues and no content information at all to situations in which ample content information is present (see Bohner, 1990), in most persuasion studies that featured both heuristic cues and persuasive arguments, the latter were more numerous. Therefore, any additional impact of the heuristic cue may have gone undetected (see Chaiken, Liberman, & Eagly, 1989).

Second, the implications of content information may call into question the validity of heuristic-based inferences (when, for example, a highly expert source presents specious arguments; Petty, Cacioppo, & Goldman, 1981). Or, judgments based on information gathered through a deliberate and effortful strategy may often just be more reliable and trustworthy than those produced by a reliance on simple decision rules. For these reasons, in settings conducive to both modes of processing, systematic processing will often attenuate the effects of heuristic processing (Chaiken, Liberman, & Eagly, 1989). There is ample support for this *attenuation hypothesis* of the model (e.g., Chaiken & Maheswaran, 1994; Maheswaran & Chaiken, 1991; for discussion see Chaiken, Liberman, & Eagly, 1989; Eagly & Chaiken, 1993).

Our discussion suggests that attenuation rather than additivity effects will be observed primarily to the extent that content information quantitatively outweighs the information conferred by an heuristic cue, and to the extent that the implications of systematic processing invalidate the heuristic-based inferences. Such invalidation is likely to occur if content information and heuristic-based inferences directly contradict each other. Of course, it may be that heuristics differ in the degree to which they trigger expectations about the validity of content information. For example, the rule that 'experts' statements are valid' is probably more likely to elicit an expectation of high argument quality than the heuristic 'I usually agree with people I like'. We will return to this possibility below in the context of our research on attributions and minority influence.

Another way in which heuristic and systematic processing may interact is expressed in the model's *bias hypothesis* (Chaiken, Liberman, & Eagly, 1989). This hypothesis asserts that heuristic processing can bias systematic processing when individuating information is ambiguous. Accordingly, under conditions of high accuracy motivation and sufficient processing resources, heuristic cues may lead people to form expectancies about message valence or strength. These expectations, in turn, should bias their message-related thoughts to the extent that message content is amenable to varying interpretations (i.e., ambiguous). This interaction hypothesis has received support in a number of studies (Bohner, 1990; Bohner *et al.*, 1992; Bohner, Chaiken, & Hunyadi, 1994; Chaiken & Maheswaran, 1994), some of which we discuss in some detail below.

A final possibility that has not been explicitly considered in the HSM framework so far may be labeled as the *contrast hypothesis*. As kind of a mirror-image of the bias hypothesis, it assumes that heuristic-based expectations may lead to a contrasting interpretation of individuating information. For example, if an individual strongly believes that 'experts' statements are valid', and if a highly salient expertise cue is present in a persuasion setting, the individual should expect the communicator's arguments to be highly convincing. If, in addition, the recipient's accuracy motivation is high and she has the capacity that is necessary to systematically process message content, she may use the initial, heuristic-based expectation as a standard against which to evaluate the actual arguments that the communicator presents. If these arguments are moderately convincing, our hypothetical recipient may think more critically about them and arrive at a more negative judgment about the communicator's position than if no expertise cue had been present at all.

What conditions determine whether direct biasing influences of heuristic information or contrast effects of such information on systematic processing are likely to occur? In both cases, the available content information must be open to varying interpretations, that is, ambiguous or moderate in strength. However, we assume that contrast effects (rather than biasing effects) should result under conditions that have been found to elicit contrast in other domains of judgment, such as *awareness* of a potential influence (e.g., Lombardi, Higgins, & Bargh, 1987) and high *extremity* of the heuristic cue (e.g. Herr, Sherman, & Fazio, 1983; for an overview see Strack *et al.*, 1993). In our example, extremity of the heuristic cue would be defined as the degree of perceived expertise. Thus, if recipients are highly accuracy-motivated and hold strong expectations on the basis of a salient heuristic cue, both their message-related thinking and their attitude judgments may reflect an impact *opposite* to the implications of the heuristic cue. While both attenuation and biasing effects have been observed under the specific conditions delineated in the HSM, the contrast hypothesis still remains to be tested. Having presented the HSM in some detail, we will now report recent experimental work that investigated some of the model's assumptions in two content areas: the impact of recipients' affective states in persuasion, and processes of social influence through minorities.

AFFECTIVE STATES AND THE CO-OCCURRENCE OF HEURISTIC AND SYSTEMATIC PROCESSING

By combining assumptions of the HSM with hypotheses drawn from affect-cognition theories, at least three ways in which moods may influence persuasion can be conceived (see Bohner, in press; Petty, Cacioppo, & Kasmer, 1988;

Schwarz, Bless, & Bohner, 1991). First, mood may itself function as an heuristic cue and may thus directly influence judgments according to a 'how do I feel about it?' heuristic (Schwarz, 1990; Schwarz & Clore, 1983, 1988), independent of available content information or thoughts generated in response to it. In other words, people with low motivation or ability to process may misidentify a pre-existing mood state as a reaction to the attitude object and form attitude judgments congruent with their mood at the time of judgment. Mood influences of this kind should be most likely in the absence of systematic processing and to the extent that the person does not attribute his current mood state to a judgment-irrelevant source (e.g., Schwarz & Clore, 1983). Second, moods may facilitate evaluatively congruent cognitive (and perhaps affective) responses to a persuasive message (Bower, 1981; Isen et al., 1978), which may then mediate mood-congruent attitude judgments. This possibility requires that some content-related thinking about the message occurs, i.e., that motivation and ability to systematically process are substantial. Third, affective states may themselves influence the extent of systematic processing, either by altering an individual's motivation to process (Schwarz, 1990) or by competing with the persuasive message for the recipient's cognitive resources (Ellis & Ashbrook, 1988; Isen, 1987).

Although some evidence for the first two possibilities (i.e., mood-congruent judgments and mood-biased systematic processing) has been reported (Petty et al., 1993), most studies on mood and persuasion provided evidence consistent with the third possibility. They demonstrated that positive mood reduced the amount of systematic processing in comparison with neutral or negative mood—i.e., happy subjects' judgments were generally less likely to reflect differences in argument strength than the judgments of subjects in a neutral or mildly depressed mood (e.g., Bless et al., 1990; Bless, Mackie, & Schwarz, 1992, Experiment 1; Bohner et al., 1992; Bohner, Chaiken & Hunyadi, 1994; Kuykendall & Keating, 1990; Mackie & Worth, 1989; Worth & Mackie, 1987).

Mood and Information Processing: The Informative Functions Approach

The most likely explanation for these mood effects assumes that *motivation* for systematic processing is dependent on a person's current mood (for an alternative, capacity-based account see Mackie & Worth, 1989, 1991; for discussion see Bohner, in press; Schwarz, 1990). According to this account, the presence of a certain affective state informs the individual about the nature of her current psychological situation (Schwarz, 1990; Schwarz & Bohner, in press). Negative affect informs us that the current situation is problematic and potentially threatening and thereby temporarily heightens our sufficiency threshold, instigating detail-oriented, analytic processing aimed at regaining control or dealing with the problematic situation. Correspondingly, positive affect informs us that the current situation is safe and our current goals are not threatened, thus lowering the sufficiency threshold, indicating no need for effortful processing and fostering simplifying, heuristic processing strategies. Recently, Sinclair, Mark and Clore (in press) provided direct evidence for this cognitive tuning hypothesis by demonstrating that sad subjects showed increased systematic processing only if they were unaware of the cause of their mood, but not if their attention was directed to an uncontrollable cause (the unpleasant weather).

While most studies on mood and persuasion found evidence for a link between affective states and the systematic processing of message *content*, only a few experiments included heuristic cues. In two studies, Mackie and Worth (1989, Experiment 2; Worth & Mackie, 1987) varied source expertise in addition to manipulating message strength and recipients' mood. Like the bulk of persuasion studies to date, this research featured extensive persuasive argumentation, and its results were in line with the HSM's attenuation hypothesis: happy subjects' attitudes were primarily influenced by source expertise but unaffected by argument strength, whereas neutral mood subjects' attitudes reflected an impact of argument strength but showed no influence of the expertise cue. However, according to the HSM, additive or interactive effects of both processing modes should also be likely if a person experiences a negative affective state that enhances accuracy motivation. We address this possibility in some detail in the following section.

Negative Mood May Enhance Both Systematic and Heuristic Processing

According to our conception of systematic processing, people in sad moods should 'access and scrutinize *all* [italics added] informational input for its relevance and importance to their judgment task, and integrate *all useful information* [italics added] in forming their judgments' (Chaiken, Liberman, & Eagly, 1989, p. 212). If message content is detailed and has unambiguous evaluative implications (as in the studies by Mackie & Worth, 1989, and Worth & Mackie, 1987), sad persons' attitudes should be essentially mediated by message- and issue-related thinking, and any impact of heuristic cues should be hard to detect, due to *attenuation* (Chaiken, Liberman, & Eagly, 1989). If, however, argumentation is ambiguous or insufficient, sad persons' systematic processing is assumed to be *biased* by heuristic processing. Under these conditions, sad subjects' attitudes should also be mediated by message-related thinking, but the valence of this thought should be biased by these sad recipients' prior processing of heuristic cues, such as consensus information or source credibility. Because happy persons generally lack motivation for systematic processing, their attitudes should primarily be mediated by heuristic processing, independent of the amount, strength, or ambiguity of message arguments. If no judgment-oriented processing goal is activated, happy individuals may even be *less* influenced by heuristic cues than their sad counterparts (see Bohner *et al.*, 1992, for discussion).

Initial evidence for the co-occurrence of systematic and heuristic processing under sad mood has been obtained in two experiments that featured insufficient and ambiguous message content, respectively. In a study by Bohner *et al.* (1992, Experiment 2), subjects who had been put in a happy or a sad mood through bogus performance feedback were later approached by a confederate who asked them to donate money to a charity. This request was insufficiently justified with only one argument, that was either plausible (the collected money would be used for the construction of ramps for wheelchairs at university buildings) or implausible (the money would be used for building a separate library for handicapped students). In addition, a salient strong or weak consensus cue (a list of contributors containing many versus few names) was presented.

As shown in Table 2.1, happy subjects' responses to the request showed no significant influence of either the heuristic cue or the content of the message, whereas sad subjects' responses were influenced by both factors in an interactive fashion: they complied with the request more frequently (and donated a greater amount) if *either* the strong cue *or* the plausible argument was present than if neither was present. Additional analyses (see Bohner, 1990) yielded results consistent with the HSM's bias hypothesis: when the request was accompanied by a strong consensus cue, sad (but not happy) subjects tended to evaluate its content more positively than when it was paired with a weak cue. Sad subjects' biased content evaluations were significantly correlated with compliance ($r = 0.64$) and with the amount donated ($r = 0.47$), whereas happy subjects' content evaluations were unrelated to behaviour ($r = 0.03$ and -0.15, *ns*, resp.).

Table 2.1 Proportion of donors and mean amount donated as a function of mood, type of request and strength of consensus cue. Adapted from Bohner *et al.* (1992), Table 2 (p. 522), © 1992 by John Wiley & Sons Ltd

	Mood			
	Positive		Negative	
	Consensus cue		Consensus cue	
Type of request	Weak	Strong	Weak	Strong
Proportion of donors				
Plausible	1.00	0.88	0.88	0.88
Implausible	1.00	0.75	0.25	0.88
Amount donated (in German Marks)[a]				
Plausible	2.25	1.94	1.75	2.34
Implausible	2.30	2.16	0.50	2.67

[a]Subjects had at least DM 5 at their disposal, because this amount, in small change, had been paid for their participation in an ostensibly unrelated experiment.

Thus, sad subjects' high motivation to process systematically in combination with the insufficient content information brought about behaviour that was clearly a function of content-related evaluations. These evaluations, however, were biased by heuristic-based expectations that were presumably formed in response to the consensus cue. The finding that happy subjects' behaviour was neither influenced by the content of the request nor by the consensus cue can be explained by these subjects' low motivation to process, in combination with the fact that no judgment-oriented processing goal had been activated; happy subjects may just have responded on the basis of a preformed 'charity script' by indiscriminately donating a small amount (see Bohner et al., 1992).[1]

In a study by Bohner, Chaiken and Hunyadi (1994), the interplay of heuristic and systematic processing under sad mood was further explored. Subjects were put in a happy or a sad mood by recalling a positive or a negative experience; later they were asked to evaluate a test report about a telephone answering machine. This report compared the target product, the 'XT-100', with two competing brands and stated that the XT-100 was best. Depending on experimental condition, this conclusion was supported by unambiguous strong, unambiguous weak, or ambiguous arguments. Importantly, all subjects learned that the message was excerpted from *Consumer Reports* magazine and were thus provided with a high credibility source cue. Bohner and colleagues predicted that happy subjects' attitudes toward the product would be primarily a function of source-related thoughts and evaluations, independent of message strength or ambiguity. Sad subjects' attitudes, on the other hand, were expected to be primarily a function of content-related thoughts. Importantly, however, for the case of ambiguous arguments, it was predicted that sad subjects' content-related thoughts would be positively biased by expectations based on the high-credibility cue.

Regression analyses confirmed the HSM-based predictions, as summarized in Table 2.2: happy subjects' attitudes were significantly influenced by source-related thoughts, but not by content-related thoughts, and this pattern was independent of message strength or ambiguity (see Table 2.2, panel (a)). Sad subjects' attitudes were significantly influenced by content-related thoughts, and additionally by source-related thoughts *if message content was ambiguous*, as evidenced by the significant interaction of valenced source-related thoughts and ambiguity (see Table 2.2, panel (b)). Further analyses revealed that sad (but not happy) subjects' content-related thoughts were significantly biased by evaluations of the source, and this influence was most pronounced in the ambiguous message conditions.

---

[1] An alternative interpretation that happy subjects' responses may reflect a ceiling effect is rendered unlikely by the amount of money data. All subjects had at least DM 5 at their disposal, because they had been paid this amount in advance for their participation.

Table 2.2 Hierarchical regression of happy and sad subjects' attitudes on message factors and valenced thought measures. Adapted from Bohner, Chaiken, and Hunyadi (1994), Table 2 (p. 216), © 1994 by John Wiley & Sons Ltd

Step	Effect	Beta	semipartial r
(a) *Happy mood conditions*			
1	Strength (1 = strong, 0 = ambiguous, –1 = weak)	0.39	0.35**
	Ambiguity (–1 = unamb., +2 = amb.)	0.03	0.03
	VAT (Valenced Attribute-Related Thoughts)	0.23	0.21
	VST (Valenced Source-Related Thoughts)	0.31	0.31**
2	VAT × VST	–0.11	–0.08
3	VST × Strength	–0.20	–0 18
	VAT × Strength	–0.07	–0.05
	VST × Ambiguity	–0.17	–0.15
	VAT × Ambiguity	–0.08	–0.06
(b) *Sad mood conditions*			
1	Strength (1 = strong, 0 = ambiguous, –1 = weak)	0.44	0.42***
	Ambiguity (–1 = unamb., +2 = amb.)	0.13	0.12
	VAT	0.36	0.35**
	VST	–0.00	–0.01
2	VAT × VST	–0.21	–0.20
3	VST × Strength	–0.02	–0.02
	VAT × Strength	–0.19	0.11
	VST × Ambiguity	0.42	0.22*
	VAT × Ambiguity	0.16	0.09

Notes: Each effect is adjusted for all other effects entered in the same step or in preceding steps.
*** $p < 0.001$; ** $p < 0.01$; * $p < 0.05$.

The two studies reviewed in this section provide further support for the HSM's bias hypothesis. They demonstrate that message recipients' mood, as other motivational variables (e.g., personal relevance: Chaiken & Maheswaran, 1994), may enhance both systematic and heuristic processing under conditions of insufficient or ambiguous message content. They further show that the heightened accuracy motivation that is elicited by sad affect (Schwarz, 1990) does not invariably lead to more valid judgments and decisions but may, under specifiable conditions, increase a person's susceptibility to bias. The HSM has thus helped to shape our understanding of affective influences in persuasion, which in recent years has dramatically changed from the overly simplistic notion that happy people are often easy to persuade (McGuire, 1985) to the more complex but probably more accurate view that affective states influence the interplay of processing strategies by changing the person's accuracy motivation (Bohner, in press; Schwarz, Bless, & Bohner, 1991).

THE HSM AS A FRAMEWORK FOR STUDYING MINORITY INFLUENCE: ATTRIBUTIONS AND THE HEURISTIC-SYSTEMATIC PROCESSING CONTINUUM

Moscovici (1976, 1980, 1985) proposed a model of minority influence whose focus is on explaining when and how minorities can influence one's private beliefs. According to Moscovici, minority positions are initially regarded as illegitimate and incorrect (e.g., Moscovici & Lage, 1976; Nemeth & Wachtler, 1974). For a minority to be influential, this initial 'rejecting' reaction must be challenged and called into doubt. A minority's behavioural style was presumed to be crucial for accomplishing this task. In particular, a consistent behavioural style was said to establish the minority as being resolute, stable, unyielding, and predictable—leading the perceiver to attribute the minority position to the fact that the minority is confident and certain that their point of view is the correct one. Such attributions were said to induce tension or doubt by creating a conflict between one's initial and heuristic response to the minority and one's current attributions. To resolve this conflict and reduce this tension, Moscovici proposed that people engage in a validation process where they reassess their own beliefs and more carefully attend to the minority position.

Thus, minority influence is said to occur through conflict with the minority's consistent behaviour leading to attributions that challenge the heuristic that 'minority positions are illegitimate'. The result on the part of majority members are feelings of doubt and increased effort toward forming a valid judgment, which finally renders them susceptible to being influenced by the minority. Moscovici's contrast between a validation process, characterized by complex cognitive appraisal, and the simpler propensity to assume that minority positions are invalid and to reject them without scrutiny, is similar to the HSM's distinction between systematic and heuristic processing. The motivating tension that Moscovici describes parallels the HSM's assumption that insufficient confidence in a judgment will result in increased processing effort. Reframing Moscovici's model in terms of the HSM, it follows that given the formation of appropriate attributions, minorities can be persuasive by influencing the extent to which the recipients of their messages engage in systematic processing.

Both models assume that an initial effortless reaction to the social environment must be challenged, and that this occurs through undermining prior beliefs, with the resulting doubt being a motivator of effortful processing. The important issue for both models is how to bring about this motivating doubt or insufficient confidence. Moscovici believed the answer was through consistent behaviour as a way in which to alter attributions. Attributions thus represent a change in one's sufficiency threshold, raising what is required to feel confident, and producing the doubt that Moscovici referred to as conflict and tension. The HSM similarly predicts that attributional logic can serve to create a confidence gap that is capable of motivating systematic processing. In the currrent section we will attempt to integrate two major attributional accounts of persuasion (Kelley, 1967, 1972; see Eagly & Chaiken, 1993), and their partial application to minority influence processes, into the HSM framework. Although causal attributions typically entail more extensive processing than relying on heuristics, attributional reasoning is, in turn, less effortful and capacity-constrained than systematic processing. Just like heuristic processing, then, attributional reasoning may affect judgments either directly or in interaction with systematic processing, depending on conditions specified in the HSM.

The Covariation Model and Minority Influence

The recipient of a persuasive communication may infer the causes of a communicator's statement by performing a subjective analysis of variance on information, arranged in a Persons × Entities × Occasions matrix (Kelley, 1967). Covariation across persons provides *consensus* information, covariation across entities (i.e., topics) furnishes *distinctiveness* information, and covariation across occasions supplies *consistency* information. According to Kelley (1967), entity attributions, and thus persuasion, should be most likely if consensus is high (i.e., most other communicators endorse the same position), if distinctiveness is high (i.e., a communicator's position is specific to the particular topic under consideration), and if consistency is high (i.e., a communicator expresses the same position across various occasions/circumstances). From this perspective, *minorities* face an essential disadvantage because, by definition, consensus for their position is low. Nevertheless, more recent attribution theories suggest that minorities' potential to exert influence should be greater if they fulfil the criteria of high distinctiveness and high consistency than if they do not, because then entity attributions will more likely and circumstance attributions will less likely be part of recipients' causal explanation (e.g., Hewstone & Jaspars, 1987; Hilton & Slugoski, 1986). However, all else being equal, minorities should still be less influential than majorities.

As we noted, the aspect of *consistency* constitutes a key concept in Moscovici's theory of minority influence (Moscovici, 1976, 1980). Research has generally supported the hypothesis that consistent minorities exert more influence than inconsistent ones (e.g., Moscovici & Personnaz, 1980; Mugny, 1982; Nemeth, Swedlund, & Kanki, 1974). Although Moscovici and colleagues have referred to Kelley's (1967) covariation principle (e.g., Moscovici & Nemeth, 1974; Moscovici & Faucheux, 1972), they did not stringently apply it. Most notably, whereas the effects of a minority's consistency over time have been extensively studied, potential effects of distinctiveness across topics have not (see Maass & Clark, 1984). This neglect of distinctiveness information may reflect the fact that Moscovici's attributional theorizing was focused on causal inferences about the *source's dispositions*, such as certainty and conviction (Moscovici & Nemeth, 1974). In Kelley's model, conversely, causal inferences about the validity of the communicator's *position* are central, and attitude change should result if personal features of the communicator can be ruled out as causes for her behaviour (Kelley, 1967). The two models thus treat *person attributions* and *entity attributions*, respectively, as the primary determinants of influence (see Eagly & Chaiken, 1993, pp. 647–9).

While positive person attributions such as conviction and determination would certainly not hinder persuasion, it is primarily negative person attributions like self-interest that must be ruled out in order for influence to occur (Maass & Clark, 1984; Mugny & Papastamou, 1980). Because a communicator's being part of a minority implies low consensus, person attributions are likely to occur. Whether these person attributions are positive or negative, however, should depend on other factors, including *distinctiveness*. Thus, the perception that a communicator's minority position is *highly distinctive* to the particular topic at hand may render unlikely certain negative person attributions such as general dogmatism. Conversely, certain positive person attributions, such as conviction or sincerity, should increase given high distinctiveness. Thus, despite the differences between Moscovici's and Kelley's approaches, distinctiveness information seems to be an important predictor of persuasion from the viewpoint of either model, albeit for different reasons.

Another difference may be conceptualized in terms of the HSM. The judgmental implications of attributional reasoning that Kelley (1967) proposed may be conceived as an (albeit elevated) form of heuristic processing, with recipients using the heuristic 'if a position is distinctive to a particular topic, it must be valid'. In contrast, Moscovici (1980) assumed that, once positive attributions about a minority source had been formed, judgments would change through a 'validation process', a form of systematic processing.

Guided by these considerations, we conducted several studies to examine the role of distinctiveness information in minority versus majority social influence. Our experiments dealt with the topic of animal experimentation, for which pre-experimental attitudes were neutral to mildly positive in the studied population. In a pilot study, subjects learned that a communicator's position against animal experimentation was either shared by most other students or not (high versus low consensus), and *expectancies* regarding distinctiveness and consistency were assessed (Bohner *et al.*, in press). We found that subjects expected that a minority (majority) communicator would hold minority (majority) views with respect to most other issues as well, and that he had expressed the same anti-experimentation view consistently on many occasions. In other words, subjects expected to find high consistency and low distinctiveness. This raises the interesting possibility that high distinctiveness may instigate attributional reasoning and, eventually, systematic processing, because of its unexpectedness (e.g., Weiner, 1985).

In the main experiment, all three dimensions of the covariation model were manipulated, and their impact on open-ended causal attributions, expected persuasiveness, liking of the communicator, and attitudes toward animal experimentation was assessed. Low distinctiveness was represented by the information that the communicator expressed either minority or majority positions with respect to both the target topic and 'most other topics' (without specifying these other topics); high distinctiveness meant that he expressed a minority or majority opinion only with respect to the target topic, but not with respect to other topics. No persuasive message was presented. The results provided partial support for both Kelley's and Moscovici's key attributional assumptions: Entity (i.e., topic-related) attributions were generally more frequent under high than low distinctiveness, and person attributions were more *positive* under high than low distinctiveness. Interestingly, both liking for the communicator and expected persuasiveness were influenced by consensus and distinctiveness information. Specifically, a distinctive minority source was liked most, whereas a non-distinctive majority source was liked least. A similar pattern emerged for expected persuasiveness.[2]

From the perspective of the HSM, the distinctiveness-based inferences that subjects made in the Bohner *et al.* (in press) study (entity attributions, positive person attributions, judgments of high persuasiveness and liking) might all be used as heuristic cues and directly influence attitude judgments when a person is faced with a persuasive message. For example, a person might form a positive attitude toward a minority's position if he inferred something about

---

[2] Two older studies included manipulations that may be reinterpreted as variations of the distinctiveness of a minority's response, even though their authors did not frame them in terms of attribution theory. In an experiment by Nemeth, Swedlund, and Kanki (1974), minority sources showed either 'straight' or 'patterned' responses in an alleged colour perception task. 'Straight' meant that they indiscriminately claimed to see blue slides as green (or, in another condition, as blue-green); 'patterned' meant that the minority's response (green or blue-green) covaried with the light intensity of the slides. In the latter condition, the minority response was thus more 'distinct' with respect to variations in the external stimuli than in the former. Consistent with our findings and predictions of the covariation model, influence was greatest for the 'patterned' condition. Also, the 'patterned' minority was rated more likeable and more competent than the minorities in the other experimental conditions. The other pertinent experiment was conducted by Bray, Johnson, and Chilstrom (1982), who studied the influence of a dissenting minority in experimental groups that discussed several topics. The minority dissented either on *all* topics, or only on the *last* topic after showing conformity on all preceding topics. Again, these conditions can be interpreted as low and high distinctiveness, respectively. It was found that under certain conditions the 'distinct' minority was more influential than the 'non-distinct' minority. It is problematic, however, that the topics used by Bray, Johnson, and Chilstrom were highly similar and therefore what we relabelled as 'high distinctiveness' might as well be interpreted as low consistency. Comparable qualifications hold for the Nemeth, Swedlund, and Kanki study. In any case, the two dimensions were not independent in these studies, and thus attributional interpretation must remain speculative.

the topic as the cause of the minority's behaviour and applied the heuristic that 'positions based on external reality are valid'. Another recipient may have inferred positive personal dispositions from the high distinctiveness of the minority's position and may have formed a positive attitude toward their position on the basis of the heuristic 'people I like are usually right.' These same inferences might, on the other hand, convey the information that systematic processing will increase judgmental confidence because message content is likely to be valid, and might thus increase systematic processing of a persuasive message if such is available.

These possibilities were first explored in an unpublished study by Bohner, Frank, and Erb (1995). Female subjects read five strong or five weak arguments against animal experimentation that were ascribed to a minority or a majority source. The source's position was again described as either distinct or non-distinct to the topic at hand. No consistency information was provided. Later subjects reported their attitudes toward animal experimentation and listed the thoughts that had come to mind while reading the message. It was found that both attitudes and the valence of subject's cognitive responses were influenced by argument strength, indicating that systematic processing had occurred. In addition, high distinctiveness led to attitudes more in line with the advocated position than low distinctiveness did, independent of argument strength and minority or majority source status. This latter effect was not paralleled by a reliable effect of distinctiveness on cognitive responding. Thus, distinctiveness information seems to have been used as an heuristic cue that *additionally* influenced attitudes. This result provides another example for the co-occurrence of systematic and heuristic processing.

Why was no *attenuation* effect observed in this study, even though ample content information was available? Above we addressed one potential explanation that should be explicitly tested in future research: Different heuristic cues may be more or less conducive to attenuation effects because their associated heuristics differ in the extent to which they elicit content-related expectations. For example, information about a source's high expertise, in combination with the heuristic 'experts statements are valid' should lead a recipient to expect that convincing arguments will be presented. It is therefore not surprising that the expertise heuristic may easily be undermined if weak arguments are presented by an expert (see Chaiken, Liberman, & Eagly, 1989, pp. 232–3). With other heuristics, inferences about message content are less likely. The rule 'I generally agree with people I like' does not necessarily imply that a likeable source (such as our 'distinctive' communicator) will present convincing arguments, and may less likely be undermined if one encounters weak arguments.

The results of our distinctiveness studies have an interesting implication for strategies that minorities might use in order to establish their innovative positions. They indicate that minorities may, as an alternative (or in addition) to displaying a consistent behavioural style, use a 'distinctiveness strategy' by pointing out that they *selectively* support unpopular positions with respect to one (or few) particular topic(s), but hold mainstream views with respect to many other topics. Such a strategy would also be expected to be successful on the basis of self-categorization theory (e.g., Turner & Oakes, 1989), which holds that a certain degree of similarity/ingroup status of the source is a prerequisite for influence.

The Multiple Plausible Causes Framework and Minority Influence

Kelley (1972) developed his ideas concerning the attribution process further with a discussion of simple strategies the perceiver can fall back on when only information regarding the single occurrence of a behaviour is available. The two central concepts in the multiple plausible causes framework are the *discounting* and *augmentation* principles. The discounting principle states that a perceiver can discount any one candidate as a potential cause for an event to the extent that other potential causal candidates are also available. Thus, the likelihood of any given cause is reduced as other plausible factors are introduced. According to the augmentation principle, there are both inhibitory conditions (which can interfere with the occurrence of an event) and facilitative conditions (which can increase the likelihood of an event). When an event occurs in the presence of an inhibitory condition, the facilitative condition is given more weight in determining attributions, or is inferred with greater certainty, because it was strong enough to overcome the interference.

For instance, if a communicator presents a message in support of a particular position, one obvious cause for advocating that position would be that it reflects *external reality*. However, there are other potential causes that may guide a person's endorsement of an issue. One may be her membership in a group that serves to gain if such positions are endorsed. Another may be that the person is paid to hold such positions, or has access to only biased information. Whether the alternative possibilities are personal (group/self benefit) or situational (biased sources) the result is the same—one can discount external reality and feel less compelled to accept the position on the issue as one's own. However, imagine if the person is a member of a group that actually serves to *lose* if the position advocated is endorsed. Such a possibility should inhibit or interfere with the communicator advocating the chosen position. The fact that it does not would then serve to augment external reality as a cause. We should be more willing to accept the validity of the message because of its ability to overcome a potential inhibitory factor.

This logic has been applied to social influence settings, and research within this attribution analysis of persuasion (e.g., Eagly and Chaiken, 1975; Eagly, Chaiken and Wood, 1982; Eagly, Wood and Chaiken, 1978; Wood and Eagly,

1981) has revealed broad support for these hypotheses. In these experiments, information that can establish an expectancy regarding what position a source will endorse is presented to subjects prior to hearing the message. This, in effect, establishes that the source will be biased in favour of one side of an issue. Reactions to the message will then be determined by whether the position advocated in the message is discrepant or consistent with the position the message recipient *expected* would be advocated. If the message discon-firms the pre-message expectancy, the message recipient will perceive the message to present an accurate description of external reality. In explaining this prediction, the augmentation principle (Kelley, 1972) is invoked. The ability to overcome the inhibitory cause (the expectancy of bias) serves to strengthen external reality as a cause. However, when the message *confirms* the pre-message expectancy, the message recipient will perceive the commu-nicator as biased. The pre-message expectancy of bias serves as a sufficient cause so that subjects can discount the viability of the message being an accurate reflection of external reality.

This attribution perspective and Moscovici's model are interesting foils. Both assert that an attribution that the message may be veridical is required for successful influence. However, Moscovici maintains that behavioural con-sistency is a key component in shaping the positive attributions that lead to influence, whereas the Eagly model maintains that a type of inconsistency— expectancy disconfirmation—is a central component in arriving at the same type of attributions.[3] This raises the interesting possibility that yet another tactic for minority influence may be to attempt to disconfirm majority group expectancies. Such a 'disconfirmation strategy' can represent an alternative means to instigate positive attributions in the minds of those who cast asper-sive glances on the minority. This becomes particularly important in light of the fact that consistency in behaviour of the sort that Moscovici advocates may take years to affect the appropriate attributions that render innovation possible, as is obvious in the examples he uses (feminists, ecologists).

However, there is a key difference between these models that perhaps limits expectancy disconfirmation as a route to minority influence. Moscovici's model explicitly refers to minority sources, whereas the Eagly model does not refer to the group status of the source. Perhaps expectancy disconfirmation is not a successful strategy for minorities. This possibility is certainly worth considering given another difference between Moscovici's approach and at-tributional accounts that we already mentioned in the context of the covaria-tion model. Whereas Moscovici maintained that positive attributions lead to influence through systematic processing (what he called a validation process), Eagly's model suggests that positive attributions lead to influence through

---

[3] In addition, as we noted, the disconfirmation of expectancies may be one of the basic condi-tions that trigger attributional activity to begin with (e.g., Weiner, 1985).

heuristic processing, by application of a simple attributional rule—augmentation. Thus, subjects are willing to accept a message without having to scrutinize its content when expectancy disconfirmation occurs. This raises the issue of whether group status information plays a role in determining the relationship between expectancy confirmation, attributions, message processing, and persuasion.

How would adding the fact that the source is a minority alter the predictions of the attribution analysis of persuasion? Knowing the source is a minority often introduces a negative expectancy, that its position is illegitimate and should be rejected. Therefore, if an expectancy of bias exists, a minority source simply should add information that can reinforce the attribution of bias; it strengthens the inhibitory cause. When the expectancy is later disconfirmed, the augmentation principle suggests that since the minority overcame an expected bias, the belief that their message is a veridical one should be enhanced. While knowing the source is a minority does not alter the initial negative attribution, it may affect message processing. Eagly, Chaiken, and Wood (1982) suggest that while expectancy disconfirmation improves chances at persuasion, it reduces the likelihood of systematic processing. Information that the source is a minority, however, should change this prediction. While disconfirmation should convey that the message is valid, the minority status should introduce doubt by revealing the position to be nonconsensual. Thus, the ability to simply follow the augmentation principle is challenged by paucity of opinion support. Therefore, for minority sources, expectancy disconfirmation should lead to positive attributions, and to persuasion, but this should occur through *systematic processing* (bringing the predictions in line with Moscovici's belief that positive attributions lead to a validation process).

Moskowitz (in press) initially examined whether in fact positive attributions formed toward a minority source were able to instigate systematic processing and subsequent minority influence. Rather than create a pre-message expectancy of bias, subjects were simply informed that they would read a message from a person who held a minority position on an issue. The issue concerned the requirements for awarding college scholarships to athletes. The negative expectancy associated with the source being a minority was then either disconfirmed or confirmed by providing subjects with some background information about the source. This information was used to provide subjects with either positive (expectancy disconfirming) or negative (expectancy confirming) attributions. Message quality was also manipulated so that systematic processing could be assessed through two separate means—by an interaction between expectancy confirmation/disconfirmation with message quality, and through open-ended thought listing measures that tapped subjects' cognitive responses.

As predicted, subjects were reliably more likely to agree with a minority source when the provided attributions disconfirmed the negative expectancies held. However, the more interesting predictions concern the type of processing that subjects used. If they processed systematically, then greater influence should be found when high-quality messages were presented (relative to low quality messages)—subjects would distinguish the features of the message and derive their opinions based on this scrutiny. A reliable interaction supported the prediction that such systematic processing occurred only when subjects' expectancies had been disconfirmed (see Table 2.3). Subjects whose expectancies had been confirmed showed relatively little agreement with the minority source, and this did not vary as a function of message quality. Subjects whose expectancies had been disconfirmed through positive attributions were reliably more influenced by strong minority messages than weak ones. Thought listing measures provided support for this finding. Minority messages that were associated with positive attributions and disconfirmed expectancies led subjects to generate a reliably greater number of message-related thoughts, the index of systematic processing used. Thus, subjects were not only more influenced by a minority after expectancy disconfirmation, but this influence occurred through the systematic route.

Moskowitz and Chaiken (1995) extended these findings by replicating the procedure used in the attribution analysis of persuasion. In this way, attributions were not directly provided to subjects, but freely formed. This allowed for a more complete test of the multiple plausible causes framework as applied to minority influence, and establishing links between these models and the HSM. In addition, conditions in which the source held a majority position were also included. Once again, the issue of college athletic scholarships was used. Subjects were provided with a pre-message expectancy that suggested that the source would be biased either in favour of or against revising the regulations governing these scholarships. It was predicted that expectancy disconfirmation should lead to external reality being seen as the cause for the advocated position. However, when such attributions are formed in response to a minority source the influence exerted should be mediated through systematic processing. In contrast, expectancy confirmation should lead to an attribution of bias, and with the reinforcement of knowing the position also lacks consensual support, rejection of the message and heuristic processing.

Table 2.3 Attitudes towards the minority proposal as a function of message quality and attributions. Data from Moskowitz (in press)

Message quality	Attribution type	
	Positive	Negative
Weak	4.30_a	3.14_a
Strong	11.44_b	5.33_a

Notes: Higher scores indicate agreement with the minority position (scale range is 1 to 15). Means with different subscripts differ at $p < 0.01$.

For the minority conditions, analyses on open-ended attribution data supported the prediction that expectancy confirmation would lead to the source being seen as relatively more biased. Subjects whose expectancies had been confirmed formed more negative attributions in general, and were particularly likely to attribute the cause of the position advocacy to the source's vested interest. In contrast, those whose expectancies were disconfirmed rated the source more positively, reliably rating him as more certain and confident, as well as more factual and fair-minded. More importantly, the issue of whether expectancy disconfirmation led to minority influence through systematic processing was examined through subjects' open-ended thought listing scores as well as the attitude data. As predicted, when expectancies were disconfirmed, high-quality messages led to more positive message-related thoughts than low-quality messages. However, when expectancies were confirmed, the difference in positive message thoughts between the high and low quality conditions were negligible. Negative message-related thoughts revealed consistent, though weaker, trends. Path analyses supported these findings by revealing a reliable impact of expectancy disconfirmation on message-related thoughts, mediated through the positivity of attributions that had been formed. Negative attributions did not predict message-related thoughts.

Interestingly, and contrary to the pattern found for the minority source, expectancy disconfirmation was *not* associated with an increase in positive attributions *when the source advocated a majority position*. Even though subjects still perceived an expectancy-confirming message to be biased, they nonetheless had an overall positive impression of the source if his position turned out to be a consensual (majority) one. Expectancy confirmation in the case of a majority source also led to more thoughts about the communicator—an index of heuristic processing—and to an overall positive attitude toward his position, which was independent of argument quality. Importantly, however, as with minority sources, an expectancy-disconfirming majority message led to more systematic processing of message content, as evidenced by a pronounced impact of argument quality on attitudes, albeit at a lower overall level. Thus, although expectancy disconfirmation led to systematic processing for both minority and majority sources, this effect was instigated by positive and negative attributions, respectively, and its resulting overall influence differed as well.

In sum, although research in this domain is limited, the findings thus far support the hypothesis that minority sources can instigate successful influence through disconfirming a prior expectancy. This influence occurs through the conflict and doubt raised by this disconfirmation serving as a motivator of systematic processing. In contrast, when a minority message confirms an expected bias it leads to relatively little influence, and heuristic dismissal. In support of this, studies on the effects of 'double minorities' also suggest the possible applicability of the multiple plausible causes framework to minority influence. A double minority is one that has minority status not only by virtue of their small numbers, but because of the social status of a group which they are a member of. Maass, Clark, and Haberkorn (1982) suggest that discounting of a minority message may take place if the source argues for a position that fosters the vested interest of a social group that she belongs to. This may reflect a tendency to attribute a minority's message to aspects other than external reality if expectations arising from a person's social category membership are confirmed.

One implication of this research is that minority groups may indeed employ an 'expectancy disconfirmation strategy' by focusing on an issue where this position is actually opposite to what one might expect on the basis of the prevalent stereotype about the minority group. In this way the minority would be fighting for a position that they truly believe, but that the majority is surprised to find them in support of. The positive attributions and resulting increased scrutiny produced by this disconfirmation could create a window for the minority, through the presentation of strong arguments, to exert influence. Once they have accomplished instigating a more systematic type of processing along this one issue, perhaps further issues will be more seriously attended to. Our preliminary results also suggest, however, that this strategy should only be efficient to the extent that the minority possesses convincing arguments; if they do not, the strategy might backfire.

For majorities, heuristic processing had the advantage of leading to simple agreement, whereas increased scrutiny, so beneficial for minorities, seemed detrimental to the majority position. Thus, for such positions an appropriate strategy for influence may be to attempt the opposite—not get people thinking too much and adopt a strategy that might increase a reliance on heuristics. While this might suggest that we endorse a dual-process view of influence in which majorities and minorities instigate different kinds of processing, this is not the case. Rather, we view social influence as a complex process in which minorities and majorities have a variety of strategies accessible to them, and that, dependent on the dictates of their situation, different strategies will be effective. We do suggest that as a more general principle the heuristic path will be more successful for majorities than minorities, given the greater likelihood of negative heuristics being in place for the minority (for further discussion, see Eagly & Chaiken, 1993; Kruglanski & Mackie, 1990).

CONCLUSIONS

In this chapter we presented the heuristic-systematic model and discussed its potential as a general model of social information processing. We reviewed recent research that applied the HSM to the areas of affect and persuasion as well as minority influence. In both domains, the model could be profitably combined with other theoretical approaches, yielding novel predictions and providing an integrative framework for further study.

In the section on mood and persuasion, we emphasized the interesting possibility that the two processing modes featured in the HSM may *co-occur* in an interactive fashion. Specifically, the motivation to systematically process that is instigated by sad affect may render people more susceptible to the biasing influence of heuristic cues if message content or other individuating information is insufficient or ambiguous. These predictions and findings go beyond those based on other existing theories of persuasion as well as affect-cognition models. Though the model's bias hypothesis has been tested primarily in the domain of persuasion (Bohner, Chaiken, & Hunyadi, 1994; Bohner *et al.*, 1992; Chaiken & Maheswaran, 1994), it applies as well to other domains of social judgment. For example, an interesting but yet untested prediction would be that the impact of stereotypes on person perception should *increase* with the degree of perceivers' accuracy motivation if the available individuating information is ambiguous. In sum, our mood and persuasion studies illustrate the potential of the HSM to model and predict a complex interplay of cognitive processes in the social context. They added to our knowledge of affective influences on information processing and provided further evidence for the HSM's co-occurrence assumptions.

While our presentation of studies in the realm of minority influence was primarily aimed at demonstrating the HSM's potential for combining and integrating distinct theoretical approaches, one of these studies also featured the co-occurrence of the model's two processing modes. Although additive effects were rarely observed in persuasion studies that featured extensive messages (see Chaiken, Liberman, & Eagly, 1989), we obtained additivity in one of our experiments (Bohner, Frank, & Erb, 1995): A distinctive minority or majority position was generally more influential than a non-distinctive one. In seeming contrast, in our studies on expectancy disconfirmation (Moskowitz, in press; Moskowitz & Chaiken, 1995) attributional inferences about the communicator had no direct impact on judgment but affected the amount of systematic message processing. However, we think that the two sets of results are compatible. Other than varying attributional information, no attempt was made in either study to manipulate subjects' processing motivation. In the distinctiveness study, subjects' motivation may have been rather high to begin with due to the involving issue of animal experimentation, whereas in the expectancy disconfirmation studies, it may have been lower. Thus, even though high distinctiveness may have been unexpected, it may not have further increased the discrepancy between desired and actual confidence, because this discrepancy was already large. Furthermore, the disconfirmation of expectancies may have been stronger in the studies by Moskowitz and Chaiken than in the study by Bohner, Frank, and Erb. In future studies, it will be interesting to delineate and test more stringently the conditions under which attributional inferences affect judgment in a direct, heuristic fashion or indirectly, by influencing the amount of systematic processing.

At the level of application, our minority influence research suggests two interesting behavioural strategies other than consistency that social minorities may effectively employ. They may either use an *'expectancy disconfirmation strategy'* or a *'distinctiveness strategy'*. One difference between these two strategies lies in the 'reality constraints' that they might face. To effectively apply the disconfirmation strategy, a minority group needs to find a focal position that it really endorses *and* that is in opposition to the existing group stereotype—a conjunction of features that may often be hard to find. The distinctiveness strategy, in contrast, is based on the disconfirmation of expectations regarding the general pattern of beliefs held by the minority that 'surround' the focal topic. Thus, this strategy may be easier to exploit because it should almost always be possible for a minority group to point to *some* topics for which they share majority views, even if the focal position they would like to promote is in line with what the majority expects from them. It is possible that the distinctiveness strategy may be employed with equal success by both minorities and majorities. In the study by Bohner, Frank, and Erb (1995), high distinctiveness was equally effective in producing attitude change for both minority and majority sources. The disconfirmation of expectancies, however, as it was featured in the studies by Moskowitz and Chaiken (1995; Moskowitz, in press), may be a more efficient means of influence for minorities than for majorities, given that they possess convincing arguments for their cause.

As our preliminary results indicate, the combination of attribution theory, minority influence models, and the HSM should provide a fertile ground for future investigations. We are confident that the heuristic-systematic model will continue to be of heuristic value for the systematic investigation of human social information processing, not only in the areas of affective processes and minority influence.

ACKNOWLEDGEMENTS

While this chapter was prepared, Gordon Moskowitz was at the University of Konstanz, Germany. The preparation of this chapter was facilitated by travel grants from the Alexander von Humboldt Foundation and the University of Mannheim to Gerd Bohner, and a research grant from the Deutsche Forschungsgemeinschaft (Bo 1248/1) to Gerd Bohner and Miles Hewstone. We gratefully acknowledge stimulating discussions we had with Herbert Bless, Hans-Peter Erb, Elisabeth Frank, Miles Hewstone, Jaques-Philippe Leyens, Marc-André Reinhard, and Michaela Wänke.

REFERENCES

Allport, G. W. (1954). *The Nature of Prejudice.* Cambridge: Addison-Wesley.

Bargh, J. A. (1982). Attention and automaticity in the processing of self-relevant information. *Journal of Personality and Social Psychology*, **43**, 425–36.

Bargh, J. A. (1989). Conditional automaticity: Varieties of automatic influence in social perception and cognition. In J. S. Uleman & J. A. Bargh (Eds), *Unintended Thought* (pp. 3–51). New York: Guilford Press.

Bargh, J. A., & Pietromonaco, P. (1982). Automatic information processing and social perception: The influence of trait information presented outside of conscious awareness on impression formation. *Journal of Personality and Social Psychology*, **43**, 437–49.

Bless, H. Mackie, D. M., & Schwarz, N. (1992). Mood effects on attitude judgments: Independent effects of mood before and after message elaboration. *Journal of Personality and Social Psychology*, **63**, 585–95.

Bless, H., Bohner, G., Schwarz, N., & Strack, F. (1990). Mood and persuasion: A cognitive response analysis. *Personality and Social Psychology Bulletin*, **16**, 331–45.

Bohner, G. (1990). *Einflüsse der Stimmung auf die kognitive Verarbeitung persuasiver Botschaften und auf nachfolgendes Verhalten* [Mood influences on the processing of persuasive messages and on subsequent behaviour]. Unpublished dissertation, Universität Heidelberg, Germany.

Bohner, G. (in press). Stimmung und Persuasion: Zum Zusammenspiel heuristischer und systematischer Verarbeitung persuasiver Botschaften [Mood and persuasion: On the interplay of heuristic and systematic processing of persuasive messages]. In E. H. Witte (Ed.), *Soziale Kognition und empirische Ethikforschung: Beiträge des 9. Hamburger Symposions zur Methodologie der Sozialpsychologie.* Special Issue of *Psychologische Beiträge*.

Bohner, G., Chaiken, S., & Hunyadi, P. (1994). The role of mood and message ambiguity in the interplay of heuristic and systematic processing. *European Journal of Social Psychology*, **24**, 207–21.

Bohner, G., Crow, K., Erb, H.-P., & Schwarz, N. (1992). Affect and persuasion: Mood effects on the processing of persuasive message content and context cues and on subsequent behaviour. *European Journal of Social Psychology*, **22**, 511–30.

Bohner, G., Erb, H.P., Reinhard, M. A., & Frank, E. (in press). Distinctiveness information in minority and majority influence: An attributional analysis and preliminary data. *British Journal of Social Psychology*.

Bohner, G., Frank, E., & Erb, H.-P. (1995). *Distinctiveness information as a heuristic cue in minority and majority influence.* Unpublished data, Universität Mannheim, Germany.

Bower, G. (1981). Mood and memory. *American Psychologist*, **36**, 129–48.

Bray, R. M., Johnson, D., & Chilstrom, J. T., Jr. (1982). Social influence by group members with minority opinions: A comparison of Hollander and Moscovici. *Journal of Personality and Social Psychology*, **43**, 78–88.

Brewer, M. B. (1988). A dual process model of impression formation. In T. K. Srull & R. S. Wyer (Eds), *Advances in Social Cognition* (Vol. 1). Hillsdale, NJ: Erlbaum.

Broadbent, D. E. (1958). *Perception and Communication.* London: Pergamon Press.

Bruner, J. S. (1957). On perceptual readiness. *Psychological Review*, **64**, 123–52.

Chaiken, S. (1980). Heuristic versus systematic information processing and the use of source versus message cues in persuasion. *Journal of Personality and Social Psychology*, **39**, 752–66.

Chaiken, S. (1987). The heuristic model of persuasion. In M. P. Zanna, J. M. Olson, & C. P. Herman (Eds), *Social Influence: The Ontario Symposium* (Vol. 5, pp. 3–39). Hillsdale, NJ: Erlbaum.

Chaiken, S., Giner-Sorolla, R., & Chen, S. (in press). Beyond accuracy: Defense and impression motives in heuristic and systematic processing. In P. M. Gollwitzer & J. A. Bargh (Eds), *Action Science: Linking cognition and motivation to behavior*. New York: Guilford Press.

Chaiken, S., Liberman, A., & Eagly, A. H. (1989). Heuristic and systematic information processing within and beyond the persuasion context. In J. S. Uleman & J. A. Bargh (Eds), *Unintended Thought* (pp. 212–52). New York: Guilford Press.

Chaiken, S., & Lutz, S. (1993). *Time pressure and social judgment*. Paper presented at the Society of Experimental Social Psychology Meeting, Santa Barbara, CA.

Chaiken, S., & Maheswaran, D. (1994). Heuristic processing can bias systematic processing: Effects of source credibility, argument ambiguity, and task importance on attitude judgment. *Journal of Personality and Social Psychology*, **66**, 460–73.

Chaiken, S., & Stangor, C. (1987). Attitudes and attitude change. *Annual Review of Psychology*, **38**, 575–630.

Dewey, J. (1938). *Logic: The theory of inquiry*. New York: Holt.

Eagly, A. H., & Chaiken, S. (1975). An attribution analysis of the effect of communicator characteristics on opinion change: The case of communicator attractiveness. *Journal of Personality and Social Psychology*, **32**, 136–44.

Eagly, A. H., & Chaiken, S. (1993). *The Psychology of Attitudes*. Fort Worth, TX: Harcourt Brace Jovanovich.

Eagly, A. H., Chaiken, S., & Wood, W. (1982). An attribution analysis of persuasion. In J. H. Harvey, W. Ickes, & R. F. Kidd (Eds), *New Directions in Attribution Theory and Research* (Vol. 3, pp. 37–62). Hillsdale, NJ: Erlbaum.

Eagly, A. H., Wood, W., & Chaiken, S. (1978). Causal inferences about communicators and their effect on opinion change. *Journal of Personality and Social Psychology*, **36**, 424–35.

Ellis, H. C., & Ashbrook, P. W. (1988). Resource allocation model of the effects of depressed mood states on memory. In K. Fiedler & J. Forgas (Eds), *Affect, Cognition and Social Behavior* (pp. 25–43). Toronto: Hogrefe.

Festinger, L. (1957). *A Theory of Cognitive Dissonance*. Stanford, CA: Stanford University Press.

Fiske, S. T. (1989). Examining the role of intent: Toward understanding its role in stereotyping and prejudice. In J. S. Uleman & J. A. Bargh (Eds), *Unintended Thought*. New York: Guilford Press.

Fiske, S. T. (1993). Social cognition and social perception. *Annual Review of Psychology*, **44**, 155–94.

Fiske, S. T., & Neuberg, S. L. (1990). A continuum model of impression formation, from category-based to individuating processes: Influences of information and motivation on attention and interpretation. In M. P. Zanna (Ed.), *Advances in Experimental Social Psychology* (Vol. 23, pp. 1–74). New York: Academic Press.

Fiske, S. T., & Von Hendy, H. (1992). Personality feedback and situational norms can control stereotyping processes. *Journal of Personality and Social Psychology*, **62**, 577–96.

Fiske, S. T., Bersoff, D. N., Borgida, E., Deaux, K., & Heilman, M. E. (1991). Social science research on trial: Use of sex stereotyping research in Price Waterhouse v. Hopkins. *American Psychologist*, **46**, 1049–60.

Gilbert, D. T. (1989). Thinking lightly about others: Automatic components of the social inference process. In J. S. Uleman & J. A. Bargh (Eds), *Unintended Thought* (pp. 189–211). New York: Guilford Press.

Heider, F. (1958). *The Psychology of Interpersonal Relations*. New York: John Wiley.

Herr, P. M., Sherman, S. J., & Fazio, R. H. (1983). On the consequences of priming: Assimilation and contrast effects. *Journal of Experimental Social Psychology*, **19**, 323–40.

Hewstone, M., & Jaspars, J. M. F. (1987). Covariation and causal attribution: A logical model of the intuitive analysis of variance. *Journal of Personality and Social Psychology*, **53**, 663–72.

Higgins, E. T. (1989). Knowledge accessibility and activation: Subjectivity and suffering from unconscious sources. In J. S. Uleman & J. A. Bargh (Eds), *Unintended Thought* (pp. 75–123). New York: Guilford Press.

Higgins, E. T. (in press). Knowledge activation: Accessibility, applicability, and salience. In E. T. Higgins & A. W. Kruglanski (Eds), *Social Psychology: Handbook of basic principles*. New York: Guilford Press.

Higgins, E. T., Rholes, W. S., & Jones, C. R. (1977). Category accessibility and impression formation. *Journal of Experimental Social Psychology*, **13**, 141–54.

Hilton, D. J., & Slugoski, B. R. (1986). Knowledge-based causal attribution: The abnormal conditions focus model. *Psychological Review*, **93**, 75–88.

Isen, A. M. (1987). Positive affect, cognitive processes, and social behavior. In L. Berkowitz (Ed.), *Advances in Experimental Social Psychology* (Vol. 20, pp. 203–53). San Diego, CA: Academic Press.

Isen, A. M., Shalker, T. E., Clark, M., & Karp, L. (1978). Affect, accessibility of material in memory, and behavior: A cognitive loop? *Journal of Personality and Social Psychology*, **36**, 1–12.

James, W. (1890). *The Principles of Psychology* (Vol. 1). New York: Dover Publications.

Jones, E. E. (1990). *Interpersonal Perception*. New York: Freeman.

Kelley, H. H. (1967). Attribution theory in social psychology. In D. Levine (Ed.), *Nebraska Symposium on Motivation* (Vol. 15, pp. 192–238). Lincoln, NB: University of Nebraska Press.

Kelley, H. H. (1972). Causal schemata and the attribution process. In E. E. Jones, D. E. Kanouse, H. H. Kelley, R. E. Nisbett, S. Valins, & B. Weiner (Eds), *Attribution: Perceiving the causes of behavior* (pp. 151–74). Morristown, NJ: General Learning Press.

Kruglanski, A. W. (1989). *Lay Epistemics and Human Knowledge: Cognitive and motivational bases*. New York: Plenum.

Kruglanski, A. W. & Mackie, D. M. (1990). Majority and minority influence: A judgmental process analysis. In W. Stroebe & M. Hewstone (Eds), *European Review of Social Psychology* (Vol. 1, pp. 229–61). Chichester: John Wiley.

Kunda, Z. (1990). The case for motivated reasoning. *Psychological Bulletin*, **108**, 480–98.

Kuykendall, D., & Keating, J. P. (1990). Mood and persuasion: Evidence for the differential influence of positive and negative states. *Psychology and Marketing*, **7** (1), 1–9.

Liberman, A., & Chaiken, S. (1992). Defensive processing of personally relevant health messages. *Personality and Social Psychology Bulletin*, **18**, 669–79.

Logan, G. D. (1980). Attention and automaticity in Stroop and priming tasks: Theory and data. *Cognitive Psychology*, **12**, 523–53.

Lombardi, W. L., Higgins, E. T., & Bargh, J. A. (1987). The role of consciousness in priming effects on categorization: Assimilation versus contrast as a function of awareness of the priming task. *Personality and Social Psychology Bulletin*, **13**, 411–29.

Maass, A., & Clark, R. D. III (1984). Hidden impact of minorities: Fifteen years of minority influence research. *Psychological Bulletin*, **95**, 428–50.

Maass, A., Clark, R. D., III & Haberkorn, G. (1982). The effects of differential ascribed category membership and norms on minority influence. *European Journal of Social Psychology*, **12**, 89–104.

Mackie, D. M., & Worth, L. T. (1989). Processing deficits and the mediation of positive affect in persuasion. *Journal of Personality and Social Psychology*, **57**, 27–40.

Mackie, D. M., & Worth, L. T. (1991). Feeling good, but not thinking straight: The impact of positive mood on persuasion. In J. P. Forgas (Ed.), *Emotion and Social Judgments* (pp. 201–19). Oxford: Pergamon Press.

Maheswaran, D., & Chaiken, S. (1991). Promoting systematic processing in low motivation settings: The effect of incongruent information on processing and judgment. *Journal of Personality and Social Psychology*, **61**, 13–25.

McGuire, W. J. (1972). Attitude change: The information-processing paradigm. In C. G. McClintock (Ed.), *Experimental Social Psychology* (pp. 108–41). New York: Holt, Rinehart & Winston.

McGuire, W. J. (1985). Attitudes and attitude change. In G. Lindzey & E. Aronson (Eds), *Handbook of Social Psychology* (3rd edn) (Vol. 2, pp. 233–346). New York: Random House.

Moscovici, S. (1976). *Social Influence and Social Change*. New York: Academic Press.

Moscovici, S. (1980). Toward a theory of conversion behavior. In L. Berkowitz (Ed.), *Advances in Experimental Social Psychology* (Vol. 13, pp. 209–39). New York: Academic Press.

Moscovici, S. (1985). Innovation and minority influence. In S. Moscovici, G. Mugny, & E. Van Avermaet (Eds), *Perspectives on Minority Influence* (pp. 9–51). Cambridge: Cambridge University Press.

Moscovici, S., & Faucheux, C. (1972). Social influence, conformity bias, and the study of active minorities. In L. Berkowitz (Ed.), *Advances in Experimental Social Psychology* (Vol. 6, pp. 149–202). San Diego, CA: Academic Press.

Moscovici, S., & Lage, E. (1976). Studies in social influence III: Majority vs. minority influence in a group. *European Journal of Social Psychology*, **6**, 149–74.

Moscovici, S., & Nemeth, C. (1974). Social influence: II. Minority influence. In C. Nemeth (Ed.), *Social Psychology: Classic and contemporary integrations* (pp. 217–49). Chicago: Rand McNally.

Moscovici, S., & Personnaz, B. (1980). Studies in social influence: V. Minority influence and conversion behavior in a perceptual task. *Journal of Experimental Social Psychology*, **16**, 270–82.

Moskowitz, G. B. (in press). The mediational effects of attributions and information processing in minority social influence. *British Journal of Social Psychology*.

Moskowitz, G. B., & Chaiken, S. (1995). *Extending the attribution analysis of persuasion to minority influence: The case of multiple plausible causes*. Manuscript submitted for publication.

Moskowitz, G. B., & Roman, R. J. (1992). Spontaneous trait inferences as self generated primes: Implications for conscious social judgment. *Journal of Personality and Social Psychology*, **62**, 728–38.

Mugny, G. (1982). *The Power of Minorities*. London: Academic Press.

Mugny, G., & Papastamou, S. (1980). When rigidity does not fail: Individualization and psychologization as resistances to the diffusion of minority innovations. *European Journal of Social Psychology*, **10**, 43–62.

Nemeth, C. J. (1986). Differential contributions of majority and minority influence. *Psychological Review*, **93**, 23–32.

Nemeth, C. J., Swedlund, M., & Kanki, B. (1974). Patterning of the minority's responses and their influence on the majority. *European Journal of Social Psychology*, **4**, 53–64.

Nemeth, C. J., & Wachtler, J. (1974). Creating the perceptions of consistency and confidence: A necessary condition for minority influence. *Sociometry*, **37**, 529–40.

Petty, R. E., & Cacioppo, J. T. (1986). *Communication and Persuasion*. New York: Springer-Verlag.

Petty, R. E., Cacioppo, J. T., & Goldman, R. (1981). Personal involvement as a determinant of argument-based persuasion. *Journal of Personality and Social Psychology*, **41**, 847–55.

Petty, R. E., Cacioppo, J. T., & Kasmer, J. A. (1988). The role of affect in the elaboration likelihood model of persuasion. In L. Donohue, H. E. Sypher, & E. T. Higgins (Eds), *Communication, Social Cognition, and Affect* (pp. 117–46). Hillsdale, NJ: Erlbaum.

Petty, R. E., Schumann, D. W., Richman, S. A., & Strathman, A. J. (1993). Positive mood and persuasion: Different roles for affect under high- and low-elaboration conditions. *Journal of Personality and Social Psychology*, **64**, 5–20.

Schlenker, B. R. (1980). *Impression Management: The self-concept, social identity, and interpersonal relations*. Monterey, CA: Brooks/Cole.

Schwarz, N. (1990). Feelings as information: Informational and motivational functions of affective states. In E. T. Higgins & R. Sorrentino (Eds), *Handbook of Motivation and Cognition: Foundations of social behavior* (Vol. 2, pp. 527–61). New York: Guilford Press.

Schwarz, N., Bless, H., & Bohner, G. (1991). Mood and persuasion: Affective states influence the processing of persuasive communications. In M. P. Zanna (Ed.), *Advances in Experimental Social Psychology* (Vol. 24, pp. 161–99). New York: Academic Press.

Schwarz, N., & Bohner, G. (in press). Feelings and their motivational implications: Moods and the action sequence. In J. Bargh & P. Gollwitzer (Eds), *Action Science: Linking cognition and motivation to behavior*. New York: Guilford Press.

Schwarz, N., & Clore, G. L. (1983). Mood, misattribution, and judgments of well-being: Informative and directive functions of affective states. *Journal of Personality and Social Psychology*, **45**, 513–23.

Schwarz, N., & Clore, G. L. (1988). How do I feel about it? The informative function of affective states. In K. Fiedler & J. Forgas (Eds), *Affect, Cognition, and Social Behavior* (pp. 44–62). Toronto: Hogrefe.

Sinclair, R. C., Mark, M. M., & Clore, G. L. (in press). Mood-related persuasion depends on misattributions. *Social Cognition*.

Strack, F., Schwarz, N., Bless, H., Kübler, A., & Wänke, M. (1993). Awareness of the influence as a determinant of assimilation versus contrast. *European Journal of Social Psychology*, **23**, 53–62.

Tetlock, P. E. (1985). Accountability: The neglected social context of judgment and choice. *Research in Organizational Behavior*, **7**, 297–332.

Thompson, E. P., Roman, R. J., Moskowitz, G. B., Chaiken, S., & Bargh, J. A. (1994). Accuracy motivation attenuates covert priming effects: The systematic reprocessing of social information. *Journal of Personality and Social Psychology*, **66**, 474–89.

68   GERD BOHNER, GORDON B. MOSKOWITZ AND SHELLY CHAIKEN

Treisman, A. M., & Geffen, G. (1967). Selective Attention: Perception or response? *Quarterly Journal of Experimental Psychology*, **19**, 1–17.

Turner, J. C., & Oakes, P. J. (1989). Self-categorization theory and social influence. In P. B. Paulus (Ed.), *Psychology of Group Influence (2nd edn)* (pp. 233–75). Hillsdale, NJ: Erlbaum.

Uleman, J. S., & Moskowitz, G. B. (1994). Unintended effects of goals on unintended inferences. *Journal of Personality and Social Psychology*, **66**, 490–501.

Weiner, B. (1985). 'Spontaneous' causal thinking. *Psychological Bulletin*, **97**, 74–84.

Wood, W., & Eagly, A. H. (1981). Stages in the analysis of persuasive messages: The role of causal attributions and message comprehension. *Journal of Personality and Social Psychology*, **40**, 246–59.

Wood, W., Kallgren, C. A., & Priesler, R. M. (1985). Access to attitude-relevant information in memory as a determinant of persuasion: The role of message attributes. *Journal of Experimental Social Psychology*, **19**, 540–59.

Worth, L. T., & Mackie, D. M. (1987). Cognitive mediation of positive affect in persuasion. *Social Cognition*, **5**, 76–94.

Chapter 3

Evaluating and Extending the Theory of Planned Behaviour

Antony S. R. Manstead
University of Amsterdam
and
Dianne Parker
University of Manchester

ABSTRACT

In this chapter we consider recent theoretical and empirical developments relevant to the theory of planned behaviour, drawing in particular on our own research in the domain of driver behaviour. The issues we focus on are the measurement of perceived control, and in particular the development of a 'belief-based' measure of perceived control; the more general issue of 'direct' versus 'belief-based' measures of constructs within the theory of planned behaviour; the advantages accruing from the addition of measures of personal normative beliefs to the existing model constructs; and the role played by affective beliefs in shaping behavioural intentions. Despite the considerable success of the theory of planned behaviour in predicting intentions and behaviours in a wide variety of behavioural domains, it is argued that significant methodological and theoretical issues remain to be resolved.

EVALUATING THE THEORY OF PLANNED BEHAVIOUR

Overview of the Theory

Ajzen's (1985, 1988, 1991) theory of planned behaviour and its predecessor, the theory of reasoned action (Ajzen & Fishbein, 1980; Fishbein & Ajzen,

European Review of Social Psychology, Volume 6. Edited by Wolfgang Stroebe and Miles Hewstone.
© 1995 John Wiley & Sons Ltd.

1975) have been the most influential and widely used models of the attitude–behaviour relationship during the last 20 years. They are intended to provide a parsimonious explanation of informational and motivational influences on behaviour and thereby to allow for its prediction and understanding. The theory of planned behaviour (TPB) represents an extension of the original theory of reasoned action (TRA) model, designed to enable it to be applied to behaviours not entirely under the volitional control of the individual. In this chapter we focus on the extended model and its performance in comparison to the original reasoned action model, and we pay particular attention to problematic issues concerning the sufficiency of the model and the way in which it is operationalised.

According to the theory of planned behaviour, the immediate determinant of human behaviour is behavioural intention. Theoretically, behaviour may be predicted from intention, providing that two conditions are met. First, both behavioural intention and behaviour must be measured with the same degree of specificity with respect to the target, action, time frame and context of the behaviour concerned. Second, there should be little opportunity for intention to change between the assessment of behavioural intention and the subsequent behavioural measure, which implies that for the purposes of prediction the time interval between the two measures should be kept to a minimum. Intention, in turn, is jointly determined by the individual's evaluations of the consequences of performing the behaviour, by his or her perceptions of normative pressure to perform the behaviour, and by the degree of control the individual perceives that he or she has over successful performance of the behaviour. These three determinants of behavioural intention are known as attitude to behaviour, subjective norm, and perceived behavioural control, respectively. Their relationship to behavioural intention, and thereby to behaviour, is illustrated in Figure 3.1.

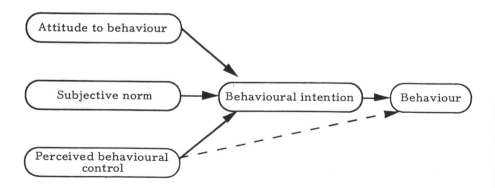

Figure 3.1   The theory of planned behaviour (after Ajzen, 1988)

The model also specifies the determinants of attitude to behaviour, subjective norms, and perceived behavioural control. In the case of attitudes, these determinants are a small set of salient *behavioural beliefs*, i.e., beliefs about the consequences of performing the behaviour, weighted by an evaluation of each of these consequences (*outcome evaluations*). For example, a respondent's score on a behavioural belief item measured on a bipolar *likely–unlikely* scale, scored from +3 to –3, would be multiplied by his or her score on the corresponding outcome evaluation item, measured on a bipolar *good–bad* scale, scored from +3 to –3. A belief-based measure of attitude may be derived from the sum of the products of behavioural beliefs and outcome evaluations. The determinants of subjective norm are said to be a small set of salient *normative beliefs*, i.e., the individual's beliefs about the perceived wishes of each of a number of significant others, weighted by the individual's *motivations to comply* with each of these other people's expectations. Thus a respondent's score on a normative belief item, measured in the same way as the behavioural belief items, would be multiplied by his or her score on the corresponding motivation to comply item, measured on a unipolar *agree–disagree* scale, scored from +1 to +7. A belief-based measure of subjective norm may be derived from the sum of the products of normative beliefs and motivations to comply.

The performance of the basic TRA model has been assessed in two meta-analytic studies. In a widely cited meta-analysis of 87 separate studies, each of which used the theory of reasoned action model, Sheppard, Hartwick, and Warshaw (1988) found a weighted average multiple correlation of 0.66 for the relationship between attitude and subjective norm, on the one hand, and behavioural intention, on the other. The average correlation between behavioural intention and behaviour was 0.53. Van den Putte's (1993) meta-analysis considered the results of 150 independent samples, reported in TRA studies published between 1969 and 1988. The weighted average correlation between attitude and subjective norm, on the one hand, and behavioural intention, on the other, was 0.68, while that between behavioural intention and behaviour was 0.62. The average correlations reported in these meta-analyses confirm that the TRA model has significantly enhanced our ability to predict intentions and behaviour on the basis of attitudes and subjective norms, as compared with the average correlations between attitude and behaviour of about 0.15 found by Wicker (1969) in his influential review.

Ajzen (1991) reviewed a number of studies testing the theory of planned behaviour, in relation to behaviours ranging from searching for a job (van Ryn & Vinokur, 1990) to limiting infant's sugar intake (Beale & Manstead, 1991) and donating a gift (Netemeyer, Andrews, & Durvasula, 1993). In the 16 studies which included measures of attitudes, subjective norms, perceived behavioural control and intentions, the multiple correlations with intentions ranged from 0.43 in the case of intention to participate in an election (Watters, 1989), to 0.94

in the case of intentions to play with video games (Doll & Ajzen, 1992). The average multiple correlation was 0.71. In each study the addition of perceived behavioural control to the regression equation predicting intentions resulted in a significant increase in the total variance explained. The regression coefficients for perceived behavioural control were significant in each study, suggesting that this construct is a reliable and significant independent predictor of behavioural intentions across a wide range of behaviours.

Madden, Ellen, and Ajzen (1992) explicitly compared the theories of reasoned action and planned behaviour across a range of 10 behaviours that had been shown in a pretest to vary with respect to controllability. The behaviours chosen ranged from sleeping and shopping, which were rated as relatively difficult to control, to renting a video and taking vitamins, which were rated as relatively easy to control. The average increase in the multiple correlation resulting from the addition of perceived behavioural control was 0.21 (sd = 0.27), a significant increase. The inclusion of perceived behavioural control also improved the model's performance in the prediction of behaviour, improved the multiple correlations by an average of 0.16 (sd = 0.17). Moreover, perceived behavioural control was shown to be most important in predicting behaviours seen as low in controllability. The correlation between the change in R^2 and the perceived controllability of the behaviour was -0.63, $p<0.05$, supporting Ajzen's contention that perceived behavioural control will be most useful as a predictor of behaviours that are lower in volitional control.

In summary, the addition of perceived behavioural control has been shown to improve the performance of the TRA model, and to extend the range of behaviours to which it can usefully be applied. However, there are several unresolved issues and problems relating to the operationalisation of the enlarged TPB model and its ability to provide a complete account of the factors which lead people to behave in a particular way. The remainder of this chapter will discuss four specific issues arising from own research, in which we applied the theory of planned behaviour to the issue of driving violations. We will begin by summarising the results of that research.

The Theory of Planned Behaviour and Driving Violations

The planned behaviour model was applied in two large-scale interview-based surveys of intentions to commit a wide range of driving violations (Parker *et al.*, 1992; Parker, Manstead, & Stradling, 1995). Before describing the studies in detail, we will comment on the fact that behavioural intention was chosen as the criterion variable in both studies. While a behavioural measure would have been the ideal criterion, there are some obvious practical and ethical problems associated with the observational measurement of driving violations. However, the findings of the meta-analyses cited above suggest that there are grounds for believing that stated driving intentions are predictive of actual driving behaviour. Furthermore, Vogel and Rothengatter (1985) observed a correlation of 0.79 between behavioural intention and reported speeding behaviour, suggesting that the intention–behaviour link is a reasonably strong one in the domain of driving violations. Given that we also have evidence that the self-reported frequency of commission of driving violations is related to accident involvement (Parker et al., in press), and that road accidents are a major cause of death (Department of Transport, 1992), we regarded the prediction and understanding of intentions to commit driving violations as constituting an important and worthwhile object of enquiry in its own right.

In the first study (Parker et al., 1992), 881 respondents were interviewed in order to measure their attitudes, subjective norms and perceived behavioural control with respect to intentions to speed, drink-drive, close follow (i.e., tailgate) and overtake in risky circumstances. In the analyses reported below, the measures of attitudes to behaviour and subjective norms are belief-based, whereas the measure of perceived behavioural control is direct. Although two items were used for the latter measure, the fact that they did not correlate very highly with each other meant that only one item was used to index this construct. Means and standard deviations for all three constructs are shown in Table 3.1. Hierarchical multiple regression analyses regressing intentions on attitudes to behaviour and subjective norm (step 1) and perceived behavioural control (step 2) indicated that the three model predictors together accounted for 23% of the variance in intentions to close follow, 32% of the variance in intentions to overtake in risky circumstances, 42% of the variance in intentions to drink-drive, and 47% of the variance in intentions to exceed the speed limit in a 30-mph zone. Each of the three model predictors had a significant regression coefficient (see Table 3.2) in each of the regression equations. The regression coefficients for perceived behavioural control were negative in each case, which reflects the fact that the behaviours concerned were regarded as socially undesirable: the more control an individual felt he or she had over the behaviour in question, the less likely he or she was to intend to perform that behaviour.

Table 3.1 Means (and standard deviations) for model predictors for four types of driving violation (Study 1)

Driving violations	Attitudes to behaviour	Subjective norm	Perceived behavioural control	Behavioural intentions
Speeding	−6.1 (14.8)	−33.0 (34.4)	0.9 (2.0)	−0.2 (2.1)
Drink-driving	−12.1 (17.7)	−48.0 (33.7)	1.9 (1.8)	−2.2 (1.5)
Close following	−14.1 (14.4)	−49.9 (32.5)	1.4 (1.9)	−2.0 (1.6)
Risky overtaking	−11.6 (15.1)	−44.8 (33.6)	0.7 (2.0)	−1.6 (1.8)

Note: This table summarises findings originally reported in Parker et al. (1992).

Table 3.2 Standardised regression coefficients (beta weights) for model predictors for intention to commit four types of driving violation (Study 1)

Driving violations	Attitudes to behaviour	Subjective norm	Perceived behavioural control	R^2
Speeding	0.13***	0.30***	−0.39***	0.47
Drink-driving	0.08**	0.26***	−0.48***	0.42
Close following	0.06*	0.40***	−0.18***	0.23
Risky overtaking	0.15***	0.33***	−0.27***	0.32

Notes: * = $p < 0.05$; ** = $p < 0.01$; *** = $p < 0.001$. This table summarises findings originally reported in Parker *et al.* (1992).

Thus the results of this study are consistent with other research on the TPB in demonstrating that the addition of perceived behavioural control improves the predictive performance of the original TRA model. However, an improvement in the predictive performance of the model, welcome though it is, is not the ultimate purpose of applying the model to a behaviour domain such as driving. The theoretical utility of the model resides in its ability to enhance our understanding of the factors that determine social behaviour, and thereby to provide a better basis on which to design effective ways of changing behaviour. In the case of perceived behavioural control, knowing that drivers' perceptions of how much control they have over the commission of violations such as speeding enhances the prediction of their intention to speed is only a first step towards understanding the relationships among perceived behavioural control, intention, and behaviour.

In our second study (Parker *et al.*, in press) we were therefore keen to use a multiple-item measure of perceived behavioural control, partly in order to establish that the findings from Study 1 could be replicated using such a measure, but mainly with a view to enhancing our understanding of the components of perceived behavioural control. In this study 598 respondents were interviewed in order to obtain both direct and belief-based measures of perceived behavioural control, in addition to direct and belief-based measures of attitudes to behaviour and subjective norms.

This study was concerned with predicting intentions to commit three violations relating to lane discipline, namely cutting across traffic lanes in order to leave a motorway (i.e., freeway), weaving in and out of lanes of slow-moving traffic in order to make faster progress, and overtaking on the inside lane of a motorway (a manoeuvre prohibited in the UK). It proved to be difficult to generate a reliable index of perceived behavioural norm measured directly. The three items used were as follows: 'My [cutting across the path of the other vehicle] in this way would be (*easy–difficult*)'; 'My refraining from [cutting across the path of the other vehicle] in this way would be (*easy–difficult*); 'It is mainly up to me whether I [cut across the path of the other vehicle] in this way (*agree–disagree*). Analysis showed that responses to these three items did not have acceptable intercorrelations. Responses to the item which required respondents to indicate on a 7-point scale how easy or difficult it would be for them to refrain from committing the violation were used as a direct measure of perceived behavioural control, since in our judgment this item has the highest face validity as a measure of perceived behavioural control. A belief-based measure of perceived behavioural control was also obtained, using a procedure that will be discussed in detail in a later section. The means and standard deviations for the key belief-based constructs are shown in Table 3.3, and the outcomes of the main regression analyses are summarised in Table 3.4. It can be seen from Table 3.4 that the findings were highly consistent with those of our first study. All three TPB constructs contributed significantly to the prediction of intentions to commit each of the three violations involved, thereby providing further evidence in support of the expanded TPB model. Moreover, the beta weights associated with the perceived behavioural control construct are all negative, just as they were in the first study, despite the fact that a direct measure was used in the first study and a belief-based measure was used in the analyses summarised in Table 3.4. Thus one key objective of the present study was achieved, in that the belief-based measure was shown to add significantly to the prediction of intentions to commit each of three driving violations.

Table 3.3 Means (and standard deviations) for model predictors for three types of driving violation (Study 2)

Driving violations	Attitudes to behaviour	Subjective norm	Perceived behavioural control	Behavioural intentions
Cutting in	−12.5 (13.9)	−63.5 (25.6)	49.2 (41.7)	−2.0 (1.5)
Reckless weaving	−13.2 (13.5)	−30.9 (19.8)	43.6 (41.6)	−1.6 (1.8)
Overtaking on inside	−17.5 (12.7)	−70.5 (34.2)	49.9 (44.1)	−2.2 (1.5)

Note: This table summarises findings originally reported in Parker, Manstead, & Stradling (in press).

Table 3.4 Standardised regression coefficients (beta weights) for model predictors for intention to commit three types of driving violation (Study 2)

Driving violations	Attitudes to behaviour	Subjective norm	Perceived behavioural control	R^2
Cutting in	0.16***	0.11*	−0.16***	0.35
Reckless weaving	0.12***	0.07*	−0.19***	0.37
Overtaking on inside	0.06*	0.20***	−0.07*	0.34

Notes: * = $p < 0.05$; *** = $p < 0.001$. This table summarises findings originally reported in Parker, Manstead, & Stradling (in press).

It is clear that the addition of a measure of perceived behavioural control can significantly enhance the predictive utility of the basic TRA model, and that in this respect alone the TPB represents a very worthwhile improvement over its predecessor. What is less clear is the extent to which the addition of this construct has enhanced our understanding of the factors that determine intentions and behaviours. What does it mean to say that a significant portion of variance in behavioural intentions is attributable to perceived behavioural control? Are drivers who report that they intend to commit violations despite having negative attitudes to behaviour and subjective norms simply trying to rationalise or justify their intentions (to themselves and/or to others) when they report that they have low control over the commission of these violations? Or, alternatively, are such drivers accurately reporting those factors that really play a part in shaping their intentions? Although it makes good sense to argue, as Ajzen (1985, 1988) does, that people will only intend to do something if they feel that there is a realistic chance that they can perform that behaviour, settling the issue of whether control perceptions have a causal impact on intentions and behaviours will require the use of either longitudinal or experimental research designs. Until such research is conducted it remains possible that the link between perceived control and intentions observed in studies such as our own reflect the respondent's attempt to rationalise or justify the fact that his or her intention does not follow 'logically' from his or her expressed beliefs. We now turn our attention to some methodological issues in conducting research using the theory of planned behaviour.

Methodological Issues in the Theory of Planned Behaviour

The Measurement of Perceived Behavioural Control

Although there has been some debate over the years concerning the best way to measure, score and combine the items which together comprise belief-based measures of attitude and subjective norm (cf. Evans, 1991; Hewstone & Young, 1988; Sparks, Hedderley, & Shepherd, 1991), the generally accepted method is the one originally advocated by Fishbein and Ajzen (1975; Ajzen & Fishbein, 1980), which involves using bipolar semantic differential scales, and summing the products of each pair of corresponding items. However, because perceived behavioural control was added to the model only relatively recently (Ajzen, 1985, 1988; Ajzen & Madden, 1986) there is as yet no real consensus about the most appropriate way in which to measure this construct on the basis of its underlying beliefs. Perceived behavioural control has typically been operationalised 'directly', by asking respondents how much control they feel they have over the behaviour of interest, or how easy or difficult they feel it would be to perform the behaviour of interest (Madden, Ellen, & Ajzen, 1992). In studies using perceived behavioural control measured in these ways, its addition to the prediction of intention or behaviour has proved useful across a range of behavioural domains (e.g., Ajzen & Driver, 1991, on leisure activities; Ajzen & Madden, 1986, on attending class and achieving an A grade; Beale & Manstead, 1991, on infant feeding; Netemeyer & Burton, 1990, on voting).

As described above, in our own research we experienced some difficulty in developing a reliable direct measure of perceived behavioural control. By the time our second study was being designed Ajzen (1991) had provided more detailed advice on the measurement of perceived behavoural control. He suggested that perceived behavioural control depends on respondents' beliefs about salient control factors, that is their beliefs about the presence or absence of resources, opportunities and obstacles which may facilitate or impede performance of the behaviour. A respondent's rating of the strength of each control factor should be multiplied by his or her rating of their perceived control over each of those factors. The sum of the resulting products provides a belief-based perceived behavioural control score. In this way, respondents' beliefs about resources and opportunities are seen as underpinning their perceived control over the behaviour in question.

A full implementation of this belief-based measure of perceived behavioural control would entail elicitation of salient control beliefs from a representative sample of the target population, so that these could be incorporated into the final questionnaire or interview schedule. Because we were unsure whether respondents would readily be able to nominate control factors influencing their commission of driving violations, and in view of the exploratory nature of this part of the investigation, we decided to generate our own set of eight control beliefs. These referred to both internal and external factors. The control factors included were as follows: in a hurry, in bad weather, in a bad mood, in a good mood, with a passenger, in heavy traffic, in a fast car, and at night.

Arriving at an appropriate format for the control belief items also posed some problems, because it is clear that in the domain of driving a given control factor may be regarded by one respondent as facilitating the commission of a driving violation and by another driver as inhibiting commission of the same violation. An example is the effect of driving at night. While one driver's inclination to speed may be inhibited at night (perhaps through his or her perceived need to exercise more caution when driving in the dark), another's inclination to speed may be facilitated (perhaps because of a sense that his or her speeding behaviour will be less visible to others). Thus the self-same factor, darkness, may inhibit a violation in one driver's eyes, yet facilitate this same violation in the eyes of another driver. The control belief items therefore had to be framed in such a way as to allow the respondent to indicate whether a particular factor facilitated or inhibited his or her own performance of the violation in question. The format of the control items as used in our study was determined following correspondence with Ajzen. The same eight control items were used for all three violations. Respondents were asked to rate both the influence of each factor (on a 7-point scale with endpoints labelled *very much more likely*, scored –3, and *very much less likely*, scored +3, and a midpoint labelled *neither more nor less likely*, scored 0), and the frequency with which they encountered that control factor in the course of their driving (on a 7-point scale with endpoints labelled *never*, scored +1, and *frequently*, scored +7).

The belief-based measure was derived by summing the products of the eight control belief items and the eight corresponding frequency items. The rationale for using frequency ratings was that the more often a facilitating or inhibiting factor is encountered, the more important it should be in contributing to the individual's perceived control over commission of the behaviour in question. Thus a respondent who reports that he or she is very much more likely to weave in and out of traffic at night (–3) and that he or she drives frequently at night (+7) would have had a product of –21, indicating that for this person driving at night is a powerful facilitating factor. On the other hand, a respondent who reports that he or she is very much more likely to weave in and out of traffic at night (–3), but who seldom drives at night (+2) would have a product of –6, indicating that for this driver darkness is a much less important facilitating factor.

The beta weights shown in Table 3.5 compare the predictive utility of direct and belief-based measures of perceived behavioural control, for the three driving violations examined in Study 2. In each case the perceived behavioural control construct was entered into the regression equation after the belief-based measures of attitude and subjective norm. As can be seen, while the belief-based measure yielded significant beta weights, making an independent contribution to the prediction of intentions across all three violations, the beta weights associated with directly measured perceived behavioural control were non-significant in all three cases. It is likely that the fact that the direct measure of perceived control was based on just one item in this study was at least in part responsible for the relatively poor predictive performance of this measure, as compared both with the direct measure used in Study 1 and the belief-based measure used in this study. Nevertheless, the fact that a belief-based measure of perceived behavioural control permits one to pinpoint specific control beliefs, coupled with the fact that such a measure yielded a significant increment in explained variance in intentions, makes it preferable to employ such a measure in future research: there is a potential gain in theoretical understanding with no loss of predictive power. We will return to this issue below, when we consider the comparative utilities of direct and belief-based measures.

Although there are some grounds for thinking that the belief-based measures that we used is preferable to a direct measure, the measurement of

Table 3.5 Standardised regression coefficients (beta weights) for direct and belief-based measures of perceived behavioural control, when entered into regression equation after belief-based measures of attitude and subjective norm (Study 2)

Driving violations	Direct perceived behavioural control	Belief-based perceived behavioural control
Cutting in	−0.01	−0.16***
Reckless weaving	−0.03	−0.19***
Overtaking on inside	−0.02	−0.07*

Notes: * = $p < 0.05$; *** $p < 0.001$. This table summarises findings from a study originally reported in Parker, Manstead, & Stradling (1995).

perceived behavioural control remains an unresolved issue in TPB research. It is still the case that most studies in which an attempt is made to assess perceived behavioural control include only a direct measure. This is probably because early statements of the TPB did not make clear recommendations about the procedures to be followed in measuring perceived behavioural control on the basis of control beliefs. As argued above, in the domain of driver behaviour the perceived power of different control factors to facilitate or inhibit performance can be translated into the frequency with which each control factor is encountered in the course of driving. It remains to be seen whether this operationalisation is equally appropriate in other behavioural domains.

A further issue in operationalising the concept of perceived behavioural control concerns the social desirability of the behaviour under study. In the case of the commission of driving violations, generally regarded as socially undesirable behaviours, a score indicating that a control factor is seen as a *facilitator* by the respondent in question would reflect a *low* level of control over the behaviour, which is typically associated with *greater* intention to enact the behaviour. This much can be seen from the negative beta weights associated with the perceived behavioural control prediction in the regression equations summarised in Tables 3.2 and 3.4. However, this will not necessarily be the case in other behavioural domains. For example, in applying the concept to preventive health care behaviours such as breast cancer screening, scores indicating that relevant control factors are perceived as *inhibiting* respondents from performing the target behaviour, e.g. attendance at a screening clinic, would reflect *low* levels of control over the behaviour, making intention to perform this desirable behaviour *less* likely.

Moreover, in the case of driving violations there is a case for arguing that the person who perceives that he or she is truly in control over the behaviour is the respondent who indicates that the various control factors listed would neither impede nor encourage commission of the violation in question. Such a respondent would score 0 on the scale, indicating that being in a bad mood, for example, would make it neither more nor less likely that he or she would weave in and out of traffic recklessly. It would be perfectly reasonable to argue that respondents who report that they would be unaffected either way by the contextual factors indicated are the ones who believe that they are truly in control of their driving. However, this approach to the interpretation of control belief responses may not be equally applicable to other behavioural domains.

In summary, the results of our two studies show that the perceived behavioural control construct is clearly an important addition to the model in the domain of driver behaviour. However, careful thought needs to be given to the question of how it should be measured. We have shown that a belief-based measure that sums the products of control beliefs and perceived frequency of encounter can result in a significant increment in predictive utility. Only when a similar measurement strategy has been used successfully in further research, addressing other behavioural domains, will there be sufficient evidence on which to base conclusions concerning the most appropriate method of measurement. Issues such as the way in which modal control beliefs should be elicited and how control belief items should be phrased also require further research.

The Use of Direct versus Belief-Based Measures

A related issue concerns the fact that where TPB constructs have been measured both directly and indirectly, the correlations between the two measures are typically rather modest, as noted by Ajzen (1991). He suggested that the reason for this may lie partly in the fact that responding to a direct question evokes a relatively automatic response, whereas more careful deliberation is required in order to respond to the individual belief and evaluation items. Some support for this contention was found in a study conducted by Ellen and Madden (1990), using the theory of reasoned action. They manipulated the degree of concentration required of respondents in two ways. First, they presented the questionnaire items organised either by behaviour (low concentration condition) or randomly (high concentration condition); second, they used either a paper-and-pencil questionnaire (low concentration condition) or a computer-administered format (high concentration condition). It was found that the prediction of intentions from attitudes and subjective norms was better under conditions assumed to require more concentration and presumably more deliberation (random ordering of items, computer-administered format) than in the other conditions, although it should be noted that concentration and deliberation were not directly measured. Thus one possible reason for the low correlations between direct and belief-based measures of constructs in the theory of planned behaviour is that subjects deliberate more carefully when answering the belief-based measures, resulting in the latter having higher predictive validity.

This does not necessarily imply, however, that attitudinal measures based on more conscious and careful deliberation will correlate more highly with behaviour than will attitudinal measures based on more 'automatic' evaluative responses to the attitude object (in this case, behaviour). This much has been demonstrated in research by Wilson on what he calls *cognitivisation*. In a series of studies, Wilson and his colleagues (Wilson & Dunn, 1986; Wilson *et al.*, 1984; Wilson *et al.*, 1989) have shown that attitudes expressed after subjects were asked to think carefully about the reasons for their attitudes were less predictive of subsequent behaviour than were attitudes expressed without such a prior requirement to think about the reasons for the attitudes. Thus although Wilson's research is consistent with the finding that direct and belief-based measures of attitude are not always highly correlated with each other (if one accepts the view that the measurement of beliefs and evaluations broadly corresponds to the cognitivisation of attitudes), it does not point to the conclusion that belief-based measures of attitude will be more predictive of behavioural intentions and behaviour.

Fazio's (e.g., 1986, 1990) research on attitude accessibility is also relevant to this issue. He argues that a crucial determinant of the strength of the attitude–behaviour relationship is the ease with which atitudes are accessed from memory, which in turn is determined by the extent to which attitudes are based on direct experience with the attitude object. The rationale is that the more accessible the attitude, the more likely it is to be activated on exposure to the attitude object or cues related to the attitude object. Furthermore, attitudes that are highly accessible will be automatically activated in the presence of the attitude object, without conscious cognitive processing. If attitudes that are more accessible are more likely to direct behaviour, and if accessible attitudes are ones that are automatically accessed on presentation of the attitude object, it may be that direct measures of attitude capture such spontaneous evaluative reactions better than do more 'deliberative' measures based on beliefs and evaluations. As with Wilson's research, Fazio's theorising points to some reasons why belief-based and direct measures are differentially related to intentions (and therefore behaviour) and, like Wilson's findings, Fazio's research suggests that belief-based measures of attitudes may be less predictive of intentions and behaviour than are direct measures. Important caveats to note in this connection are that the research programmes of Wilson and of Fazio are concerned with attitudes to objects, rather than attitudes to behaviour, and that they focus on an attitude–behaviour relationship unmediated by intentions (since questions about intentions presumably elicit the very deliberative processes that automatic activation of attitudes presumably shortcuts). As a result there is some doubt about the degree to which one can simply generalise from their research to the TPB.

We were able to address this issue of the relationship between direct and belief-based measures in our second study (Parker, Manstead, & Stradling, 1995), since we took both direct and belief-based measures of all three key constructs in the TPB. The correlations between direct and belief-based measures are reported in Table 3.6. It is evident that the correlations between direct and belief-based measures vary as a function of which construct and which behaviour is being measured. The correlations involving the assessment of perceived behavioural control were consistently low. As we have already seen (Table 3.5), the direct and belief-based measures of perceived behavioural control performed differently in the prediction of intentions to commit each of three driving violations. It is interesting to consider why this should be the case. One possibility, as mentioned earlier, is that the poorer predictive performance of the direct measure simply reflects its lower reliability. However, we are inclined to think that there are more than measurement issues at stake here. How well a direct measure of perceived behavioural control captures the essence of the underlying construct will depend to an important extent on the individual's awareness of his or her control perceptions. It may be that respondent's perceived control can be more effectively measured via the component control beliefs, insofar as they have greater awareness of the facilitating or inhibitory roles played by specific factors than of their overall sense of control over the behaviour in question.[1]

The correlations between direct and belief-based measures of attitude were also relatively low, at least for the 'cutting in' and 'overtaking on the inside' violations. This may be due to the fact that the two sorts of measure capture different underlying processes, with the direct measure reflecting automatic reactions to the behaviour, and the belief-based measures tapping a more deliberative reaction. The correlations *among* the directly measured constructs and those *among* the belief-based constructs are compared in Tables 3.7–3.9. It is evident that the correlations among the belief-based constructs (shown above the diagonal in Tables 3.7–3.9) tended to be lower than those among the directly measured constructs. In particular, the correlations between the belief-based measures of attitude to behaviour and subjective norm, on the one hand, and behavioural intentions, on the other, were consis-

Table 3.6 Correlations between direct and belief-based measures (Study 2)

Driving violations	Attitudes to behaviour	Subjective norm	Perceived behavioural control
Cutting in	0.35	0.56	0.30
Reckless weaving	0.52	0.45	0.33
Overtaking on inside	0.37	0.56	0.21

Notes: All correlations significant ($p < 0.001$). This table summarises findings originally reported in Parker, Manstead, & Stradling (1995).

---

[1] This possibility was suggested to us by Bas Verplanken.

tently lower than were the equivalent correlations involving the direct measures, despite the fact that the belief-based indices of attitudes to behaviour and subjective norms were based on a larger number of items (12 in each case) than were the direct measures (four and two items, respectively). Thus measurement error would have been lower for the belief-based indices; and yet these were the ones which correlated less strongly with behavioural intentions.

One explanation for the weaker correlations between belief-based measures and intentions and/or behaviour is that the procedures used by investigators to identify which beliefs should be included in such measures somehow fail to capture all the beliefs that in practice underlie constructs such as attitudes to behaviour and subjective norms. This issue will be taken up below in the section on affective versus instrumental beliefs. Another explanation would draw on Wilson *et al.*'s (1989) notion of cognitivisation, or on Fazio's (1986, 1990) notion of attitude accessibility, as discussed earlier, although such an account is not of course mutually exclusive with the 'failure to capture all relevant beliefs explanation', just discussed.

Table 3.7 Zero-order correlations among theory components: Cutting in (Study 2)

Measure	Attitudes to behaviour	Subjective norms	Perceived behavioural control	Behavioural intentions
Attitudes to behaviour	—	0.33	−0.24	0.44
Subjective norms	0.56	—	−0.23	0.42
Perceived behavioural control	−0.30	−0.34	—	−0.39
Behavioural intentions	0.50	0.54	−0.40	—

Notes: All correlations significant ($p < 0.01$). Coefficients above the diagonal relate to *belief-based components*, those below the diagonal to *directly measured* constructs. This table summarises findings originally reported in Parker, Manstead, & Stradling (1995).

Table 3.8 Zero-order correlations among theory components: Reckless weaving (Study 2)

Measure	Attitudes to behaviour	Subjective norms	Perceived behavioural control	Behavioural intentions
Attitudes to behaviour	—	0.37	−0.34	0.50
Subjective norms	0.61	—	−0.20	0.35
Perceived behavioural control	−0.28	−0.27	—	−0.46
Behavioural intentions	0.62	0.54	−0.35	—

Notes: All correlations significant ($p < 0.01$). Coefficients above the diagonal relate to *belief-based components*, those below the diagonal to *directly measured* constructs. This table summarises findings originally reported in Parker, Manstead, & Stradling (1995).

Table 3.9 Zero-order correlations among theory components: Overtaking on the inside (Study 2)

Measure	Attitudes to behaviour	Subjective norm	Perceived behavioural control	Behavioural intentions
Attitudes to behaviour	—	0.38	−0.19	0.40
Subjective norms	0.56	—	−0.17	0.51
Perceived behavioural control	−0.36	−0.32	—	−0.29
Behavioural intentions	0.56	0.53	−0.38	—

Notes: All correlations significant ($p < 0.01$). Coefficients above the diagonal relate to *belief-based components*, those below the diagonal to *directly measured* constructs. This table summarises findings originally reported in Parker, Manstead, & Stradling (1995).

It is tempting to conclude on the basis of the foregoing that directly measured constructs of attitudes to behaviour and subjective norms are preferable to belief-based ones. However, only using direct measures necessarily limits the applicability of the findings to any subsequent attempts at interventions. Knowing the global attitude to behaviour and the general subjective norm does not provide any guidance concerning how best to modify these constructs. By contrast, knowing the beliefs and associated variables on which these constructs are based indicates where social influence attempts should be targeted.

These findings raise another issue of some importance to the way in which the TPB is evaluated via empirical research. If direct measures of the constructs specified by the theory of planned behaviour are generally more strongly associated with the behavioural intentions and behaviour than are belief-based measures, tests of the sufficiency of the model (i.e., the extent to which the influence of any other factors on intentions and behaviour is statistically redundant) need to be conducted with some caution. Belief-based measures may allow more scope for variables external to the theory of planned behaviour to exert an impact on intentions and behaviour. It therefore seems advisable to test the extent to which such external variables add to the variance accounted for by the constructs within the model by using both direct and belief-based measures of these constructs.

EXTENDING THE THEORY OF PLANNED BEHAVIOUR

Introduction

One of the central tenets of the TRA and the TPB has been the claim that these models are 'sufficient', in the sense that variables external to the model fail to account for variance in intentions of behaviour, once the effects of attitudes to behaviour, subjective norms and (in the case of the TTB) perceived behavioural control have been taken into account. Over the years there have been a number of attempts to challenge this claim of sufficiency, and these are admirably summarised by Eagly and Chaiken (1993, pp. 177–93). It is not our objective here to review each of these challenges. Instead we will review two groups of constructs which do not fall within the TRA/TPB model components, but which show some promise in accounting for variance in behavioural intentions, over and above what is accounted for by the TPB. The two constructs concerned are what we will refer to as (1) 'personal norms' and (2) 'affective evaluations of behaviour'.

What these two constructs have in common is that they depart from the rational, cost–benefit analysis of behavioural choice that lies at the heart of the TRA and TPB. The Fishbein–Ajzen approach is rooted in expectancy-value models of attitudes and decision-making. In the belief-based measure of attitudes to behaviour, behavioural beliefs represent 'expectancies' and outcome evaluations represent 'values'; likewise, in the belief-based measure of subjective norms, normative beliefs represent 'expectancies' and motivations to comply represent 'values'. The underlying logic is that the intention to behave in a certain way depends on the expected utilities (personal and social) of the action in question. Such an approach does not easily embrace beliefs that are not directly related to the immediate costs and benefits of the behaviour. While in principle all conceivable outcomes of a behaviour could be included under the headings 'behavioural beliefs' and 'normative beliefs', in practice the kinds of beliefs that Fishbein and Ajzen had in mind in developing these constructs is revealed by the questions recommended for use in pilot research in order to elicit the beliefs that would be salient for subjects. In the case of behavioural beliefs, pilot subjects are asked about the 'advantages' and 'disadvantages' of behaving in a specified way; in the case of normative beliefs, pilot subjects are asked about people who might 'approve' or 'disapprove' if the subject acted in that way. Personal beliefs about the inherent rightness or wrongness of behaving in a certain way, founded on more abstract principles than short-term advantages or disadvantages or immediate social approval or disapproval, may not be adequately represented within the TRA/TPB framework. Associated with such personal beliefs might be anticipated affective reactions to having behaved in a certain way, such that the individual would expect to feel pleasant or unpleasant affective reactions if the behaviour in question had been executed. Together, beliefs about moral norms and anticipated affective reactions can be seen as representing 'personal norms' regarding the behaviour in question. There is a second group of affective responses to behaviour that is conceptually distinct from those just discussed, in that they concern the affects that the individual expects to experience while performing the behaviour in question, such as the 'thrill' that a driver might expect to experience while driving in a risky fashion (as opposed to the guilt that he or she expects to experience having driven in that way). We will refer to these as affective evaluations. Both types of anticipated affect might help to shape intentions and behaviour without being adequately captured by TRA/TPB model constructs.

Personal Norms

In the current formulation of the TPB no special account is taken of the individual's personal beliefs about what it is right and wrong to do. The distinction between personal and social normative beliefs, dropped from the earliest version of the TRA, has continued to find favour with other researchers, particularly with reference to behaviours that have a clear moral component (e.g., Gorsuch & Ortberg, 1983; Pomazal & Jaccard, 1976; Schwartz & Tessler, 1972; Zuckerman & Reis, 1978).

Ajzen has recently reconsidered the usefulness of measures of personal norms. In a study examining predictors of cheating on a test, shoplifting and lying, Beck and Ajzen (1991) used a three-item measure of perceived moral obligation to refrain from performance of the behaviour, in addition to measures of the three constructs of the theory of planned behaviour. It was found that entering the index of perceived moral obligation into the regression equation after the TPB constructs significantly increased the amount of variance explained by between 3% and 6%. Similarly, Boyd and Wandersman (1991), in a study of condom use by undergraduates, found that a single item measuring the respondent's sense of moral responsibility to use a condom significantly increased the explanatory power of the theory of reasoned action model.

The concept of anticipated regret is distinct from, but related to, moral norm. The concept was first used in regret theory (Loomes & Sugden, 1982, 1984), one of several challenges to classical expected utility theory which have emerged in economics in recent years. Regret theory has been used by researchers seeking to explain the failure of utility theories to predict accurately decisions made under conditions of uncertainty, and is concerned with the psychological and affective consequences of making decisions. In conventional expected utility theories the consequences of each possible decision are evaluated independently. In contrast, regret theorists postulate that the utility associated with any possible outcome depends crucially on the value attached to the rejected alternatives. The theory holds that the comparison of the chosen alternative with other possible decisions will result in either regret or rejoicing. Decision makers are familiar with this phenomenon, and so take such feelings into account when making a decision (Josephs et al., 1992). The underlying assumptions is that people are motivated to avoid feeling regretful, and there is empirical support for the contention that people will attempt to avoid regret even if it means losing a measure of financial return (Bell, 1982).

In social psychology anticipated regret has also been shown to be an important predictor of behavioural expectations in the context of sexual and contraceptive behaviour (Richard, 1994; Richard, van der Pligt, & de Vries, 1995). Used in this way, anticipated regret can be seen as reflecting the anticipated affective consequences of breaking internalised moral rules. In formulating an intention to commit a driving violation, we might reasonably expect issues of the morality of such behaviour to be taken into consideration. Therefore, we (Parker, Manstead, & Stradling, 1995) investigated the usefulness of moral norm and anticipated regret as additions to the TPB. To our knowledge, no other research has examined the joint utility of moral norm and anticipated regret in enhancing the prediction of behavioural intentions.

To assess the role played by moral norms and anticipated regret in the formation of an intention to commit a driving violation, we added three measures to the standard battery of TPB measures. Moral norm was assessed by the single item: 'It would be quite wrong for me to cut across the path of the other vehicle in this way' (strongly agree–strongly disagree). Anticipated regret was measured by two items: 'Having cut across the path of the other vehicle would make me feel very sorry for doing it' (strongly likely–strongly unlikely), and 'My cutting across the path of the other vehicle would make me feel good' (strongly likely–strongly unlikely). The latter two items were combined (after reverse-scoring the second item) to form a single index of anticipated regret.

The addition of measures of these two variables improved the predictive performance of the model by substantial amounts, ranging from 10.6% in the case of 'cutting in', to 15.3% in the case of 'overtaking on the inside'.[2] As shown in Table 3.10, the beta weights for moral norm were positive for all three violations, indicating that the more respondents felt that it would be inherently wrong to commit a driving violation, the less likely they were to report intending to do so. The beta weights for anticipated regret were all negative, suggesting that the more that respondents anticipated feeling regret if they were to commit a driving violation, the less likely they were to report intentions to do so. Thus the predictive power of the model was significantly increased by the addition of the two predictors of personal or moral norm, in the case of each of the three driving violations. Together with the results of Beck and Ajzen's (1991) study, these findings illustrate the importance of internalised notions of right and wrong in the formation of attitudes towards the commision of antisocial behaviours, such as driving violations, which are actually or potentially the subject of public opprobrium. The importance of personal moral norms may also give a clue as to how the problem of irresponsible driving could be tackled in the future, for example by fostering among pre-drivers the development of a stronger sense of the immorality of careless driving.

---

[2] Although the figures given here relate to analyses using belief-based measures of the TPB constructs, moral norm and anticipated regret also added significantly to the amount of explained variance when direct measures were used.

Table 3.10 Standardised regression coefficients (beta weights) for additional predictors (Study 2)

Measure	Cutting in	Reckless weaving	Overtaking on inside
Moral norm	0.27	0.33	0.34
Anticipated regret	−0.18	−0.15	−0.22

Notes: All coefficients significant ($p < 0.001$). This table summarises findings originally reported in Parker, Manstead, & Stradling (1995).

It is interesting to note that with the addition of measures of personal norm to the TPB the diffreence between this model and the Triandis (1977) model of attitude–behaviour relations further narrows. Triandis' model has attracted considerably less attention than the TRA/TPB model (for exceptions, see Boyd & Wandersman, 1991; Jaccard & Davidson, 1975; Valois, Desharnais, & Godin, 1988). The addition of perceived behavioural control to the basic TRA model already enhanced its similarity to Triandis' model, which includes under the umbrella term 'facilitating conditions' notions of perceived control and self-efficacy, thereby anticipating concern with volitional control over performance. Triandis' model also incorporates *affect towards the behaviour* as a theoretical construct, which could be regarded as potentially including the notions of *anticipated regret* and *affective evaluations* (see below). Furthermore, Triandis' model includes the concept of *personal normative beliefs*, which is typically operationalised as *moral obligation*, and therefore has strong similarities to *moral norm* as measured in our own research.

Affective Evaluations and Behavioural Beliefs

As we have seen when considering the notion of anticipated regret, there is some reason to believe that the role played by affective factors in determining intentions and behaviours has been underestimated in research using the TRA or TPB. In common with many other social-cognitive models, the TRA/TPB does not pay much attention to affective processes. Thus the theory assumes that the decision to behave in a given way is based primarily on a rational assessment of salient information, and makes no distinction between the feelings one has concerning a behaviour and one's evaluations of the costs and benefits of performing that behaviour. Outside the realm of attitude–behaviour research, it has been argued and demonstrated that affective reactions to attitude objects have an influence on attitude formation that is to some degree independent of the influence exerted by beliefs about the attributes of that object. Although this argument is not without controversy (see Eagly & Chaiken, 1993, pp. 10–17), there is in our view sufficient evidence to be able to conclude that under certain conditions measures of evaluative response based on affective reactions to an attitude object are empirically distinguishable from measures of evaluative response based on beliefs about that attitude object (e.g., Breckler & Wiggins, 1989; Eagly, Mladinic, & Otto, 1994; Pfister & Bohm, 1992). If affective and cognitive measures of attitudes towards objects are empirically as well as conceptually distinguishable, there seems no reason to assume that the same would not be true of attitudes to behaviour.

We will use the term 'affective evaluations of behaviour' to refer to an individual's positive or negative feelings about his or her performance of that behaviour. In the context of driver behaviour an example would be 'Driving very fast is exciting'. In contrast the behavioural beliefs typically tapped by a TRA/TPB questionnaire concern the individual's assessments of the costs and benefits entailed in performance (e.g., 'Driving very fast increases the likelihood of having an accident'). The usefulness of this distinction between affective evaluations and behavioural beliefs was assessed in relation to the theory of planned behaviour by Ajzen and Driver (1991), in a study of five leisure activities. Although the convergent and discriminative validities of the measures of affective evaluations and behavioural beliefs were established, using the two measures separately did not result in a significant improvement in the prediction of behavioural intentions. When an overall attitude measure was used, a multiple correlation of 0.85 was obtained; when the subscales measuring affective evaluations and behavioural beliefs were entered into the regression equation separately, the resulting multiple correlation coefficient was 0.86.

Despite this evidence, it seems intuitively reasonable to distinguish between the feelings engendered by speeding and the perceived costs and benefits arising from speeding, and it also seems likely that drivers vary with respect to the relative importance of affective evaluations versus behavioural beliefs in the formation of attitudes towards the commission of driving violations. In order to explore this issue further, it is necessary to change the way in which modal behavioural beliefs are identified in TPB research. The normal method used to identify modal salient beliefs about a given behaviour at the pilot stage involves asking a sample of people from the population of interest what they see as the advantages and disadvantages of behaving that way. This type of question lends itself to a relatively dispassionate and thoughtful consideration of the consequences of the behaviour. In the two large-scale pilot studies we carried out in preparation for our own TPB studies (Parker et al., 1992; Parker, Manstead, & Stradling, 1995), this form of questioning only gave rise to instrumental outcomes of the type usually used to assess behavioural beliefs.

In preparation for further TPB research on driving violations, participants in pilot studies were therefore specifically prompted for their affective evaluations of committing various driving violations, such as speeding in different physical contexts, flashing lights at the vehicle in front in order to persuade it to travel faster, and deliberately driving through a traffic light that has just turned to red. In order to determine positive affective evaluations, they were asked 'What do you like/enjoy about [speeding]?'. Negative affective evaluations were elicited by asking 'What do you dislike/hate about [speeding]?'. The data derived from these pilot studies suggest that behavioural beliefs about and affective evaluations of speeding can be distinguished, in that the responses to the affective evaluation items did not overlap at all with the behavioural beliefs derived from the more usual questions, which asked about the perceived advantages and disadvantages of speeding. When asked what they liked or disliked about speeding, respondents variously indicated that speeding made them feel exhilarated, or nervous, or powerful, or frightened, and so on. When asked the 'standard' questions about the advantages and disadvantages of speeding, respondents indicated that speeding reduces journey times, can cause an accident, might result in being stopped by the police, and so on. These responses were used to devise items tapping affective as well as behavioural outcomes of the different violations concerned, together with corresponding measures of evaluations of these outcomes. These items have been incorporated into the interview schedules used in two further studies, one concerned with 'flashing (head)lights' and 'shooting (traffic) lights', the other with speeding on different types of road.

Analysis of the results of this research is still in progress, but it is already clear that measures of attitudes to driving violations based on affective evaluations are far from perfectly correlated with attitudes to the same violations based on behavioural beliefs weighted by outcome evaluations. For example, an affective measure of attitudes to the 'flashing lights' violation correlates only 0.29 with a typical belief-based measure, while the corresponding correlation for the 'shooting lights' violation is 0.14. To the extent that affectively-based and cognitively-based measures of attitudes to behaviour are only modestly correlated with each other, it is possible that they will be differentially related to intentions and behaviours, and that the inclusion of affective evaluations, alongside the more usual belief-based measures of attitudes to behaviour, will result in significant improvements in the ability of the TPB to predict intentions to commit driving violations. It remains to be seen whether the findings bear out these conjectures and, if they do, whether similar findings can be obtained in other behavioural domains. To the extent that the affective evaluations–behavioural beliefs distinction proves to enhance the predictive utility of the TPB, several interesting questions will arise. For example, are some types of intentions and behaviours shaped more powerfully by affective than by instrumental considerations? Or are some types of individuals' intentions and behaviours shaped more powerfully by affective than by instrumental considerations? Addressing questions such as these should help to develop the TPB beyond its current status as an effective but unduly rational model of social behaviour.

SUMMARY AND CONCLUSIONS

In this chapter we have considered recent theoretical and empirical developments relevant to the theory of planned behaviour, drawing mainly on our own research in the domain of driver behaviour. We first evaluated the model, focusing initially on the extent to which the addition of the construct of perceived behavioural control to the basic theory of reasoned action model enjoys empirical support. Both previous research and our own work provides ample evidence of the superior predictive utility of the TPB model over the TRA model. However, the psychological significance of the role played by perceived behavioural control in shaping intentions and behaviours remains unclear. Taken at face value, the research findings support Ajzen's contention that intentions to perform a behaviour will (unless the behaviour is highly controllable) be determined partly by the individual's sense that he or she can perform the behaviour in question. The rationale is that people are unlikely to intend to perform behaviours over which they think they have no control. However, the correlational nature of the research evidence leaves it open to an alternative interpretation, namely that measures of perceived behavioural control enable respondents to rationalise or justify, either to themselves or to others, sensed inconsistencies between their beliefs and their intentions. Ruling out this alternative explanation will require longitudinal and/or experimental research designs. We continued our evaluation of the theory of planned behaviour by examining methodological problems in conducting TPB research. Two such problems were discussed: the measurement of perceived control; and the use of direct versus belief-based measures of TPB constructs. With regard to the measurement of perceived behavioural control, we focused on issues concerning the development of belief-based measures of this construct and showed that while such a measure does have predictive utility, there is a pressing need for further research on the optimal method of measuring this construct both directly and via control beliefs. The issue of direct versus belief-based measures of TPB constructs was examined both empirically and theoretically. While the relatively modest relationships between these two types of measure can always be 'explained' by arguing that the belief-based measures somehow fail to capture all of the relevant beliefs, it was also contended that there may be theoretical reasons for these weaker-than-expected relationships. Specifically, direct measures of attitudes may be better at reflecting the 'automatic' evaluations of behaviour that have more impact on intentions and behaviours than the 'deliberative' evaluations tapped by belief-based measures. Conversely, belief-based measures of perceived behavioural control may be better able than direct measures to assess control perceptions, insofar as respondents do not have readily accessible 'stored summaries' of perceived control over behaviour.

Finally, we considered theoretical and empirical grounds for extending the theory of planned behaviour. Two such extensions were considered, one involving 'personal norms' and the other relating to 'affective evaluations'. Personal norms were defined as including moral norms and anticipated regret and it was shown that adding measures of these variables to the standard TPB constructs significantly improves the predictive utility of the model, thereby suggesting that intentions (to commit driving violations, at least, and possibly other behaviours that carry moral implications) are shaped by more than perceptions of the costs and benefits of such behaviour, coupled with perceived social normative pressure. Affective evaluations were defined as beliefs about the affects that would be experienced while enacting the behaviour, weighted by evaluations of those affects, and it was argued that attitudes to behaviour may be determined by these affective evaluations, as well as by the more instrumental considerations normally captured by behavioural beliefs and outcome evaluations. Preliminary evidence suggests that measures of attitudes to behaviour based on affective evaluations are only moderately corrrelated with more traditional measures of attitudes to behaviour, raising the issue of when and why one of these two aspects of attitudes to behaviour will be dominant in determining intentions and behaviour. In short, although the theory of planned behaviour is undoubtedly a very useful model for predicting and understanding social behaviour, there is a great deal of scope for further development of the model.

ACKNOWLEDGEMENT

The authors wish to thank Icek Ajzen, Bas Verplanken, an anonymous reviewer, and the Editors for their helpful comments on an earlier version of this chapter.

REFERENCES

Ajzen, I. (1985). From intentions to actions: A theory of planned behaviour. In J. Kuhl and J. Beckman (Eds), *Action Control: From cognition to behaviour* (pp. 11–39). Berlin: Springer-Verlag.

Ajzen, I. (1988) *Attitudes, Personality and Behaviour*. Milton Keynes: Open University Press.

Ajzen, I. (1991). The theory of planned behavior. *Organizational Behavior and Human Decision Processes*, **50**, 179–211.

Ajzen, I., & Driver, B. E. (1991). Prediction of leisure participation from behavioral, normative, and control beliefs: An application of theory of planned behavior. *Leisure Sciences*, **13**, 185–204.

Ajzen, I., & Fishbein, M. (1980). *Understanding Attitudes and Predicting Social Behavior*. Englewood Cliffs, NJ: Prentice Hall.

Ajzen, I., & Madden, T. J. (1986). Prediction of goal-directed behavior: Attitudes, intentions and perceived behavioral control. *Journal of Experimental Social Psychology*, 22, 453–74.

Beale, D.A., & Manstead, A. S. R. (1991). Predicting mothers' intentions to limit frequency of infants' sugar intake: Testing the theory of planned behaviour. *Journal of Applied Social Psychology*, 21, 409–31.

Beck, L., & Ajzen, I. (1991). Predicting dishonest actions using the theory of planned behavior. *Journal of Research in Personality*, 25, 285–301.

Bell, D. E. (1982). Regret in decision making under uncertainty. *Operations Research*, 30, 961–81.

Boyd, B., & Wandersman, A. (1991). Predicting undergraduate condom use with the Fishbein and Ajzen and the Triandis attitude-behavior models: Implications for public health interventions. *Journal of Applied Social Psychology*, 21, 1810–30.

Breckler, S. J., & Wiggins, E. C. (1989). Affect versus evaluation in the structure of attitudes. *Journal of Experimental Social Psychology*, 25, 253–71.

Department of Transport (1992). *Road Accidents Great Britain: The casualty report.* London: HMSO.

Doll, J., & Ajzen, I. (1992). Accessibility and stability of predictors in the theory of planned behavior. *Journal of Personality and Social Psychology*, 63, 754–65.

Eagly, A. H., & Chaiken, S. (1993). *The Psychology of Attitudes.* Fort Worth, TX: Harcourt Brace Jovanovich.

Eagly, A. H., Mladinic, A., & Otto, S. (1994). Cognitive and affective bases of attitudes toward social groups and social policies. *Journal of Experimental Social Psychology*, 30, 113–37.

Ellen, P. S., & Madden, T. J. (1990). The impact of response format on relations among intentions, attitudes and social norms. *Marketing Letters*, 1, 161–70.

Evans, M. (1991). The problem of analyzing multiplicative composites: Interactions revisited. *American Psychologist*, 46, 6–15.

Fazio, R. H. (1986). How do attitudes guide behavior? In R. M. Sorrentino & E. T. Higgins (Eds), *Handbook of Motivation and Cognition: Foundations of social behavior* (pp. 204–43). New York: Guilford Press.

Fazio, R. H. (1990). Multiple processes by which attitudes guide behavior: The MODE model as an integrative framework. In M. P. Zanna (Ed.), *Advances in Experimental Social Psychology* (Vol. 23, pp. 75–109). San Diego, CA: Academic Press.

Fishbein, M., & Ajzen, I. (1975). *Belief, Attitude, Intention and Behavior: An introduction to theory and research.* Reading, MA: Addison-Wesley.

Gorsuch, R. L., & Ortberg, J. (1983). Moral obligation and attitudes: Their relation to behavioural intentions. *Journal of Personality and Social Psychology*, 44, 1025–8.

Hewstone, M., & Young, L. (1988). Expectancy-value models of attitude: Measurement and combination of evaluations and beliefs. *Journal of Applied Social Psychology*, 18, 958–971.

Jaccard, J. J., & Davidson, A. R. (1975). A comparison of two models of social behavior: Results of a survey sample. *Sociometry*, 38, 497–517.

Josephs, R. A., Larricks, R. P., Steele, C. M., & Nisbett, R. E. (1992). Protecting the self from the negative consequences of risky decisions. *Journal of Personality and Social Psychology*, 62, 26–37.

Loomes, G., & Sugden, R. (1982). Regret theory: An alternative theory of rational choice under uncertainty. *The Economic Journal*, 92, 805–24.

Loomes, G., & Sugden, R. (1984). The importance of what might have been. In O. Hagen and F. Wenstop (Eds), (pp. 219–35). *Progress in Utility and Risk Theory.* London: D. Reidel.

Madden, T. J., Ellen, P. S., & Ajzen, I. (1992). A comparison of the theory of planned behavior and the theory of reasoned action. *Personality and Social Psychology Bulletin*, **18**, 3–9.

Netemeyer, R. G., Andrews, J. C., & Durvasula, S. (1993). A comparison of three behavioral intention models: The case of Valentine's day gift-giving. *Advances in Consumer Research*, **20**, 135–41.

Netemeyer, R. G., & Burton, S. (1990). Examining the relationships between voting behavior, intention, perceived behavioral control, and expectation. *Journal of Applied Social Psychology*, **20**, 661–80.

Parker, D., Manstead, A. S. R., & Stradling, S. G. (1995). Extending the theory of planned behaviour: The role of personal norm. *British Journal of Social Psychology*, **34**, 127–37.

Parker, D., Manstead, A. S. R., Stradling, S. G., Reason, J. T., & Baxter, J. S. (1992). Intentions to commit driving violations: An application of the theory of planned behaviour. *Journal of Applied Psychology*, **77**, 94–101.

Parker, D., Reason, J. T., Manstead, A. S. R., & Stradling, S. G. (in press). Driving errors, driving violations, and accident involvement. *Ergonomics*.

Pfister, H., & Bohm, G. (1992). The function of concrete emotions in rational decision making. *Acta Psychologica*, **80**, 105–16.

Pomazal, R. J., & Jaccard, J. J. (1976). An informational approach to altruistic behaviour. *Journal of Personality and Social Psychology*, **33**, 317–26.

Richard, R. (1994). *Regreat is what you get: The impact of anticipated feelings and emotions on human behaviour.* Unpublished doctoral dissertation, University of Amsterdam.

Richard, R., van der Pligt, J., & de Vries, N. (1995). Anticipated affect and behavioural choice. *British Journal of Social Psychology*.

Schwartz, S. H., & Tessler, R. C. (1972). A test of a model for reducing measured attitude–behavior inconsistencies. *Journal of Personality and Social Psychology*, **24**, 225–36.

Sheppard, B. H., Hartwick, J., & Warshaw, P. R. (1988). The theory of reasoned action: A meta-analysis of past research with recommendations for modifications and future research. *Journal of Consumer Research*, **15**, 325–43.

Sparks, P., Hedderley, D., & Shepherd, R. C. (1991). Expectancy-value models of attitudes: A note on the relationship between theory and methodology. *European Journal of Social Psychology*, **21**, 261–71.

Triandis, H. C. (1977). *Interpersonal Behavior.* Monterey, CA: Brooks/Cole.

Valois, P., Desharnais, R., & Godin, G. (1988). A comparison of the Fishbein and Ajzen and Triandis models for the prediction of exercise intention and behavior. *Journal of Behavioural Medicine*, **11**, 459–72.

Van den Putte, B. (1993). *On the theory of reasoned action.* Unpublished doctoral dissertation. University of Amsterdam, The Netherlands.

van Ryn, M., & Vinokur, A. D. (1990). *The role of experimentally manipulated self-efficacy in determining job-search behavior among the unemployed.* Unpublished manuscript, Institute for Social Research, University of Michigan.

Vogel, R., & Rothengatter, J. A. (1985). *Motieven van snelheidsgedrag op autosnelwegen: Een attitude onderzoek.* [Motives for speeding behaviour on motorways: An attitudinal study]. Report VK 84-09. Traffic Research Centre, University of Groningen, The Netherlands.

Watters, A. E. (1989). *Reasoned/intuitive action: An individual difference moderator of the attitude–behavior relationship in the 1988 U.S. presidential election.* Unpublished master's thesis, Department of Psychology, University of Massachusetts at Amherst.

Wicker, A. W. (1969). Attitudes versus actions: The relationship of verbal and overt behavioral responses to attitude objects. *Journal of Social Issues*, **25**, 41–78.

Wilson, T. D., & Dunn, D. S. (1986). Effects of introspection on attitude–behavior consistency: Analyzing reasons versus focusing on feelings. *Journal of Experimental Social Psychology*, **22**, 249–63.

Wilson, T. D., Dunn, D. S., Bybee, J. A., Hyman, D. B., & Rotondo, J. A. (1984). Effects of analyzing reasons on attitude–behavior consistency. *Journal of Personality and Social Psychology*, **47**, 5–16.

Wilson, T. D., Dunn, D. S., Kraft, D., & Lisle, D. J. (1989). Introspection, attitude change, and attitude–behavior consistency: The disruptive effects of explaining why we feel the way we do. In L. Berkowitz (Ed.), *Advances in Experimental Social Psychology* (Vol. 22, pp. 287–343). San Diego, CA: Academic Press.

Zuckerman, M., & Reis, H. (1978). Comparison of three models for predicting altruistic behavior. *Journal of Personality and Social Psychology*, **36**, 498–510.

Chapter 4

Outcome Frames in Bilateral Negotiation: Resistance to Concession Making and Frame Adoption

Carsten K. W. De Dreu
University of Groningen
Peter J. D. Carnevale
University of Illinois at Urbana-Champaign
Ben J. M. Emans and Evert van de Vliert
University of Groningen

ABSTRACT

This chapter reviews research and theory concerned with outcome frames in negotiation—the negotiator's conception of the dispute as involving gains (gain frame) or losses (loss frame). We argue that because losses are more aversive than equivalent gains are attractive, loss framed negotiators should display greater resistance to concession making and settle less easily than negotiators with a gain frame. A review of frame research supports this argument. Furthermore, we propose that during negotiations, disputants communicate about their frame, and tend to adopt the frame communicated by their opponent. Several experiments are reviewed that show this frame adoption effect to be likely especially when the negotiators themselves have a gain rather than a loss frame. The chapter concludes with a discussion of the importance of outcome frames to the escalation of social conflict.

European Review of Social Psychology, Volume 6. Edited by Wolfgang Stroebe and Miles Hewstone.
© 1995 John Wiley & Sons Ltd.

INTRODUCTION

The stability of international relations, organizational effectiveness, and marital satisfaction all depend on how participants solve their social conflicts. Many conflicts are resolved through negotiation which occurs when two or more individuals try to settle a mutual conflict of interest, and have an incentive to cooperate with each other in an attempt to reach agreement, as well as an incentive to compete with each other in an attempt to obtain the largest share of the joint outcome (Carnevale & Pruitt, 1992; Rubin & Brown, 1975). Whether negotiators tend to cooperate or compete is affected by their subjective representation of the situation, of the issues at stake, and of the outcomes involved (Deutsch, 1973; Kelley & Thibaut, 1978; Neale & Bazerman, 1991). This chapter deals with one such subjective representation, namely the negotiators' *outcome frame*—the negotiators' conception of the dispute as involving gains and profits (gain frame), or as involving losses and costs (loss frame) (cf. Tversky & Kahneman, 1981). For example, if you wish to sell the car you bought for $8,000 two years ago, you can evaluate someone's offer of $3,500 as a gain relative to $0. Conversely, you can evaluate the $3,500 as a $4,500 loss relative to the car's original value of $8,000. Similarly, one can think about labor–management negotiations where a union claims an 8% raise whereas management argues for a 0% raise, both parties may view settlement at 4% as a gain (i.e. more than their opponent's initial position), but also as a loss (i.e. less than their own initial position) (Bazerman, 1983).

Research shows that, in general, negotiators with a gain frame demand less, concede more and settle more easily than those with a loss frame (for reviews, see Carnevale & Pruitt, 1992; Neale & Bazerman, 1991; Thompson, 1990). This chapter is a review of research and theory dealing with these and other effects of outcome frames in bilateral negotiation. Our goal is three-fold. First of all, there is the issue of what explains frame effects in bilateral negotiation. Why do gain framed negotiators demand less, concede more, and settle more easily than loss framed negotiators? Current research and theory tends to rely on either one of two explanatory constructs—loss framed negotiators' heightened risk-tolerance, and loss framed negotiators' heightened concern for own outcomes. We will critically discuss the evidence for each of the two potential explanations, in an attempt to determine whether both are really needed, or whether one or the other suffices. Second, we will discuss the accumulating evidence that negotiator frame and behavior are influenced by information about their opponent's gain or loss frame (De Dreu, Emans, & Van de Vliert, 1992a; Putnam & Holmer, 1992). Third we will delineate the relationship between outcome frames and conflict escalation, and examine the circumstances under which the loss frame leads to more conflict escalation than the gain frame.

NEGOTIATOR FRAMES: DEFINITIONS AND EXPLANATIONS

Negotiation may be conceived of as a complex decision making task (Neale & Bazerman, 1991; Raiffa, 1982), and although some decisions are made after careful scrutiny of the decision alternatives, most are made intuitively and on heuristic bases (cf. Chaiken, Liberman, & Eagly, 1989; Dawes, 1988). Consequently, negotiator judgment and decision making is likely to be affected by rules of thumb, and by simplyfing mental representations. In particular judgments and decisions concerning one's own prospective outcomes may be affected by the negotiator *outcome frame*. As mentioned, the negotiator's outcome frame can be defined as the negotiator's cognitive representation of the potential outcomes associated with the negotiation. Specifically, the outcome frame indicates whether the negotiator views the dispute as positive involving gains and profits (gain frame), or as negative involving losses and costs (loss frame) (Kahneman & Tversky, 1979; Tversky & Kahneman, 1981). Gain framed negotiators then are more or less focused on the maximization of their gains, and they evaluate their own concessions as decreases in their gains. Loss framed negotiators are more or less focused on the minimization of their losses, and they evaluate their own concessions as increases in their losses (Bazerman, 1983; Carnevale & Pruitt, 1992).[1]

Central to the frame concept is the *reference outcome* from which all other potential own negotiation outcomes are described. Negotiators have a gain frame when they rely on a relatively low reference-outcome, so that all possible outcomes are coded positively and evaluated as gains. When, in contrast, a relatively high reference-outcome is taken, possible outcomes will be coded negatively and evaluated as losses. According to Tversky and Kahneman (1981), the reference-outcome is judged neutral. It is supposed to correspond to a level of aspiration, or to a state to which one has adapted. Liebrand and Messick (1993), for example, assumed a person's reference-outcome to be the average of the outcomes of several people close to this particular person. Thus, when a negotiator anticipates outcomes that fall at or above the average

---

[1] The outcome frame is but one variant of a larger class of framing phenomena outlined by Kahneman and Tversky (1979; Tversky & Kahneman, 1981). Other frames relate to probabilities and expectancies as opposed to outcomes, or to the decomposition of the decision process into a coding stage and an evaluation stage. These decision making frames have yet not been exported into negotiation research, and are not discussed any further. However, negotiation research has discovered that in addition to the outcome frame other frames may affect negotiation and conflict management. Pinkley (1990; Pinkley & Northcraft, 1994) observed that disputants tend to frame the conflict in terms of task versus relationship, emotion versus intellect, and cooperative versus win conflicts. In line with Pinkley's cooperative versus win frame, Putnam (1990) distinguishes between integrative and distributive frames. These frames tend to deal primarily with the negotiation process and with the relational aspects of the conflict, and thus complement the outcome frame discussed and reviewed here.

outcome of his or her six colleagues, he or she is predicted to adopt a gain frame; if outcomes fall below the average outcome of his or her six colleague negotiators, he or she is predicted to have a loss frame.[2]

Unlike Prospect Theory (Kahneman & Tversky, 1979), negotiation theory tends to conceive of the level of aspiration as the goal for which one strives (Kelley & Thibaut, 1978; Rubin, Pruitt, & Kim, 1994; Siegel & Fouraker, 1960). This goal may change during negotiation, for example as a function of the opponent's behavior (Siegel & Fouraker, 1960; Yukl, 1974). In this chapter, we assume that the *level of aspiration* as conceived in negotiation theory does not determine the frame, but exists *within the frame*. To put it another way, it is assumed that gain framed negotiators have an aspiration about the amount of gains they attempt to achieve. Loss framed negotiators have an aspiration regarding the amount of loss they attempt to avoid. Likewise, both gain and loss framed negotiators have a *limit*—the minimum gain (or maximum loss) below (or above) which they refuse to concede (Pruitt, 1981). That is, in the example of the $8,000 car you attempt to sell, with either the gain frame ($0 as the reference-outcome) or the loss frame ($8,000 as the reference-outcome), your level of aspiration may be $7,000 (i.e., to gain at least $7,000, or to lose $1,000 at most). Similarly, your limit may be $6,000, or, to put it another way, your limit is a $6,000 gain, or a $2,000 loss.

Explanations of Frame Effects in Negotiation

Although perhaps a dozen different explanations may be put forward, negotiation research tends to rely on either one of two general explanatory constructs—heightened *risk-tolerance* (Bazerman, 1983; Bottom & Studt, 1993; Lax & Sebenius, 1986; Neale & Bazerman, 1991; Olekalns & Frey, 1994), and heightened *concern for outcomes* (Carnevale & Pruitt, 1992; De Dreu et al., 1995; Kahneman, 1992; Ross & Nisbett, 1991). Both explanations assume that framing outcomes as gains or as losses has important implications for the evaluation of prospective outcomes in terms of subjective utility and

---

[2] We assume that negotiators operate on the basis of one reference-outcome, not two or more, and thus adopt either a gain frame or a loss frame (cf. Kahneman & Tversky, 1979). This assumption is inspired by Prospect Theory and parallels similar assumptions made in the domain of schemata (e.g., Fiske & Taylor, 1991). Recent research tends to challenge this assumption by showing that people may use multiple reference-outcomes in judging satisfaction with a particular outcome (Boles & Messick, in press). These studies show that a loss (compared to the status quo) evokes more satisfaction than a gain (compared to the status quo) when a relevant comparison other incurs a greater loss, or a larger gain, respectively. It should be noted, however, that this evidence pertains to *observers* judging how (dis)satisfied an *actor* would be given a particular outcome. That observers use multiple reference-outcomes in evaluating an actor's outcome does not necessarily mean that the actor is doing the same thing. Rather, we expect the actor to rely on one reference-outcome, either the status quo, or the outcome obtained by the relevant comparison other. Further research is needed, however, to settle this issue.

thus for subsequent decision making. How objective outcomes represented as either gains or losses relate to subjective utility is depicted in Figure 4.1, which is based on Kahneman and Tversky's (1979) value function. The value function is part of Prospect Theory, which was developed basically to deal with risky decision making, but which also incorporates important propositions about human behavior when no risk is at stake.

The value function incorporates two variables that may explain the effect of frame on negotiator motivation and behavior. First, frame affects risk-tolerance. This derives from the fact that the value function is *concave* in the case of a gain frame, and *convex* in the case of a loss frame. In other words, the growth in positive (or negative) subjective utility is larger when the increase in gains (or losses) is from $0 to $4,000, than from $4,000 to $8,000. This decreasing sensitivity has an important implication for decision making under uncertainty in general. Imagine that someone faces the choice between a sure $4,000 gain on the one hand, and a fifty–fifty chance on $0 or $8,000 on the other. As can be seen in Figure 4.1, the $4,000 gain yields more positive utility than the sum of 50% on a $0 gain and 50% on a $8,000 gain. To put it another way, the risky option is less attractive than the sure gain. Provided that decision makers attempt to maximize their subjective utility, they will, in the case of a gain frame, choose the certain alternative. Conversely, a certain $4,000 loss yields more negative subjective utility than the sum of 50% on a $0 loss and 50% on a $8,000 loss. Now the risky option is more attractive than the certain loss. The value function thus predicts that in case of a choice between a sure thing and an uncertain alternative *with equivalent expected value*, gain framed decision makers are risk-averse, whereas loss framed decision makers are risk-seeking (for evidence and discussions, see Budescu & Weiss, 1987; Fagley, 1993; Fagley & Miller, 1990; Hershey & Schoemaker, 1980; Kahneman & Tversky, 1979; Schneider, 1992; Schneider & Lopes, 1986; Van der Pligt & Van Schie, 1990).

In addition to risk-tolerance, frame impacts on the concern for own outcomes. Figure 4.1 shows that the value function is steeper for losses than for gains, reflecting the well-documented fact that losses are more aversive than equivalent gains are attractive. Thus, whether a loss or a gain frame is adopted may affect decision making because losses are more aversive than gains are attractive (Budescu & Weiss, 1987; Kahneman & Tversky, 1979; Tversky & Kahneman, 1991). In the realm of union–management negotiations, Ross and Nisbett (1991, p. 64) illustrated this loss–gain asymmetry by noting that 'union militancy was spurred less by promises of gain than by the threat and experience of loss. In particular . . . the most stormy epoch in the history of organized labor, came in the early part of the twentieth century at a time when the influx of jobless immigrants prompted employers to cut wages'. Tversky and Kahneman (1991, p. 1045) argued on the basis of more experimental material that 'a given difference between two options will generally have greater

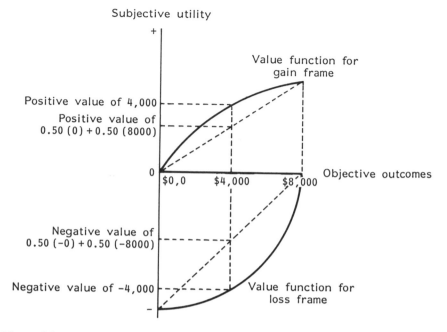

Figure 4.1   An example of the value function based on Prospect Theory

impact when it is evaluated as a difference between two losses . . . than when it is viewed as a difference between two gains'.

This second component of Prospect Theory captures additional differences in the way people deal with losses as opposed to gains, such as the fact that losses are to be avoided whereas gains are attracted. This parallels the fact that negative stimuli such as losses evoke more causal analysis, deeper processing, and more intense emotions (for reviews, see Taylor, 1991; Peeters & Czapinski, 1990). Research indeed shows that compared to prospective gains, prospective losses evoke more 'inner conflict', as exemplified by lower decision speed (De Dreu, Emans, & van de Vliert, 1992a; Dehue, McClintock, & Liebrand, 1993; Smith & Epstein, 1967), higher arousal (Losco & Epstein, 1977), and lower consistency over decision trials (e.g., Schneider, 1992). In line with this, Schneider (1992, p. 1054) argued that 'people have a stronger desire to minimize losses than to maximize gains'.

When its components are taken together, Prospect Theory suggests that the outcome frame may affect decision making in general, and negotiation in particular because the loss frame leads to more tolerance toward risky strategies, and because the loss frame enhances the negotiator's concern for own outcomes. Although both explanations may very well co-exist, there is tendency in the current literature to rely upon either one or the other. In the following sections, we will review the theoretical and empirical issues underlying both explanations, in an attempt, for reasons of parsimony, to determine whether both explanations are needed, or whether one or the other suffices.

Risk-Tolerance Explaining Negotiator Frame Effects

Originally, scholars assumed frame effects in bilateral negotiation to be due to the fact that frame affects risk-tolerance (e.g., Bazerman, 1983; Bazerman, Maggliozzi, & Neale, 1985; Neale & Bazerman, 1985; see also Lax & Sebenius, 1986; Olekalns & Frey, 1994). For example, Bazerman (1983) assumed that negotiation involves decisions between options varying in their degree of uncertainty. He conceived of negotiation as a choice between, for instance, the adversary's current proposal (e.g., $4,000) and the possible outcomes that an arbitration would yield in the case of non-agreement (e.g., a 50/50 chance on $0 or $8,000). Whereas other's current offer is a sure thing, arbitration in case of non-agreement is uncertain: depending on the arbitrator's decision, it either yields higher or lower outcomes than other's offer. On the basis of Prospect Theory's value function, Bazerman (1983) argued that gain framed negotiatiors are more aversive of this risky arbitration and thus of non-agreement than loss framed negotiators. The former consequently demand less, concede more and settle more easily than the latter.

Results of several studies were originally interpreted as supporting this *risk-hypothesis*. In an experimental study of union–management negotiations, Neale and Bazerman (1985) instructed half of their subjects to attempt to maximize their gains, and the other half to attempt to minimize their losses. Subjects were told that in case of non-agreement, arbitration would decide whether the subject's or the opponent's position would be settled upon. Subjects all assuming the role of the management representative thereafter negotiated settlement on vacation pay, medical plan, wages, paid sick days, and night shift differential with a confederate assuming the role of the union representative. The confederates always pursued a reciprocal strategy, that is, they mimicked the subject's negotiation behavior. Subjects were given twenty minutes to reach agreement, and if they failed to settle within this time allotted, they were asked to submit a final offer to the arbitrator. This arbitrator then chose the final offer that represented the greatest overall concession. Results indicated that in case of a gain rather than loss frame, negotiators made larger concessions, resolved a greater number of issues, reported higher perceived fairness of the contract, settled more often, and reported lower perceived level of competition.

Neale and Bazerman concluded that their results supported the risk-hypothesis. They stated 'individuals are more likely to choose a certain outcome—the negotiation settlement—when evaluating the prospects of perceived gains. But when individuals evaluate the prospect of losses, they behave in a more risk-seeking manner—they are more likely to choose the risky option of arbitration rather than to take what appears to be a certain loss' (Neale & Bazerman, 1985, p. 45). Unfortunately, however, this conclusion may have been somewhat premature. It is unclear what exact outcomes and probabilities were associated with the risky arbitration, making it difficult to interpret settlement as risk-aversive behavior. That is, has risky arbitration indeed an expected value equivalent to other's offer, which represented the riskless option? Furthermore, the experimental design did not include a control condition in which no risky arbitration was to be anticipated and, according to the risk-hypothesis, no frame effects should have been found.

Other studies supposedly supporting the risk-hypothesis were conducted by Bazerman, Magliozzi, and Neale (1985), and Neale, Huber, and Northcraft (1987). Subjects in these studies participated in a competitive market negotiation—a room full of buyers and sellers trying to complete as many transactions as possible in the time allotted. One half of them negotiated over net profits regarding such issues as warranty, delivery time, and price (gain frame); the other half bargained over expenses that would cut into their gross outcomes (loss frame) (the objective outcomes were the same in both conditions). Negotiators were allowed to exchange any information they wished, but were not allowed to exchange their issue charts with their opposing party. Hence, parties were basically unaware of each other's frame. In addition, subjects in these studies were told that if they failed to reach agreement with a particular party, their outcome would be a definite zero. Results showed that gain framed negotiators settled more often than loss framed negotiators, and the authors concluded that this supports the risk-hypothesis. For example, the researchers stated that the study 'suggests that positively (gain) framed negotiators will be more risk averse . . . than negatively (loss) framed negotiators' (Bazerman, Magliozzi, & Neale, 1985, p. 298). Aside from uncertainty about finding a new opponent in case of non-agreement, however, negotiators in these studies anticipated absolute certainty about their outcomes in case of non-agreement. That is, they were told they would receive a zero outcome in case of non-agreement. Thus, because there was little or no risk involved, these data seem to violate one of the basic premises of the risk-hypothesis, namely that frame effects occur when uncertainty is associated with non-agreement.

We would argue, therefore, that the empirical evidence for the risk-hypothesis is not yet very convincing. Furthermore, this research relied on an early version of Prospect Theory in its infancy. More recent theoretical developments identified particular problems with, and limitations to Prospect Theory (e.g., Fagley, 1993; Schneider, 1992; Schneider & Lopes, 1986; Tversky & Kahneman, 1991). Relevant to the current discussion is that in order to explain negotiation as risk-seeking/avoiding, all decision alternatives should have equivalent expected value and vary only in their degree of uncertainty

(Lopes, 1987). Often this condition is not met. Also, the risk-hypothesis implies that negotiators should have complete information about both outcomes and associated probabilities, a situation that may be rare in most negotiations. Despite these problems, however, current research still tends to rely upon the risk-hypothesis (e.g., Bottom & Studt, 1993; Olekalns & Frey, 1994). In the next section, we discuss a potential alternative to explain frame effects in bilateral negotiation.

Concern for Own Outcomes Explaining Negotiator Frame Effects

The concurrent and perhaps more parsimonious explanation for frame effects in bilateral negotiation is, as mentioned earlier, based on the robust observation that the negative subjective utility of a loss exceeds the positive subjective utility of an equivalent gain. The implication is that it is more difficult and more painful to incur losses, and to lose resources, than to forgo gains and resources. In line with this, Kahneman (1992) argued that there exists 'concession aversion': The losses incurred by making concessions loom larger than the gains one makes by receiving other's concessions, and therefore, concessions are difficult to make. Research on the Endowment Effect (e.g., Kahneman, Knetsch, & Thaler, 1990; Tversky & Kahneman, 1991) similarly shows that when given the opportunity to trade one's resouces (e.g., a coffee mug, or five dollars) for those of someone else (e.g., five dollars, or a coffee mug), people tend to perceive their own resources as twice as valuable as those of the other party. Thus, people ask for twice as much as they are willing to pay, regardless of what goods are traded. Apparently, losing something one possesses is much harder and more painful than receiving it is pleasant and satisfying.

These arguments can be combined to form a *resistance-hypothesis:* compared to a loss framed negotiator, a gain framed negotiator has lower resistance to concession making, and will therefore demand less, concede more and settle more easily (cf. Carnevale & Pruitt, 1992). Notice that, contrary to the risk-hypothesis, the resistance-hypothesis assumes the negotiator frame to affect the negotiator's concern for own outcomes, and predicts frame effects to occur regardless of the presence or absence of uncertainty in the case of non-agreement. The data originally seen as supporting the risk hypothesis (Bazerman, Magliozzi, & Neale, 1985; Neale, Huber, & Northcraft, 1987; Neale & Bazerman, 1985) may be readily interpreted as confirming this more parsimonious resistance-hypothesis. In addition, the resistance-hypothesis may nicely account for the recent finding (explained by the authors in terms of risk-tolerance) that negotiators with a gain frame are sensitive to being more or less powerful than their opponent, whereas loss framed negotiators are not (Olekalns & Frey, 1994). Since the gain framed negotiators have less internal resistance to concession making, having less power than the opponent leads to much more concession making than having more power. But the loss framed negotiators' high resistance to concession making may counteract to some extent the tendency to yield in case of a disadvantaged bargaining position.

Both the risk-hypothesis and the resistance-hypothesis may be equally valid, and both may co-exist. However, the preceding sections revealed some important shortcomings of the risk hypothesis. The explanation in terms of concern for own outcomes does not appear to suffer from such drawbacks, is more generally applicable (i.e. to situations with and without uncertainty), and appears to be more parsimonious. On top of this, the evidence presented in favor of the risk-hypothesis can be easily understood in terms of the resistance-hypothesis, whereas the reverse is not always true. The pivotal question thus is whether we need the risk-hypothesis to explain effects of outcome frames in bilateral negotiation. In an attempt to answer this question, Carnevale, Gentile, and De Dreu (1993) tested the risk-hypothesis and the resistance-hypothesis simultaneously. Since this experiment used a methodology typically used in our research, we will discuss its methods and procedures in some detail.

Subjects in the Carnevale, Gentile, and De Dreu (1993) experiment were undergraduate students assuming the role of sellers in a buyer–seller negotiation. Each subject was seated in front of a personal computer, connected to a central server. All instructions, the negotiation task, and a post-negotiation questionnaire appeared on the computer screen; responses to questions, written statements to the opposing negotiator, and counter-offers during negotiation all had to be communicated through the keyboard connected to the computer. Subjects were told that they would negotiate with another participant (the buyer), who in fact was simulated by a pre-programmed computer. Subjects then received some task-instructions, including an issue chart listing three issues (discount, delivery time, and financing terms, for a series of home appliances) with eight different settlement levels per issue (i.e., for discount, settlement could be reached on 10% discount, on 15% discount, on 20% discount, and so on). In the gain frame conditions, the issue chart contained positive numbers reflecting one's net profit at a particular settlement level (e.g., settling on a 15% discount resulted in a net profit of 1,800 whereas settling on a 20% discount would result in a net profit of 1,500). The minimum net profit summed over the three issues was 0, the maximum was 8,000. In the loss frame conditions, the issue chart contained negative numbers reflecting costs cutting into one's Gross Outcomes of 8,000. Thus, settling on a 15% discount resulted in a loss of 600, whereas settling on a 20% discount would result in a loss of 900. The maximum loss summed over the three issues was 8,000, the minimum was 0.

To ensure sufficient motivation to negotiate seriously, subjects were told that at the end of the study, their personal earnings from the negotiation would be converted into lottery tickets giving them a chance at winning one of five 20-dollar prizes. After some practice rounds to familiarize themselves with the computer and the task, subjects received a first (quite unattractive) offer from their opponent. Subjects were prompted to make a counter-offer, and, if they wanted, to create and send a written message to their opponent. This procedure continued for a maximum of six rounds. The pre-programmed strategy pursued by the buyer was non-contingent upon the subjects' concession pattern, and also constant over experimental conditions. After six exchanges of offers, the negotiation was interrupted and some questions had to be answered. Hereafter, subjects were debriefed, and thanked for their time.

Carnevale, Gentile, and De Dreu (1993) tested the risk-hypothesis in the following way. Besides outcome frame, they manipulated the absence versus presence of risk by telling the subjects that, in the case of non-agreement, there would be a coin flip yielding a 50/50 chance on $6,000 or $0 (risky condition), or by telling them that in the case of non-agreement, they would get $3,000 for sure (riskless condition). If the risk-hypothesis is valid, that is, if outcome frame affects negotiation because it affects risk-tolerance, outcome frame should have an impact on negotiation behavior only in the risky condition, and not in the riskless condition (where variations in risk-tolerance do not matter). According to the resistance-hypothesis, presence or absence of risk should not matter, and hence outcome frame should impact negotiation irrespective of the presence or absence of risk. This is exactly what was found: negotiators demanded more and conceded less when they had a loss rather than a gain frame, and this effect was not qualified by a two-way interaction between risk and frame. Thus, these data can be well understood in terms of the resistance-hypothesis, and the risk-hypothesis seems to be additional at best.

In addition to this, the Carnevale, Gentile, and De Dreu (1993) study provided rather compelling evidence for the resistance-hypothesis. Besides frame and risk, the experiment manipulated time pressure as a third independent variable. This was done by telling one half of the subjects prior to negotiation that 'you have 21 rounds of negotiation, which is plenty of time to reach agreement' (low time pressure condition), or that 'you have 7 rounds of negotiation, which is very little time to reach agreement' (high time pressure condition). Negotiation research has shown that negotiators with high resistance to concession making, for example due to high levels of aspiration, tend to be less affected by time pressure than negotiators without such strong resistance to making concessions (e.g., Carnevale, O'Connor, & McCusker, 1993; Smith, Pruitt, & Carnevale, 1982; Yukl et al., 1976). Thus, if the resistance-hypothesis for effects of outcome frames is valid, one should expect loss framed negotiators to demand more and to concede less than gain framed negotiators, especially in case of high rather than low time pressure. This is exactly what Carnevale, Gentile, and De Dreu observed. Table 4.1 gives the cell means for negotiator demand and concession making (both averaged over

Table 4.1 Negotiator demand and concessions (averaged across rounds) as a function of time pressure and outcome frame

	Time pressure			
	High		Low	
	Gain frame	Loss frame	Gain frame	Loss frame
Concession	11.37$_a$	9.55$_b$	8.22$_b$	8.15$_b$
Demand	5,443$_a$	6,043$_b$	6,457$_b$	6,315$_b$

Note: For concessions, means could range between 0 and 27, with lower numbers indicating smaller concessions. For demand, means could range between 0 and 8,000, with higher numbers indicating higher demands. Cell means in each row with unequal subscripts are significantly different at $p < 0.05$.
Source: Carnevale, Gentile, and De Dreu (1993).

six rounds of negotiation). As can be seen, the loss frame leads to higher demands and smaller concessions, but especially in case of high time pressure.

Summary and Conclusion

The previous section reviewed the theoretical substance, and the empirical evidence for the two most popular explanations for effects of outcome frames on negotiation—risk-tolerance and concern for outcomes. This review strongly suggests that the older explanation—risk-tolerance—is theoretically problematic, and empirically not well supported. This conclusion is important since some recent research tends to continue to interpret frame effects in negotiation in terms of variations in risk-tolerance (Bottom & Studt, 1993; Olekalns & Frey, 1994). At the same time, our review suggests that the second explanatory construct—concern for outcomes—is theoretically sound and empirically validated. Moreover, concern for outcomes is a more parsimonious construct than risk-tolerance. Finally, concern for outcomes explains the data originally seen as supporting the risk-hypothesis, whereas the reverse is not always the case. In the following sections of this chapter, we therefore assume effects of outcome frames on negotiation to be due to the fact that the loss frame produces higher concern for outcomes than the gain frame.

DYNAMICS OF OUTCOME FRAMES

So far, the discussion focused on the effects of negotiators' own frame on their own motivation and behavior other than verbal communication. As such, there was the implicit assumption that frames are static and do not change easily. However, Bartlett (1932) described frames as dynamic, changing patterns. Donnelon and Gray (1990) postulated that negotiation is a process of framing and reframing the parameters and definition of a dispute. Pinkley and Northcraft (1994, p. 195) further note that, just as past experiences help determine the cognitive frames that opponents bring into the dispute, new experiences during conflict management and negotiation, such as interaction and exchange of information with the opposing party, should also influence the opponent's frame. In the following sections, we argue that one's own outcome frame affects one's own communication, which in turn impacts the other party's frame and behavior, and vice versa. Furthermore, we assume that negotiators may have foreknowledge about their opponent's frame, for example through third-party communications, or through information conveyed in the mass media. Experiments centred around these two sources of frame influence—opponent's frame communication and foreknowledge about other's frame—will be reviewed.

Frame Communication

Negotiators may be motivated to talk about gains and profits, for example in an attempt to induce a more desirable frame in their opponent (cf. Kahneman, 1992; Putnam & Holmer, 1992; Russo & Schoemaker, 1989). Furthermore, there is good evidence that other's cognitions affect one's choice of linguistic labels and verbal categories (Glucksberg, 1988; Markus & Zajonc, 1985). Ross and Nisbett (1991) nicely illustrate how different perspectives on, for example, the issue of abortion are reflected in public statements about these issues ('reproductive freedom' versus 'murder of the fetus'). They furthermore suspect that spokespersons may actively frame issues in a particular way in order to persuade the opposing party, or some neutral bystander.

   In negotiations, matters may be similar, and the outcome frame may affect the way negotiators verbally evaluate outcomes in either gain or loss terms. Thus negotiators may consciously or unconsciously communicate their own gain or loss frame to the other party. The language and cognition literature cited above would suggest the hypothesis that gain framed negotiators more often communicate about gains and profits (e.g., 'this concession really decreases my gains and profits, you know') than about losses and costs (e.g., 'this concession really increases my losses and costs, you know'), whereas loss framed negotiators do the reverse. An experiment by De Dreu and Carnevale (1992, fully reported in De Dreu, 1993) tested this prediction. The study used the previously described computer-paradigm with undergraduate students assuming the role of seller, and supposedly playing against another participant assuming the role of buyer (in fact a standardized computer program). The subject's own frame was induced using the issue-charts manipulation discussed above. Thus, one half of the subjects negotiated over net profits (gain frame), whereas the other half negotiated the costs they would incur in their gross outcomes (loss frame). The opponent sent offers to the subject, but never a verbal message. The subjects, in contrast, could respond with both counter-offers and self-created messages. Analyses of subjects' offers replicated the classical frame effect, with loss framed subjects demanding more and conceding less than gain framed subjects (see also row 1 of Table 4.2).

The messages sent by the subjects were scored for (a) communicated gain frame, when the message contained terms such as 'profits', 'benefits' or 'gains', or (b) communicated loss frame, when the message contained terms like 'expenses', 'costs' or 'losses'. Messages that could not be classified as either communicated gain or loss frame were classified as 'communicated no frame'. No message potentially reflected both a gain and a loss frame (e.g., 'loss in profit'). Furthermore, no subject communicated both a gain and a loss frame in the messages across rounds. Table 4.2 shows the number of subjects who communicated at least once a gain or loss frame as a function of the gain and loss frame conditions. In the gain frame condition, significantly more subjects communicated a gain frame than a loss frame (i.e., 35 and 11). In the loss frame condition, this pattern was reversed. Here, more subjects communicated a loss frame than a gain frame (i.e., 24 and 4).

Frame Adoption

The findings reported above suggest that during negotiation, disputants exchange frame-relevant pieces of information. This is important since people are generally inclined to reciprocate communication styles (Giles & Smith, 1979). Moreover, people tend to converge toward similar definitions of the situation, a phenomenon assumed to be crucial for effective negotiation and reaching settlement (Lewicki & Litterer, 1985; Putnam, Wilson, & Turner,

Table 4.2 Demand (averaged across rounds) and number of subjects communicating a gain frame or a loss frame as a function of outcome frame

	Outcome frame	
	Gain ($N = 119$)	Loss ($N = 106$)
1. Demand	5,498	5,986
2. Communicates gain frame	35	4
3. Communicates loss frame	11	24
4. Communicates no frame content	80	71

Note: For demand, means could range between 0 and 8,000, with higher numbers indicating higher demands. Cell means for demand level are significantly different at $p < 0.05$. Numbers in row 2 through 4 reflect the number of subjects, ranging between 0 and 119 in the gain frame condition, and between 0 and 106 in the loss frame condition.
Source: De Dreu and Carnevale (1992).

1990). More specifically, Donnelon and Gray (1990) argued that negotiators exposed to the dispute interpretation of the other party are likely to alter their own interpretations to incorporate the other disputant's frame. As disputants share information and raise the salience of the issues important to each other, disputants' cognitive frames may become more similar. Pinkley and Northcraft (1994) tested this proposition. Subjects were asked both before and after a negotiation what they thought the dispute was actually about (i.e. their 'conflict frame'). Both the pretest and the post-test measures were categorized on a task–relationship dimension, an emotional–intellectual dimension, and a cooperate–win dimension. Analyses revealed that within-dyad differences in conflict frame were substantially greater before than after dispute resolution. Pinkley and Northcraft (1994, p. 201) concluded that disputants' frames mutually influenced each other, converging during the process of negotiation.

Things may be no different in the case of outcome frames. The opposing negotiator's communicated gain or loss frame may substantially influence the focal negotiator's representation of the dispute as involving gains, or as involving losses. If so, the focal negotiator's communication should reflect his or her opposing negotiators communicated frame at least as well as the own frame (as manipulated through issue charts), and in addition, other's communicated gain frame should induce less resistance to concession making than other's communicated loss frame.

For three reasons, however, this frame adoption may occur especially when negotiators themselves have a gain rather than loss frame. First, some scholars have argued that in social conflict, people tend to focus on their losses more than on their gains (Brockner & Rubin, 1985). Similarly, Kelley and Thibaut (1978, p. 200) argued that people more easily focus on the highest rather than the lowest outcome possible. They suspect some tendency for people to compare all prospective outcomes available to the highest outcome known, rather than to compare all prospective outcomes available to the lowest outcome known. This would imply that outcomes tend to be coded negatively, rather than positively. Thus, referring to the highest outcome (when one communicates a loss frame) may be more natural, more fitting with what the recipient is tempted to do, than referring to the lowest outcome (when one communicates a gain frame).

Second, there is some evidence that loss framed decision makers scrutinize incoming information to a greater extent than gain framed decision makers (e.g., Dunegan, 1993; Schneider, 1992). Thus, loss framed negotiators may be less easily 'tricked' by variations in their opponent's communicated frame. Third, there is increasing evidence that loss framed decision makers are particularly scrutinizing information regarding their own outcomes (e.g., De Dreu, Emans, & van de Vlicrt, 1992a; De Dreu, Lualhati, & McCusker, 1994; Dehue, McClintock, & Liebrand, 1993), probably making other's frame communication relatively unimportant and uninteresting. Thus, the ultimate *Frame Adoption Hypothesis* is that negotiators tend to adopt their opponent's communicated frame, especially when they themselves have a gain rather than a loss frame. Consequently, other's communicated gain frame should induce less resistance to concession making than other's communicated loss frame, but less so when the focal negotiator has a loss frame rather than a gain frame.

Evidence for the Frame Adoption Hypothesis was obtained in three experiments (De Dreu, Emans, & van de Vliert, 1992b; De Dreu & Carnevale, 1992; De Dreu *et al.*, 1994). All experiments used the computer-simulation paradigm outlined above. In addition to the offers the preprogrammed buyer sent on each of the six negotiation rounds, there was a message to the seller (the subject) on each round of the negotiation. This message either evaluated the buyer's outcomes in terms of gains and profits (other's communicated gain frame), or in terms of losses and costs (other's communicated loss frame). An example is: 'I cannot make more concessions since my gains are really too small' (. . . my losses are really too large). Another example would be: 'I really have to make some profit out of this transaction' (. . . cut some losses in this transaction). Pretest data always revealed that the gain versus loss-frame messages did not differ in terms of cooperativeness and persuasiveness. During negotiation, subjects were not only prompted to make counter-offers, but also to create messages to their buyer. As in the study by De Dreu and Carnevale (1992) reported above, the subjects' messages were coded for frame content. Since subjects could refer to both other's, and own outcomes, we ensured that only explicit references to own outcomes were coded. Thus, a message containing statements such as 'my profits', 'my benefits' or 'my gains', was coded as communicated gain frame (but a message only containing a statement like 'your gains' was not). Likewise, a message containing statements such as 'my expenses', 'my costs' or 'my losses' was coded as communicated loss frame, but a message only containing a statement like 'your expenses' was not. Ambiguous messages, i.e., those reflecting both a gain and loss frame, were rare, and left out of the analyses. Note that the fact that ambiguous messages were rare corroborates our assumption (footnote 2, p. 100) that negotiators adopt either a gain or a loss frame.

In all three experiments, these content-analyses of the messages subjects sent to their buyer revealed support for the Frame Adoption Hypothesis. To illustrate this, Figure 4.2 summarizes the cell means (i.e., the number of frame-related messages divided by the total number of messages the subject sent during negotiation) from the study by De Dreu and Carnevale (1992; data patterns for the other two experiments closely matched this figure). The top figure shows that negotiators with a gain frame communicated a gain frame much more often than a loss frame when their opponent communicated a gain frame, but a loss frame much more than a gain frame when their opponent communicated a loss frame. Thus, negotiators with a gain frame tended to reciprocate their opponent's communicated frame; they started to talk about their own outcomes in the way their opponent referred to his own outcomes. Things were different for loss framed negotiators, however. The bottom figure shows that loss framed negotiators communicated a loss frame much more than a gain frame, irrespective of the gain or loss frame communicated by the opponent. Thus, negotiators with a loss frame tended to stick to their interpretation of own outcomes as losses, and appeared insensitive to their opponent's communicated frame. On top of this, analyses of negotiator demands averaged over the six rounds of negotiation revealed that other's

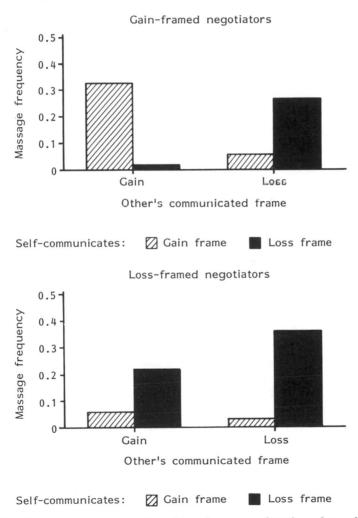

Figure 4.2 Own communicated gain and loss frame as a function of own frame and opponent's communicated frame (based on De Dreu & Carnevale, 1992)

Table 4.3 Demand (averaged across rounds) as a function of outcome frame and opponent's communicated frame

| | Outcome frame | | | |
| | Gain | | Loss | |
Communicates	Gain frame	Loss frame	Gain frame	Loss frame
1.	4,440[a]	5,275[b]	4,890[ab]	5,006[ab]
2.	4,747[x]	5,074[y]	5,124[y]	5,128[y]
3.	5,109[a]	5,820[b]	5,628[b]	5,454[ab]

Note: Data in row 1 ($N = 141$) are based on De Dreu, Emans, and van de Vliert (1992b); those in row 2 ($N = 103$) on De Dreu and Carnevale (1992), and those in row 3 ($N = 107$) on De Dreu *et al.* (1994). Means could range between 0 and 8,000, with higher numbers indicating higher demands. [a,b] Means in each row not sharing equal superscripts are significantly different at $p < 0.05$; [x,y] Means in each row not sharing equal superscripts are significantly different at $p < 0.10$.

communicated frame interacted with the negotiator's own frame to influence negotiator demand as predicted. Consistent with the Frame Adoption Hypothesis, results repeatedly demonstrated that negotiators with a gain frame demand less when their opponent communicates a gain rather than loss frame. When negotiators have a loss frame, other's communicated gain or loss frame does not affect negotiator demand. Table 4.3 summarizes the cell means obtained by De Dreu, Emans, & van de Vliert (1992b), De Dreu and Carnevale (1992), and De Dreu *et al.* (1994).

Foreknowledge about Other's Frame

The preceding section showed that negotiators may become aware of other's frame through other's communication, and how this exchange of information leads to convergence of frame. In addition to communication, negotiators often have foreknowledge about their opponent's frame, for example due to information search prior to the negotiation, or to information conveyed in the mass media. Also, negotiators may have some assumptions about their opponent's frame, for example based upon their own gain or loss frame (De Dreu, Emans & van de Vliert, 1991). Two distinct lines of research studied the influence of foreknowledge about other's frame. The first line of research studied its effects in the realm of negotiations and shows that other's loss frame compared to other's gain frame enhances competitive responses. The second line of research studied effects of foreknowledge about other's frame in the realm of allocation behavior and satisfaction with distributions of outcomes between oneself and some other party, and tends to show that other's loss frame elicits more cooperative responses than other's gain frame. Thus, at least at first sight, results of these two lines of research appear to be inconsistent. Besides reviewing these two lines of research, the current section attempts to reconcile these apparent differences.

Recall that losses loom larger than equivalent gains, and that increasing one's losses is considered to be more painful than decreasing one's gains. An interesting implication is that another party's concession may be perceived as larger and as more painful to the opponent when he or she is assumed to have a loss rather than gain frame. Put differently, a conceding other party may be perceived as more cooperative when the other supposedly has a loss rather than gain frame. De Dreu et al. (1994) tested this hypothesis. Using the computerized buyer–seller paradigm, they provided subjects with information about other's issue-charts in such a way that other's concessions implied an increase in other's losses (other's loss frame condition), or a decrease in other's gains (other's gain frame condition). As in all previous experiments, the buyer was simulated by a computer-program, and pursued a concession strategy that was independent of what the subject did, and that was similar in every experimental condition. However, consistent with the hypothesis that losses loom larger than equivalent gains, the other party was perceived as more cooperative and less competitive in the other's loss rather than gain frame condition. Moreover, subjects tended to exploit this apparent cooperativeness by making smaller concessions themselves when the opponent had a loss frame (and was perceived as relatively cooperative) rather than a gain frame (and was perceived as relatively competitive). On the basis of these results, De Dreu et al. (1994) concluded that foreknowledge about other's outcome frame may substantially bias the perception of other's behavior, and thereby affect the perceiver's negotiation behavior considerably.[3]

As noted, these data, although consistent with predictions derived from Prospect Theory, appear inconsistent with data obtained in a second line of research. De Dreu, Emans, and van de Vliert (1992a) provided subjects with outcome-matrices (i.e., Decomposed Prisoner's Dilemma Games; Pruitt, 1967). These matrices provided subjects with either positive outcomes (own gain frame) or negative outcomes (own loss frame), and the other party with either positive outcomes (other's gain frame) or negative outcomes (other's loss frame). Subjects were then asked to make decisions between a cooperative alternative and a non-cooperative alternative (no information about other's choice-behavior was provided). Results showed more cooperation when subjects were informed that the other party had a loss frame, than when

---

[3] It should be noted that in this experiment, the opponent also communicated a gain or a loss frame. Thus, in addition to having foreknowledge about other's frame, subjects also received frame-related communication from their opponent. Interestingly, however, foreknowledge of frame and communicated frame did not interact, and whereas foreknowledge did affect perception of cooperativeness but not own frame-related communication, other's communicated frame affected own frame-related communication but not the perception of cooperativeness. Thus, foreknowledge about other's frame seems to evoke rather different processes than other's communicated frame. That is, foreknowledge about other's frame affects the perception and interpretation of other's behaviors, and communicated frame affects one's own frame and motivation.

they were informed that the other party had a gain frame. De Dreu, Lualhati, and McCusker (1994) obtained a conceptual replication of this finding. This study provided subjects with a series of distributions of outcomes between the subject and a co-worker. Some distributions provided subjects with advantageous inequality, some with equality, and the rest with disadvantageous inequality. Subjects were informed that the outcomes to the other party either were less than the other expected (other's loss frame condition) or more than the other expected (other's gain frame condition). Results showed that subjects rated advantageous inequality (getting more than the other) as more dissatisfying when the other party had a loss rather than a gain frame. We explained these data by arguing that people feel more inclined to help someone reducing his or her losses, than to increase his or her gains (De Dreu, Emans, & van de Vliert, 1992a; De Dreu, Lualhati, & McCusker, 1994).

Taken together, some research on foreknowledge about other's frame tends to indicate that other's loss frame enhances cooperative responses more than other's gain frame. Other research, in contrast, suggests that other's loss frame enhances cooperative responses more than other's gain frame. Closer examination of the differences between these studies reveals that (1) in the first line of research, information about other's behavior was provided, whereas the second line of research did not give any such information, and that (2) the first line of research may have used subjects with rather selfish attitudes, whereas the second line of research may have used more pro-socially oriented subjects. Especially the second difference may prove to be important in explaining the different results obtained. That is, in the negotiation study by De Dreu *et al.* (1994), the other party was perceived as more cooperative when he had a loss rather than gain frame, and subjects tended to exploit this apparent cooperativeness. There is ample evidence, however, that at times negotiators may have more pro-social attitudes toward their opposing negotiator (Carnevale & Pruitt, 1992; De Dreu & Van Lange, in press), and one may speculate that more pro-social negotiators reciprocate rather than exploit the other party's perceived cooperativeness. Thus, the subjects' low versus high concern for the other party may be the key variable in explaining why some studies found other's loss frame to enhance competitive action, whereas other studies tended to find the reverse. Research is needed, however, to affirm these speculations.

OUTCOME FRAMES AND CONFLICT ESCALATION

The research discussed so far indicated that (1) the loss frame induces more resistance to concession making than the gain frame, and (2) the loss frame is more easily adopted and less readily changed into a gain frame than vice versa. This might suggest that, as a rule, the loss frame should be avoided since it enhances the probability of mutual hostility, conflict escalation and stalemate rather than settlement (De Dreu, Emans, & van de Vliert, 1992b; De Dreu, Lualhati, & McCusker, 1994; McCusker & Carnevale, in press; Neale & Bazerman, 1991). In contrast with this, however, research has begun to show that the loss frame may, compared to the gain frame, enhance the quality of decision making and negotiator performance.

To understand this, it is important to realize that most negotiations involve *integrative potential*. The term 'integrative' has its origins in the concepts of *integration* (of both parties' interests; Follett, 1940), *integrative bargaining*, which refers to the process through which high joint benefit is developed (Walton & McKersie, 1965), and *integrative agreement* meaning that participants are all satisfied with their outcomes and feel that they have gained as a result of the negotiation (Deutsch, 1973; Pruitt, 1981). Integrative potential thus refers to the mere possibility of integration, and of reaching integrative agreement. To illustrate this, imagine a brother and a sister negotiating the division of an orange (Follett, 1940). After some discussion, they decide to split the orange in two equal parts—they accept a fifty–fifty compromise. Ironically, however, the sister now drinks the juice from her half, and throws away the peel, whereas the brother squeezes his half to use the peel for a cake he is baking. Clearly, this negotiation between brother and sister had integrative potential, in that both parties could have been better off than they were by splitting the orange. The perfect solution here was, of course, to give the brother the whole peel, and the sister all the juice.

The example shows that negotiations may involve integrative potential, that is not always easily discovered and may require substantial information exchange in addition to creative problem solving, but which imply much better joint outcomes than the more obvious fifty–fifty compromise (Lax & Sebenius, 1986; Walton & McKersie, 1965). According to Dual Concern Theory (Pruitt & Carnevale, 1993; Rubin, Pruitt, & Kim, 1994), negotiators use the integrative potential better when they have a high rather than low concern for their opponent's goals and interests, but especially when this high concern for other's outcomes is combined with a high rather than low resistance to concession making. This is because integrating own and other's interests satisfies both the high resistance to concession making, and the high concern for other's outcomes (for some empirical evidence, see Ben-Yoav & Pruitt, 1984; Pruitt & Lewis, 1975; for a critique, see Thompson, 1990). From Dual Concern Theory it thus follows that compared to gain framed negotiators, loss framed negotiators may engage in more contending when they have a low concern for other's outcomes, but in more integrative bargaining when they have a high concern for other's outcomes.

Carnevale *et al.* (1994) noted that most prior research on effects of outcome frames induced a rather low concern for the other party. Usually, subjects were told that they could make some real money from the negotiation, based on how well they would perform, irrespective of their opponent's performance. Some studies went even further, by explicitly instructing subjects 'to disregard the buyer's needs and interests' (for a more detailed analysis, see De Dreu & McCusker, 1994). To test the hypothesis that, compared to gain framed negotiators, loss framed negotiators would contend more in case of low concern for other's outcomes, but engage in more integrative bargaining in case of a high concern for other's outcomes, Carnevale *et al.* (1994) simultaneously manipulated outcome frame (gain versus loss) and the negotiator's concern for other's outcomes. As to the latter, negotiators were instructed to be concerned for other's needs and interests (high concern for other), or to disregard other's needs and interests (low concern for other). Results supported the hypothesis: in the low concern for other condition, loss framed negotiators had lower settlement rates than gain framed negotiators, reflecting the now classical observation that the former engaged in more contending than the latter. In the high concern for other condition, however, loss framed negotiators reach settlement as frequently as gain framed negotiators, but with higher joint benefit, reflecting more integrative bargaining. Thus, Carnevale *et al.* (1994) showed that resistance to concession making due to frame may lead to enhanced hostility when paired to a low concern for other's outcomes, but to more problem solving and increased quality of settlement when paired to a high concern for other's outcomes. A similar conclusion was reached by De Dreu and McCusker (1994) in their research on frame effects in Prisoner's Dilemma games. This series of experiments showed that the loss frame induced more competition than the gain frame when decision makers had individualistic motives (i.e. low concern for other's outcomes), but more cooperation when decision makers had pro-social motives (i.e. high concern for other's outcomes).

The provocative message these more recent studies seem to send is that framing outcomes in negative terms, as losses, may turn out to be very profitable, in the sense that loss framed negotiators seem more 'consistent' negotiators. That is, negotiators with a loss frame cooperate more than those with a gain frame when joint outcomes are at stake (high concern for other), but they compete more when personal outcomes are at stake (low concern for other). In a sense, these data are consistent with other findings in the domain of negotiation and social interdependence. First, as mentioned, there is quite some evidence suggesting that loss framed decision makers take more time to make decisions (De Dreu, Emans, & van de Vliert, 1992a; Schneider, 1992). Second, there is some evidence that loss framed negotiators scrutinize decision alternatives better than gain framed decision makers (De Dreu, Emans, & van de Vliert, 1992a; Dunegan, 1993). Third, there is increasing evidence that loss framed negotiators are less concerned about equality than gain framed negotiators (De Dreu, Lualhati, & McCusker, 1994). Especially in bilateral negotiations, striving for equality is satisficing rather than optimizing (Rubin, Pruitt, & Kim, 1994).

Together, these pieces of evidence suggest that loss framed negotiators are, in a sense, 'better' decision makers: they scrutinize alternatives in a more systematic and thoughtful way, and they are less preoccupied with satisficing rather than optimizing heuristics like the equality rule. Of course, all this leads to more thorough decision making, which may enhance decision quality at the expense of efficiency. When time is precious, outcomes should perhaps be framed as gains rather than as losses.

SUMMARY OF THE CONCLUSIONS

The goal of this chapter was to review research on the impact of outcome frames on negotiator cognition, motivation, concession making and communication processes. The review boils down to five conclusions. The *first conclusion* is that negotiator frames affect the negotiator's resistance to concession making: negotiators with a gain frame demand less, concede more, and settle easier than negotiators with a loss frame. This conclusion alters the assumption early theorists made, and some researchers continue to make, namely that the outcome frame affects negotiation because of variation in risk-tolerance. Although research so far has not really falsified the risk-tolerance hypothesis, it can be rejected nevertheless because an equally plausible, yet more parsimonious, explanation is available.

The *second conclusion* is that negotiator frames affect the choice of linguistic labels to describe and evaluate overtly the anticipated or obtained outcomes: gain framed negotiators communicate more about gains and profits (communicated gain frame) than about losses and costs (communicated loss frame), whereas loss framed negotiators do the reverse. An important implication of this conclusion is that third parties such as mediators or constituents may detect the negotiator's frame through careful reading. For example, mediators wishing to settle the dispute quickly and thus to reduce resistance to concession making may, via careful scrutiny of the parties' communications, detect whether concession making is slowed down due to one or both parties' loss frame.

The *third conclusion* builds upon the second one. It is that negotiators are influenced by their opponent's communicated gain or loss frame, in that they adopt other's communicated frame, albeit especially when they themselves have a gain rather than loss frame. Frame adoption goes hand in hand with the negotiator's low versus high resistance to concession making and subsequent low versus high demands. An important implication of the Frame Adoption Effect is that because loss framed negotiators are less subject to frame adoption than gain framed negotiators, it requires only one negotiator to communicate in loss terms for both to end up with a loss frame and its concomitant high resistance to concession making. It thus appears that the loss frame is the dominant perspective in negotiation and, most likely, in other forms of social conflict.

The *fourth conclusion* deals with effects of foreknowledge about other's frame. Foreknowledge about other's frame appears to evoke two distinct processes. First, foreknowledge appears to affect helping motives, with other's loss frame eliciting stronger inclination to help than other's gain frame. This process is likely to occur especially when there is high concern for other's outcomes. When there is low concern for other's outcomes, no effects of other's frame on intentions to help are to be expected. In addition to helping motives, foreknowledge about other's frame appears to bias the perception of other's concessionary behavior, in that the other party looks more cooperative when he or she has a loss rather than gain frame. When negotiators have a low concern for other's outcomes, this perception of other's cooperativeness may evoke exploitation. But one might speculate that in case of a high concern for other's outcomes, this tendency to exploit may be replaced by a tendency to reciprocate perceived other's cooperativeness (cf. Pruitt & Carnevale, 1993).

The *fifth and last conclusion* of this review is that although the loss frame more than the gain frame predisposes the negotiator to act in ways that trigger escalation rather than de-escalation of the social conflict, research commences to show that this effect is especially true when the loss frame comes hand in hand with low concern for the other party's needs and interests. When the loss frame is paired to high concern for other, there may be even more constructive problem solving and integrative negotiation than in the case of a gain frame.

Before closing, two limitations to these conclusions should be mentioned. First of all, we explained effects of outcome frames in bilateral negotiation in terms of the loss framed negotiators heightened concern for own outcomes. We cannot, however, exclude the possibility that entirely different processes at least contribute to explaining the fact that loss framed negotiators demand more, concede less, and settle less easily than gain framed negotiators. Second, our conclusions pertaining to frame communication and frame adoption may have restricted generalizability due to the subject samples we used (undergraduate students), and due to the computerized buyer–seller paradigm we relied upon. Future research should corroborate our findings at least with different samples, such as professional negotiators, and with different methodologies, such as negotiations over land-use, or over social contracts, rather than over the sales transaction of home appliances.

Despite these potential limitations, the current chapter informs us that the negotiator frame is dynamic because it is subject to revision following frame-related communication by the negotiators themselves. It underscores Kahneman's (1992, p. 310) argument that 'it is useful to view messages that negotiators exchange as attempts by each side to communicate its reference point and to affect the other side by inducing anchors and norms'. More generally, this chapter indicated how the opponent's communications affect the individuals' representation of outcomes which—in interaction with the disputants' concern for other—determines constructive versus destructive conflict management.

ACKNOWLEDGEMENTS

Preparation of this chapter was facilitated by financial support from a Royal Netherlands Academy of Sciences Fellowship awarded to Carsten de Dreu, a Dutch National Science Foundation Grant 575-271-011 awarded to Evert van de Vliert and Carsten de Dreu, and a United States National Science Foundation Grant BNS-8809263 awarded to Peter Carnevale. We thank Wolfgang Stroebe and Miles Hewstone for their editorial guidance, and three reviewers for their insightful and constructive comments and suggestions.

REFERENCES

Bartlett, F. C. (1932). *Remembering: A study in experimental and social psychology.* Cambridge: Cambridge University Press.

Bazerman, M. H. (1983). Negotiator judgment: A critical look at the rationality assumption. *American Behavioral Scientist*, **27**, 211–28.

Bazerman, M. H., Magliozzi, T., & Neale, M. (1985). Integrative bargaining in a competitive market. *Organizational Behavior and Human Decision Processes*, **35**, 294–313.

Ben-Yoav, O., & Pruitt, D. (1984). Resistance to yielding and the expectation of cooperative future interaction in negotiation. *Journal of Experimental Social Psychology*, **34**, 323–35.

Boles, T. L., & Messick, D. M. (in press). A reverse outcome bias: The influence of multiple reference points on the evaluation of outcomes and decisions. *Organizational Behavior and Human Decision Processes*.

Bottom, W. P., & Studt, A. (1993). Framing and the distributive aspects of integrative negotiation. *Organizational Behavior and Human Decision Processes*, **56**, 459–74.

Brockner, J., & Rubin, J. Z. (1985). *Entrapment in Escalating Conflicts: A social psychological analysis.* New York: Springer-Verlag.

Budescu, D. V., & Weiss, W. (1987). Reflection of transitive and intransitive preferences: A test of Prospect Theory. *Organizational Behavior and Human Decision Processes*, **39**, 184–202.

Carnevale, P. J., Gentile, S., & De Dreu, C. K. W. (1993). *Frame and time pressure in bilateral negotiation.* Unpublished manuscript, University of Illinois at Urbana-Champaign.

Carnevale, P. J., O'Connor, K., & McCusker, C. (1993). Time pressure in negotiation and mediation. In O. Svensson & J. Maule (Eds), *Time Pressure in Human Judgment and Decision Making* (pp. 117–27). New York: Plenum Press.

Carnevale, P. J., & Pruitt, D. G. (1992). Negotiation and mediation. *Annual Review of Psychology*, **43**, 531–82.

Carnevale, P. J., De Dreu, C. K. W., Rand, K., Keenan, P., & Gentile, S. (1994). *Frames in bilateral negotiation: Loss aversion versus risk attitude.* Unpublished manuscript, University of Illinois at Urbana-Champaign.

Chaiken, S., Liberman, A., & Eagly, A. H. (1989). Heuristic and systematic information processing within and beyond the persuasion context. In J. S. Uleman & J. A. Bargh (Eds), *Unintended Thought* (pp. 212–52). New York: Guilford Press.

Dawes, R. M. (1988). *Rational Choice in an Uncertain World.* San Diego, CA: Harcourt Brace Jovanovich.

De Dreu, C. K. W. (1993). *Gain and loss frames in bilateral negotiation.* Unpublished dissertation, University of Groningen.

De Dreu, C. K. W., & Carnevale, P. J. (1992). *Communication of frame and cooperation in bilateral negotiation: The frame adoption effect.* Unpublished manuscript, University of Groningen.

De Dreu, C. K. W., Emans, B. J. M., & van de Vliert, E. (1991). De invloed van referentiekader op de utiliteit van verdeling van geld [The impact of frame of reference upon the utility of outcome-distributions]. *Gedrag en Organisatie*, **4**, 429–43.

De Dreu, C. K. W., Emans, B. J. M, & van de Vliert, E. (1992a). Frames of reference and cooperative social decision making. *European Journal of Social Psychology*, **22**, 297–302.

De Dreu, C. K. W., Emans, B. J. M., & van de Vliert, E. (1992b). The influence of own cognitive and other's communicated gain or loss frame on negotiation behavior. *International Journal of Conflict Management*, **3**, 115–32.

De Dreu, C. K. W., Lualhati, J., & McCusker, C. (1994). Effects of gain-loss frames on satisfaction with self-other outcome differences. *European Journal of Social Psychology*, **24**, 497–510.

De Dreu, C. K. W., & McCusker, C. (1994). A transformational analysis of frame effects in mixed-motive interdependence. Manuscript under review.

De Dreu, C. K. W., & Van Lange, P. A. M. (in press). Impact of social value orientation on negotiator cognition and behavior. *Personality and Social Psychology Bulletin*.

De Dreu, C. K. W., Carnevale, P. J., Emans, B. J. M., & van de Vliert, E. (1994). Gain-loss frames in negotiation: Loss aversion, mismatching, and frame adoption. *Organizational Behavior and Human Decision Processes*, **60**, 90–107.

Dehue, F., McClintock, C., & Liebrand, W. (1993). Social values and their influence on cognitive processing time. *European Journal of Social Psychology*, **23**, 273–94.

Deutsch, M. (1973). *The Resolution of Conflict: Constructive and destructive processes.* New Haven, CT: Yale University Press.

Donnelon, A. E., & Gray, B. (1990). *An interactive theory of reframing in negotiation.* Unpublished manuscript, Pennsylvania State University.

Dunegan, K. J. (1993). Framing, cognitive modes, and image theory: Toward an understanding of a glass half full. *Journal of Applied Psychology*, **78**, 491–503.

Fagley, N. S. (1993). A note concerning reflection effects versus framing effects. *Psychological Bulletin*, **113**, 451–2.

Fagley, N. S., & Miller, P. M. (1990). The effect of framing on choice: Interactions with risk-taking propensity, cognitive style, and sex. *Personality and Social Psychology Bulletin*, **16**, 496–510.

Fiske, S. T., & Taylor, S. E. (1991). *Social Cognition.* New York: McGraw-Hill.

Follett, M. (1940). Constructive Conflict. In H. C. Metcalf & L. Urwick (Eds), *Dynamic Administration: The collected papers of Mary Parker Follett*. New York: Harper.

Giles, H., & Smith, P. M. (1979). Accommodation theory: Optimal levels of convergence. In H. Giles and R. N. St. Clair (Eds), *Language and Social Psychology* (pp. 45–65). Oxford: Basil Blackwell.

Glucksberg, S. (1988). Language and thought. In R. J. Sternberg and E. E. Smith (Eds), *The Psychology of Human Thought* (pp. 214–42). Cambridge: Cambridge University Press.

Hershey, B., & Schoemaker, P. J. D. (1980). Prospect Theory's reflection hypothesis: a critical examination. *Organizational Behavior and Human Decision Processes*, **25**, 395–418.

Kahneman, D. (1992). Reference points, anchors, norms, and mixed feelings. *Organizational Behavior and Human Decision Processes*, **51**, 296–312.

Kahneman, D. T., Knetsch, J. L., & Thaler, R. (1990). Experimental tests of the endowment effect and the Coase Theorem. *Journal of Political Economy*, **158**, 1325–48.

Kahneman, D., & Tversky, A. (1979). Prospect Theory: an analysis of decision making under risk. *Econometrica*, **47**, 263–91.

Kelley, H. H. & Thibaut, A. (1978). *Interpersonal Relations*. New York: John Wiley.

Lax, J., & Sebenius, R. (1986). *The Manager as Negotiator*. New York: Free Press.

Lewicki, R. J., & Litterer, J. A. (1985). *Negotiation*. Homewood, IL: Irwin.

Liebrand, W. B. G., & Messick, D. M. (1993). Computer simulations of the relation between individual heuristics and global cooperation in prisoner's dilemmas. In U. Schulz, W. Albers, & U. Mueller (Eds). *Social Dilemmas and Cooperation* (pp. 327–40). New York: Springer-Verlag.

Lopes, L. L. (1987). Between hope and fear: The psychology of risk. In L. Berkowitz (Ed.), *Advances in Experimental Social Psychology* (Vol. 20, pp. 255–95). New York: Academic Press.

Losco, J., & Epstein, S. (1977). Relative steepness of approach and avoidance gradients as a function of magnitude and valence of incentive. *Journal of Abnormal Psychology*, **86**, 360–8.

Markus, H., & Zajonc, R. B. (1985). The cognitive perspective in social psychology. In G. Lindzey and E. Aronson (Eds), *The Handbook of Social Psychology*, 3rd edn (pp. 137–230). New York: Random House.

McCusker, C., & Carnevale, P. J. (in press). Frame and loss aversion in social dilemmas. *Organizational Behavior and Human Decision Processes*.

Neale, M., & Bazerman, M. H. (1985). The effects of framing and negotiator overconfidence on bargaining behavior and outcomes. *Academy of Management Journal*, **28**, 34–49.

Neale, M., & Bazerman, M. H. (1991). *Rationality and Cognition in Negotiation*. New York: Free Press.

Neale, M., Huber, V., & Northcraft, G. (1987). The framing of negotiations: Contextual versus task frames. *Organizational Behavior and Human Decision Processes*, **39**, 228–41.

Olekalns, M., & Frey, B. F. (1994). Market forces, negotiator frames, and transaction outcomes. *European Journal of Social Psychology*, **24**, 403–16.

Peeters, G., & Czapinski, J. (1990). Positive–negative asymmetry in evaluations: The distinction between affective and informational distinctivity effects. In W. Stroebe and M. Hewstone (Eds), *European Review of Social Psychology* (Vol. 1, pp. 33–60). Chichester: John Wiley.

124   C. DE DREU, P. CARNEVALE, B. EMANS AND E. VAN DE VLIERT

Pinkley, R. (1990). Dimensions of conflict frame: Disputant interpretations of conflict. *Journal of Applied Psychology*, **75**, 117–26.

Pinkley, R., & Northcraft, G. (1994). Conflict frames of reference: Implications for dispute processes and outcomes. *Academy of Management Journal*, **37**, 193–205.

Pruitt, D. G. (1967). Reward structure and cooperation: The decomposed prisoner's dilemma game. *Journal of Personality and Social Psychology*, **7**, 21–7.

Pruitt, D. G. (1981). *Negotiation Behavior*. New York, Academic Press.

Pruitt, D. G., & Carnevale, P. J. (1993). *Negotiation in Social Conflict*. Buckingham: Open University Press.

Pruitt, D. G., & Lewis, S. A. (1975). Development of integrative solutions in bilateral negotiation. *Journal of Personality and Social Psychology*, **31**, 621–30.

Putnam, L. L. (1990). Reframing integrative and distributive bargaining: A process perspective. In B. H. Sheppard, M. H. Bazerman, & R. J. Lewicki (Eds), *Research on Negotiation in Organizations* (Vol. 2, pp. 3–30). Greenwich, CT: JAI Press.

Putnam, L. L., & Holmer, M. (1992). Framing, reframing and issue development. In L. L. Putnam, and M. E. Roloff (Eds), *Communication Perspectives on Negotiation*, Newbury Park, CA: Sage.

Putnam, L. L., Wilson, S. R., & Turner, D. B. (1990). The evolution of policy arguments in teachers' negotiations. *Argumentation*, **4**, 129–52.

Raiffa, H. (1982). *The Art and Science of Negotiation*. Cambridge, MA: Harvard University Press.

Ross, L., & Nisbett, R. (1991). *The Person and the Situation*. New York: McGraw-Hill.

Rubin, J. Z., & Brown, B. R. (1975). *The Social Psychology of Bargaining and Negotiation*. New York: Academic Press.

Rubin, J. Z., Pruitt, D. G., & Kim, S. (1994). *Social Conflict: Escalation, stalemate, settlement*. New York: McGraw-Hill.

Russo, J. E., & Schoemaker, P. J. H. (1989). *Decision Trap: ten barriers to brilliant decision making*. New York, Simon & Schuster.

Schneider, S. (1992). Framing and conflict: Aspiration level contingency, the status quo, and current theories of risky choice. *Journal of Experimental Psychology: Learning, Memory, and Cognition*, **18**, 1040–57.

Schneider, S., & Lopes, L. L. (1986). Reflection in preferences under risk; who and when may suggest why. *Journal of Experimental Psychology: Human Performance and Perception*, **12**, 535–48.

Siegel, S., & Fouraker, L. E. (1960). *Bargaining and Group Decision Making: Experiments in bilateral monopoly*. New York: McGraw-Hill.

Smith, B., & Epstein, S. (1967). Influence of incentive on adequacy and mode of conflict resolution. *Journal of Experimental Psychology*, **75**, 175–9.

Smith, D. L., Pruitt, D., & Carnevale, P. J. (1982). Matching and mismatching: the effect of own limit, other's toughness, and time pressure on concession rate in negotiation. *Journal of Personality and Social Psychology*, **42**, 876–83.

Taylor, S. E. (1991). Asymmetrical effects of positive and negative events: The mobilization–minimization hypothesis. *Psychological Bulletin*, **110**, 67–85.

Thompson, L. L. (1990). Negotiation behavior and outcomes: empirical evidence and theoretical issues. *Psychological Bulletin*, **108**, 515–32.

Tversky, A., & Kahneman, D. (1981). The framing of decisions and the rationality of choice. *Science*, **211**, 453–8.

Tversky, A., & Kahneman, D. (1991). Loss aversion in riskless choice: A reference-dependent model. *Quarterly Journal of Economics* (November), 1039–61.

Van der Pligt, J., & Van Schie, E. (1990). Frames of reference, judgment and preference. In: W. Stroebe and M. Hewstone (Eds), *European Review of Social Psychology* (Vol. 1, pp. 61–80). Chichester: John Wiley.

Walton, R., & McKersie, R. (1965). *A Behavioral Theory of Labor Negotiations.* New York: McGraw-Hill.

Yukl, G. A. (1974). The effects of situational variables and opponent concessions on a bargainer's perception, aspirations, and concessions. *Journal of Personality and Social Psychology*, **29**, 227–36.

Yukl, G. A., Malone, M. P., Hayslip, B., & Pamin, T. A. (1976). The effects of time pressure and issue settlement order on integrative bargaining. *Sociometry*, **39**, 277–81.

Chapter 5

Social Remembering: Individual and Collaborative Memory for Social Information

N. K. Clark and G. M. Stephenson
University of Kent at Canterbury

ABSTRACT

The study of individual memory and remembering has a very long history in experimental psychology. However, it was not until recently that experimental studies systematically investigated social aspects of remembering. In particular, relatively few studies have examined remembering (a) as both an individual and group phenomenon, and (b) when the stimulus material to be recalled is a purposive social interaction. The present chapter reviews the theoretical implications of a continuing series of social remembering studies which compare individual with social (or collaborative) remembering in terms of both the *quantity* (accuracy and error) and the *quality* of what was recalled, and particular attention is paid to the relationship between accuracy and confidence. The applied implications of this research in the area of the social psychology of law are also discussed.

INTRODUCTION

Despite the efforts of some researchers (e.g., Neisser, 1976, 1982) to persuade cognitive psychologists of the inadequacies of theoretical explanations of memory and remembering based purely on intra-individual processes, many

European Review of Social Psychology, Volume 6. Edited by Wolfgang Stroebe and Miles Hewstone.
© 1995 John Wiley & Sons Ltd.

still relegate social influences on cognition to the status of 'context effects'. A consideration of the justification for such dismissals of the importance of social phenomena in cognition suggests that many cognitive psychologists still hold to the belief that the true vocation for their discipline is the development of theoretical models of 'pure' cognition, often supported by appeals to the scientific method and reductionism. However, as Neisser has forcefully pointed out (e.g., 1976), theories of so-called 'pure' cognition are of very little utility in explaining or predicting everyday cognitive phenomena.

The emphasis on intra-individual processes also has a long tradition in social psychological studies. Even when group processes have been under investigation, some researchers have argued that such phenomena are ultimately reducible to intra- and inter-individual processes (e.g., Allport, 1962). While many researchers today would argue for the legitimacy and importance of levels of explanation beyond the individual, some areas of social psychology are predominately still investigated at the individual level. The investigation of cognitive processes in social psychology, or social cognition, is one area particularly marked by the emphasis of researchers on individual cognitive processes. Indeed, Fiske and Taylor (1991, p. 1) defined the area of social cognition as 'the study of how people make sense of other people and themselves . . . [how they] think about people and how they think they think about people'.

In a recent review of the group problem solving literature, Larson and Christansen (1993, p. 5) point out that most social cognition researchers use the word 'social' 'to refer either to the contents of cognition, or to a class of factors that affect cognition. Cognition itself, however, is construed in strictly non-social terms. It is something that happens inside the individual'. As they point out, social cognition shares both the individual perspective and many of the basic assumptions of cognitive psychology. They claim that investigating social cognitive phenomena solely at the individual level ignores, or assumes to be either irrelevant or of minor importance, group-level social phenomena such as group decision making and group problem solving. They argue for the theoretical and practical importance of developing an understanding of cognitive phenomena at the group level by reviewing the contributions of a substantial number of studies in the general area of group problem solving. Larson and Christensen then propose a new 'meaning' for *social cognition*:

> We suggest that the term . . . can be usefully applied at the group level of analysis to refer to those social processes (e.g. introducing information into a group discussion) that relate to the acquisition, storage, transmission, manipulation and use of information for the purpose of creating a group-level intellective product. In this context, social cognition is not merely cognition 'about', it is cognition 'by', with the word 'social' referring to the way in which cognition is accomplished. At the group level of analysis, cognition is a social phenomenon. (p. 6)

It should, however, be noted that many important insights into the social nature of memory are not new, and have a long history in psychology, philosophy and sociology (e.g., Halbwachs, 1950). Indeed, many acute observations on the social nature of memory were made some sixty or more years ago by Frederic Bartlett in *Remembering: A Study in Experimental and Social Psychology* (1932). Bartlett's contribution to contemporary cognitive psychology was initially appreciated by cognitive psychologists when interest began to grow in understanding and developing theoretical models of story and discourse comprehension (e.g., Kintsch & van Dijk, 1978; Rumelhart, 1978). However, there is far more to *Remembering* than the notion of schemata, as Bartlett's conception of cognitive schemata is clearly distinguishable from modern information-processing based conceptions in that he considered schemata to be essentially *social* both in nature and function. Bartlett's theory of memory is unique in its claim that remembering is essentially a *social* phenomenon—information is encoded for social purposes and remembered to facilitate and fulfil social needs and ends. Implicit in this is a rebuttal of the value of attempting to investigate 'pure' memory processes, including remembering, in isolation from the social context within which the processes were employed. From the viewpoint of our own research Bartlett's theory provided us with an initial appreciation of the possible relationships between the cognitive and social aspects of cognition which we could investigate empirically. This allowed us to design a series of studies which sought to address these relationships systematically.

The close relationship between individual and group levels of analysis is also implicit in the philosophical writings of Wittgenstein (1953), in relation to the social nature and functions of language and its relation to social action. Wittgenstein argued that we remember primarily in order to promote particular kinds of social order and action through the medium of social interaction; remembering to represent our experiences to ourselves was of secondary importance. Wittgenstein's constructionist theme has since provided the underpinning for some more recent social psychological studies of the social construction of social behaviour and communication (e.g. Gergen, 1982; Shotter, 1984), and psychological–philosophical accounts of collective remembering in particular (Shotter, 1987, 1990).

In addition to our own experimental approach to studying social remembering, a wide variety of approaches and methodologies have been brought to bear on the study of social memory. Perhaps the most important of these are represented in two edited collections of papers on collective memory (Carraher *et al.*, 1987), and collective remembering (Middleton & Edwards, 1990). The papers in these collections illustrate the very diverse and eclectic approach to the phenomenon of social remembering that has emerged over the last decade.

EMPIRICAL STUDIES OF SOCIAL REMEMBERING

The research programme reviewed below addresses one particular area of social cognition termed by Larson and Christensen (1993), *informational retrieval*, although the area is more commonly known by the terms social remembering (Clark, Stephenson, & Kniveton, 1990), group recall (Stephenson *et al.*, 1986), or group remembering (Clark & Stephenson, 1989). Clark (1987) defined social remembering as recall which takes place within the context of social interactions between people who have experienced the same (or similar) social events, resulting in either the production of a joint account of the event, or an agreed response to direct questions about the event, and/or the modification of subsequent individual remembering. Stephenson *et al.* (1986) also included situations in which group discussion occurs at one stage or another between the encoding and recall of an event. Social remembering differs from Wegner's (1986) notion of *transactive memory*, which involves the sharing of individual knowledge through social networks, as there is no requirement that members of transactive memory networks experience the same social events.

A small number of earlier empirical studies of social remembering provide some useful, if partial, indicators of the effects of group remembering on what is remembered by both a group, and its individual members. Almost invariably, within-subjects studies comparing group recall with the recall of single individuals have found that groups recall a greater *quantity* of stimulus material accurately regardless of whether group recall preceded (Dashiell, 1935; Yuker, 1955) or followed individual recall (Hoppe, 1962; Lorge & Solomon, 1962; Perlmutter, 1953; Perlmutter & de Montmollin, 1952; Ryak, 1965), or individual and group recall was performed by subjects in independent groups (Warnick & Sanders, 1980). Group remembering has also been reported as quantitatively superior to the recall of the most accurate individual group member (Yuker, 1955). Moreover, the superiority of group over individual remembering holds even in circumstances where individual performance is known to be generally poor (e.g., in immediate recall experiments) (Hartwick, Sheppard, & Davis, 1982). Hartwick, Sheppard, and Davis (1982) also suggested that the superior recall of groups was likely to be due to the group possessing greater cognitive resources than individuals—there is a greater probability of at least one member of a group recalling a fact than there is of one individual recalling the fact alone.

In order to compare the *potential* productivity of groups with actual productivity, several studies have compared actual group performance with that predicted by *nominal* groups or algebraic models. Interestingly, the recall performance of *real*, face-to-face, groups (with *n* members) has been consistently reported as inferior to that of *nominal* groups (fictitious groups created by randomly combining the products of *n* subjects who have recalled individually) (Lorge & Solomon, 1962; Perlmutter & de Montmollin, 1952; Ryak, 1965). Studies have also reported attempts to extrapolate group recall from individual recall performance, most frequently using the probabilistic model of group productivity proposed by Lorge and Solomon (1955). This model predicts the probability of a group recalling a particular item of information given that the probability of an individual recalling that item is known, and the model assumes no process loss. Only studies which have employed nonsense syllables as stimulus material have reported that predictions from individual recall were achieved by groups (Hoppe, 1962; Perlmutter & de Montmollin, 1952; Ryak, 1965). Studies which have employed meaningful words or three-digit numbers as stimulus material have found that predictions from individual performance consistently over-predict actual group performance significantly (Lorge & Solomon, 1962; Morrissett, Crannell, & Switzer, 1964). The under performance of groups in comparison to what might be expected by individual performance is generally referred to as *process loss* (Steiner, 1972).

Another example of process loss is provided by studies which have investigated the effects of recalling initially as an individual and then as a group member (Alper *et al.*, 1976; Dashiell, 1935; Perlmutter, 1953; Yuker, 1955). Although these studies have generally revealed that groups produced more accurate recall than did individuals, in some cases comparisons between individual and group recall have revealed that some individuals produced more accurate recall than did their own group, suggesting that some process loss may well be due to either 'social loafing' (Latané, Williams, & Harkin, 1979), or coordination loss if a group rejects the (accurate) account of a member. Alper *et al.* (1976) also found that group estimates of the duration of a staged crime subjects had witnessed were significantly better than individual estimates. However, they also reported that on average groups produced some 40% more errors of commission (fabrications) in their recall protocols than did individuals. In other studies, individual recall has followed either group discussion (Warnick & Sanders, 1980) or group recall (Bekhterev & de Lange, 1924; Yuker, 1955), and individual recall accuracy has been found to have been enhanced, and become less variable when it followed collaborative recall.

THE SOCIAL REMEMBERING RESEARCH PROGRAMME

The general focus of our own research on social remembering has been to investigate experimentally the ways in which a group-level of analysis is appropriate to explain and predict remembering by face-to-face task-oriented groups, in comparison to the performance of individuals. At the outset of the programme it was clear that all of the small number of published studied of group remembering had serious theoretical and methodological limitations. For example, stimulus materials used had often been very artificial and simplistic (e.g., nonsense words and three-digit numbers), and where more complex stimulus material had been used (short stories: Perlmutter, 1953; Yuker, 1955; classroom incidents: Dashiell, 1935), the decision criteria for accuracy were often vague and subjective (see Clark, 1987, for a critical review).

Moreover, earlier studies had almost exclusively focused only on one aspect of social remembering—quantitative comparisons of accurate recall and errors production by individuals and groups. Despite Bartlett's (1932) early work on the reconstructive nature of remembering, particularly in relation to the recall of connected discourse (e.g., stories or events), few of the studies mentioned above went beyond a simple analysis of the quantity of accurate/inaccurate reproduction. In addition, most studies examined only free-recall measures of recall—little was known of the effects of social remembering on cued-recall or recognition measures (i.e., where individuals/groups are required to either answer direct questions about, or recognise information from, the stimulus material). While an analysis of free-recall errors for nonsense words and lists of numbers is unlikely to provide us with any useful insights into the nature of either individual or social remembering, such error analyses may provide extremely useful information about the nature of both individual and social remembering when the stimulus material being recalled is more realistic, and particularly when it is in the form of a connected discourse (e.g., a story or a social interaction).

In addition, none of the above studies had ever addressed the issue of the *quality* of what was accurately recalled by either individuals and groups. The *quality* of what is recalled is not, of course, an issue where each 'item' of stimulus material has an equal value (e.g., word or number lists), but quality is of great importance when the stimulus material is a connected discourse of any kind. All discourses, from the most simple to the most complex, must by their nature contain details which are *central* to the meaning (or *gist*) of the discourse and details which are peripheral to that meaning (Kintsch, 1974). In a *coherent* or comprehensible discourse the structure of the discourse itself normally provides strong indications about how information should be processed and the main elements identified (see Kintsch & van Dijk, 1978; van Dijk & Kintsch, 1983). It is essential, therefore, that when individuals or groups recall a coherent discourse we are able to distinguish between accurate recall that clearly represents the gist of the discourse and that which only represents peripheral details. For example, if the stimulus material was a story, it is both theoretically and pragmatically important to be able to distinguish between the recall protocols of two individuals (or groups) who have the same accuracy score, when one individual has accurately reproduced the gist of the story, while the other has reproduced a jumble of unconnected peripheral details, albeit accurately. To summarise, the *quality* of what is recalled refers to the degree to which a recall protocol contains the gist or main points of an interaction or other discourse. When comparing individual and social remembering it is therefore important to investigate in what ways social remembering systematically affects both the quantity and the quality of what is recalled.

It is not surprising that early studies of social remembering failed to address this issue as the necessary methodology for developing models of discourse comprehension only began to appear in the late 1970s. These macropropositional models of discourse comprehension (e.g., Kintsch & van Dijk, 1978) have allowed us to perform a variety of psycholinguistic analyses of both individual and group free-recall protocols which were unavailable to earlier researchers. While it is relatively easy to achieve fairly high levels of inter-rater reliability when analysing recall protocols of simplistic stimulus materials such as word lists, prior to Kintsch and van Dijk's (1978) introduction of macropropositional analysis the analysis of recall protocols containing connected discourse was often haphazard, even when short stories were employed as stimulus material. Researchers tended to adopt their own, often idiosyncratic, definitions of what constituted the 'units' into which a protocol should be decomposed in order to be analysed. Although researchers tended to apply their own analysis rules consistently across their own studies (giving fairly high inter-rater reliability), making valid comparisons between studies conducted by different researchers was extremely difficult.

Kintsch and van Dijk's (1978; van Dijk & Kintsch, 1983) methods of analysis for connected discourse had much to recommend them. Firstly, they offered methods by which both a stimulus discourse and recall protocols could be decomposed into psychologically 'real' units—propositions (the 'idea units' actually contained within the discourse itself) and macropropositions (higher-order propositions representing the gist of the discourse, which may be explicitly contained within the discourse or inferred from the discourse). This allows for precise quantitative analyses of accuracy and error to be conducted which can be readily and consistently applied across discourses (and across researchers) with high levels of inter-rater reliability. Secondly, macropropositional analysis allowed researchers to systematically investigate the *quality* of what was recalled in relation to the original discourse. As noted above, the *quality* of what is accurately recalled may in some cases be virtually independent of the *quantity* of accurate recall. For example, the testimony of a witness to a crime who recalls many accurate details may not be as valuable in evidence as a second witness who recalls fewer accurate details if the former only recalled peripheral details (e.g., physical details of several other witnesses) while the latter recalled details that were central to the event (e.g., physical details of a perpetrator).

In order to assess the quality of free-recall, a multi-stage, hierarchical model of a stimulus discourse is generated which relates its constituent individual propositions (idea units) to the structure of the discourse (macropropositions), and then relates this to individual cognitive processes occurring during the encoding and comprehension of the discourse. Such models are *predictive* as well as descriptive as they allow for the probabilistic prediction of individual recall based on the analysis of the stimulus discourse. Indeed, such models have proved highly predictive of individual free-recall for fairly long pieces of written discourse (e.g., stories, newspaper articles, research reports etc.—see van Dijk & Kintsch, 1983). Our studies sought to extend the use of macropropositional analysis in two ways: firstly, by the novel application of the analysis method to social interactional rather than story stimulus material; and, secondly, by assessing the value of such predictive models of accurate free-recall for predicting both individual and *group* recall.

Two additional issues were also of interest to us: firstly, as noted above, earlier comparisons of individual and social remembering had almost entirely examined only free-recall measures. We were also interested in investigating the relationship between individual and social remembering using cued-recall measures where subjects are required to respond to direct questions regarding aspects of the stimulus discourse. Secondly, employing cued-recall measures also allowed us to investigate a second important issue—the relationship between accuracy and confidence in cued-recall answers for both individuals and groups, an issue which will be discussed in detail in the next section.

To summarise, we set out to investigate the social remembering of complex purposive social interactions with two general orientations:

(a) *Quantitative*—investigating the relationship between individual and social remembering in terms of recall accuracy, different types of errors, confidence in recall, and the relationship between accuracy and confidence. Both free-recall and cued-recall methods were generally employed; and

(b) *Qualitative*—investigating the quality of accurate individual and group free-recall using modified versions of Kintsch and van Dijk's (1978; van Dijk & Kintsch, 1983) macropropositional model of discourse comprehension and recall both to analyse and to *predict* accurate recall.

In addition, we also wished to extend the study of social remembering beyond the comparisons of individual versus dyadic recall to which earlier studies had been limited. In several of our studies we therefore compared individual and dyadic recall with that of four-person groups.

During the initial planning of our programme we became aware that an investigation of social remembering could have both theoretical and applied implications. Moreover, we realised that social remembering could have long-term (and potentially negative) consequences for some members of society—

those that are suspected or accused of criminal activity. Our programme has, therefore, focused on the social psychological aspects of a forensic psychological problem—social remembering in eyewitness contexts.

SOCIAL REMEMBERING AND THE LAW

There are some social situations where accurate social remembering is of the utmost importance, and many of the best examples are in the area of criminal investigations and proceedings in courts of law. For example, more than one police officer may witness a crime being committed, or be present when a suspect is interrogated or a witness interviewed. In such situations it is possible, and indeed likely, that officers will informally discuss the case together, if not produce a joint report of the event. Although social remembering has generally been neglected as a research area by psychologists, there have been occasional studies of collaborative remembering for everyday discourse (Edwards & Middleton, 1986, 1987), and some psycho-legal studies of, for example, jurors' group recall (Hartwick, Sheppard, & Davis, 1982) and collaborative eyewitness testimony (Alper et al., 1976; Hollin & Clifford, 1983; Rupp et al., 1976; Warnick & Sanders, 1980) where social remembering has been a focus. However, it is surprising that no psychological investigations of individual and group remembering by police officers had been conducted until we began our research programme (e.g. Clark, Stephenson, & Kniveton, 1987; Stephenson, Kniveton, & Wagner, 1991). This is despite the fact that testimony presented by the police in British courts may be based on such discussions and recollections, after the event, of criminal acts or social interactions that they have witnessed either individually or jointly.

To understand the importance of social remembering to the police it is necessary to outline briefly the current situation in England and Wales regarding the admissibility of collaborative evidence in court. Reports, usually made in police officers' notebooks, frequently form the basis of an officer's testimony during court proceedings. In English courts it has historically been the case that officers swore under oath that they wrote their notes 'as soon as possible' after an event, and that they did not collaborate with other officers in their preparation. Such statements have, however, occasionally led to incredulity from judges and defence lawyers (and sometimes juries) when several officers presented the same evidence, almost word-for-word, while swearing that they compiled their evidence separately.

Collaboratively based testimony raises several legal problems. For example, if testimony is based on collaborative recall, how do officers resolve disagreements on matters of fact? If an officer agrees to include facts in a joint account because others assert them, although he or she believes them to be false, a jury would be (at least partially) deprived of its right to decide the case on all the available facts, and the officer might be accused of perjury. More-over, if an officer agrees to a joint account that he or she does not know to be true from the evidence of his or her senses it is, strictly, only hearsay evidence. Finally, if an officer presents testimony on behalf of him or herself and other officers, and some of the testimony originates from the observations of the other officers, how can such a witness be fully cross-examined in court as to the truth of those observations?

Regardless of these possible legal objections to the admission of collabora-tive testimony, police officers (but not members of the public) in England and Wales have had the option of presenting collaborative testimony in court since an Appeal Court ruling in 1953 (*R. v. Bass*). However, the use of collaboratively produced police testimony in court has not gone unchallenged. Heaton-Armstrong (1987, p. 472), in a swingeing critique of the acceptability of collaborative testimony, 'condemned uncompromisingly the insidious and dangerous practice of pre-note making collaboration by police officers over anything other than the spoken word'. In contrast, Baines (1987, p. 1869), a serving police officer, presented a different view:

> Collaboration is designed to produce a clear overall picture of what has occurred and not as [Heaton-Armstrong] suggests—that the officers should agree a 'com-mon version' of the incident . . . A clear overall picture of the incident will assist not only the prosecution case but can also assist the defence in that, as far as possible, no particulars will be left out of the officer's records, particulars which could assist one or more of the defendants at a subsequent trial.

It was against this background of anecdotal legal 'wisdom' that we identi-fied social remembering as essentially an applied social cognition problem where the accuracy (or inaccuracy) of recall, and the quality of what was recalled, may have severe and long-lasting consequences, particularly for the accused. As testimony based on social remembering was being admitted as evidence in court, we considered that a detailed investigation of several as-pects of the phenomenon would be of both theoretical and applied importance.

OVERVIEW OF DESIGN AND METHODOLOGY

The studies reviewed here investigated the recall of a particular type of pur-posive social interaction: *remembering what was said, and by whom, during police interrogations*. All the studies employed a similar type of stimulus discourse and general methodology, as a brief summary will illustrate. Two stimulus discourses were employed: (i) a fictional police interrogation of a woman who alleged that she had been raped, in two formats: a dramatised audio recording (Clark, 1987; Stephenson, Clark, & Wade, 1986); and a slide presentation of a transcript of the interrogation (Clark, 1987; Clark, Stephenson, & Kniveton, 1990; Stephenson, Kniveton, & Wagner, 1991); and (ii) a video recording of part of a real interrogation of a woman alleging rape (Stephenson et al., 1986; Stephenson & Wagner, 1989).

Two subject populations were employed for these studies (often in comparison with each other): university undergraduate students and experienced serving police officers. Both free-recall and cued-recall measures were used as (a) no earlier comparisons of individual and group recall had compared both memory measures (although the literature on individual recall suggests that the two types of recall tap different recall strategies which may lead to significant differences in the quality and quantity of accurate recall); and (b) British police officers generally employ both methods when interviewing witnesses and interrogating suspects. The general strategy adopted during questioning by police officers is, firstly, to ask a witness or suspect to give an account in their own words of what had taken place (i.e. a free-recall), and then to ask a series of detailed questions about the incident, often to elicit further potentially relevant details not included in the initial free-recall account (i.e., a cued-recall). In addition, police interviewers regularly ask witnesses and suspects how confident they are in the answers they are providing. We therefore required subjects to rate their confidence in the accuracy of each cued-recall response they made. No ratings of confidence in free-recall material were required, as a pilot study indicated that individuals experienced difficulty in systematically dividing their protocol into separate statements in order to rate them for confidence.

In all of the studies, a brief general introduction was followed by exposure of the subjects to the stimulus discourse. Subjects then completed a distractor task individually for several minutes. Subjects would then be randomly assigned to either individual or dyadic recall conditions (all studies) and, in some studies, an additional four-person group condition (Clark, 1987; Clark, Stephenson, & Rutter, 1986; Clark, Stephenson, & Kniveton, 1990; Stephenson, Clark, & Wade, 1986). Dyads and four-person groups would then be assigned to individual experimental rooms to work in. Subjects in the individual recall conditions would generally complete the recall tasks together in one room. Subjects were required to produce a free-recall account of the stimulus discourse and then to answer specific factual questions about the interrogation in the form of a cued-recall questionnaire. The questionnaire also required them to rate their confidence in each answer they gave on a four-point scale (guessing – doubtful – fairly certain – certain). In dyads and four-person groups all group members had to agree on the material included in their free-recall protocol, and on all cued-recall answers and confidence ratings. In some studies additional measures were taken after the recall tasks had been completed (see below). The reason for individual subjects undertaking their recall together was that we wished to avoid confounding two variables when comparing individual and group recalls—the effects of actual group discussion and simple co-action (i.e., mere presence of another subject). Our studies do not, then, compare group recall with *isolated* individual recall. This issue is also important from a forensic viewpoint as when a witness or suspect is interviewed by the police, by definition there must always be at least two persons present when recall occurs.

In general, the text of the stimulus discourse and all free-recall protocols were analysed using a modified version of Kintsch and van Dijk's (1978; van Dijk & Kintsch, 1983) macropropositional model of discourse analysis (see Clark, 1987; Clark, Stephenson, & Rutter, 1986). This allowed us to score each protocol very precisely for accuracy and error. In addition, in some studies we developed a probabilistic, predictive model of free-recall of the original, and compared this with actual free-recall by both individuals and groups. This allowed us to investigate the relationship between the quality of individual recall and that of dyadic and four-person group recall.

RESEARCH FINDINGS

We have divided the review of our research findings into sections which address different aspects of the relationship between individual and social remembering. Firstly, we compare individual and social remembering when independent groups of subjects have participated in the individual and group recall conditions (i.e., purely between-subjects designs). We then consider the individual/group relationship in studies where subjects have participated in both individual and social remembering in the same experiment (using both between- and within-subjects designs). In the latter studies we review the effects of social remembering when it occurs prior to, or following, individual remembering.

Individual and Group Narrative Recall

Two studies have compared individual and group free-recall narratives in detail for a variety of measures of accuracy and error: Stephenson, Clark, and Wade (1986) and Clark, Stephenson, and Kniveton (1990). Stephenson, Clark, & Wade (1986) compared individual, dyadic and four-person group accuracy in a student sample, while Clark, Stephenson, and Kniveton (1990) compared the performance of a student sample with that of a sample of serving British police officers. Our findings and conclusions regarding the relationship between individual and social remembering are summarised in terms of effects on (a) the quantity and quality of reproductive recall, (b) the incidence of various types of errors; and (c) the willingness of individuals and groups to make evaluative comments on the stimulus discourse.

The Initial Study (Clark, Stephenson, & Rutter, 1986; Stephenson, Clark, & Wade, 1986)

Reproducing the original—quantity. Stephenson, Clarke, and Wade (1986) defined reproductive recall as: 'recalled propositions that are accurate reproductions or semantic equivalents of (macro)propositions appearing in the original text'. They found that with student subjects the quantity of reproductive recall in protocols increased significantly from individual, to dyad to four-person group (see Table 5.1 and Figure 5.1), and this was true for both the *content* of what was said and for assigning specific utterances to particular speakers. On average, dyads produced significantly more reproductive recall than did individuals, and four-person groups significantly more than both dyads and individuals. However, even though four-person groups reproduced almost twice as much of the original as did individuals, on average they only reproduced approximately a fifth of the content of the original.

Reproducing the gist of the original—quality. As noted above, it is both theoretically and pragmatically important to be able to distinguish in terms of *quality*, between recall protocols which contain the same *quantity* of reproductive recall. While the issue of quality has been extensively investigated by

Table 5.1 Stephenson, Clark, and Wade (1986)—summary of free- and cued-recall measures: conditional means

	Individual	Dyad	Four-person group
Free-recall measures			
Total reproductive recall (including correctly identified speakers)	36.3	53.9	70.6
Reconstructive (implicational) errors	21.5	14.4	16.1
Confusional errors	1.4	1.7	1.0
Metastatements	46.2	19.4	10.6
Cued-recall measures			
Accurate answers	8.2	10.9	13.7
Confidence (accurate answers)	3.2	3.5	3.8
Confidence (inaccurate answers)	2.0	2.3	3.1

Note: The data in this table is extracted from 'Meetings make evidence? An experimental study of collaborative and individual recall of a simulated police interrogation' by G. M. Stephenson, N. K. Clark, and G. S. Wade, 1986, *Journal of Personality and Social Psychology*, **50**, 1113–22.

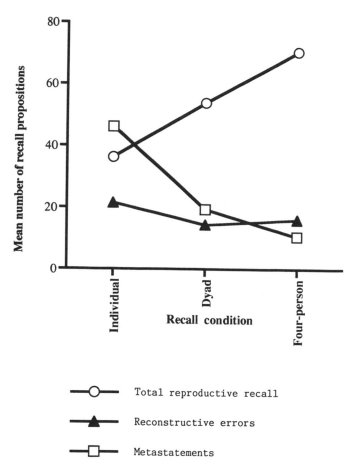

Figure 5.1 The effect of social remembering on free-recall: reproductive recall, reconstructive errors and metastatements (Stephenson, Clark, & Wade, 1986)

cognitive psychologists interested in the recall of written discourse, particularly stories (e.g., Kintsch, 1974), no studies had systematically investigated the quality of individual reproductive recall for a social interaction, nor had any qualitative comparisons between individual and group recall been made. Clark, Stephenson, and Rutter (1986) reported the first qualitative analysis of reproductive recall by individuals and groups for a social interaction, using the protocols produced by student subjects in Stephenson, Clark, and Wade (1986). As noted above, a modified version of Kintsch and van Dijk's (1978) model of story comprehension was employed to develop models of recall for the stimulus discourse (Clark, 1987). Such models, based on mechanistic assumptions regarding individual cognitive processes involved in encoding, comprehension and recall, allowed us to test various assumptions about the strategies employed in working memory to select and retain particular propositions from a discourse for further processing in order to develop a coherent representation in long-term memory of the gist of the discourse. In our studies models derived from several possible processing strategies (e.g. random selection, primacy, recency) were compared. Interestingly, we consistently found that the most predictive model of recall for a social interaction was one based closely on the processing model found to be most predictive of story recall tested by Kintsch and van Dijk (1978). This finding suggests that subjects appear to employ fairly similar mechanistic cognitive processing strategies when they attempt to comprehend information from both written stories and heard social interactions.

In terms of social remembering, the important issue was whether or not group recall had any systematic effects on the quality of what was recalled and, if so, in what ways. In other words, in what ways is social remembering *qualitatively* different from individual recall? Clark, Stephenson, and Rutter (1986) found that their model of recall quality was almost equally predictive of both individual and dyadic recall, and to a lesser, but still significant degree, of four-person group recall. Table 5.2 summarises the correlations between our model of recall quality and actual recall by individuals and groups. It should, however, be noted that these correlations between predicted and

Table 5.2 Quality of recall: getting the gist. Comparisons of predicted and actual recall

Recall condition		Correlation (r)	Variance explained
Clark, Stephenson, and Rutter (1986)			
Individual		0.57	30.3%
Dyad		0.52	27.3%
Four-person group		0.44	19.3%
Clark (1987)			
Individual	Student	0.50	24.9%
	Police	0.48	23.0%
Dyad	Student	0.53	29.5%
	Police	0.48	23.1%
Four-person group	Student	0.52	26.9%
	Police	0.51	25.8%

Note: The data in this table is extracted from 'Memory for a complex social discourse: The analysis and prediction of individual and group recall' by N. K. Clark, G. M. Stephenson, and D. R. Rutter, 1986, *Journal of Memory and Language*, **25**, 295–313, and from 'The analysis and prediction of individual and group remembering' by N. K. Clark, 1987, Unpublished doctoral thesis, University of Kent at Canterbury, UK.

actual recall of an interaction are strikingly lower than those achieved by other researchers who have compared predicted and actual recall for short story material (see van Dijk & Kintsch, 1983, for a review), suggesting that some of the complexities involved in comprehending a social interaction are not currently adequately accounted for in the mechanistic assumptions of the current macropropositional model.

The propensity to err. Two types of error were examined in our studies: *reconstructive* (or implicational) errors and *confusional* errors. Reconstructive (or implicational) errors were defined by Stephenson, Clark, and Wade (1986) as 'recalled propositions giving either (a) the addition of normal properties and plausible detail, (b) particularization, or (c) specification of normal conditions, components, or consequences of events'. In other words, recalled information which did not appear in the original, but which did *not* contradict anything in the original. In contrast, confusional errors were defined by Stephenson, Clark, and Wade (1986) as 'recalled propositions that clearly contradict (macro)propositions in the original text'—that is, recalled information which directly contradicted material in the original. Earlier studies comparing individual and group recall have tended to confabulate these two types of error in one error category (e.g., Alper *et al.*, 1976, who analysed what they termed 'errors of commission' or 'fabrications'). However, the literature on the recall of written discourse provides strong theoretical and empirical support for distinguishing between these two types of error (see Clark, 1987, for a detailed discussion of this issue, or Kintsch & van Dijk, 1978).

In terms of *reconstructive* (or *implicational*) errors Stephenson, Clark, and Wade (1986) found a clear pattern: individuals included a significantly greater number of reconstructions in their protocols than did groups, but there was no difference in the numbers of reconstructions in dyadic and four-person protocols (Table 5.1 and Figure 5.1). Group recall appeared to lead to the suppression of reconstructive errors. In contrast, the level of *confusional errors* (i.e., recall propositions which directly contradicted material in the original) was surprisingly low, varying between 1.5% and 2.8% of the total content of protocols, and there was no significant effect of recall condition on the number of confusional errors in protocols.

Making evaluative comments. Metastatements were defined by Stephenson, Clark, and Wade (1986) as 'recalled propositions that make comment on (a) the content or organization of the text, (b) expressions of the subject's own attitudes/opinions towards the text, or (c) the attribution of motives/ intentions to characters that are not explicitly stated in the text'. Examples of metastatements from Stephenson, Clark, and Wade (1986) included such statements as 'I [the subject] believe the woman was hiding something', and 'I think the police could have been more understanding towards the woman'. Such statements cannot legitimately be coded as either reproductive recall or as errors as they simply express the subject's own views and opinions on the characters in the interaction. None of the early studies of social remembering reviewed above examined the effects of collaboration on the number of meta-statements included in protocols. This is not a serious omission as subjects tend not to make such comments when the stimulus material to be recalled is, for example, a word list. However, when stimulus material is lifelike, stimulating and controversial, a significant proportion of the content of a protocol may be metastatement. Indeed, the absence of metastatements in individual protocols might be interpreted as an indication of a lack of self-involvement with the stimulus discourse. Stephenson, Clark, and Wade (1986) found a substantial and highly significant effect for group recall on the inclusion of metastatements in protocols. Dyads produced significantly fewer metastatements than did individuals, while four-person groups produced significantly fewer than individuals and dyads (Table 5.1 and Figure 5.1).

Individuals and Groups Answering Questions

Accuracy.   Several of our studies have compared individual and social remembering using cued-recall measures. Typically, following a free-recall task individuals and groups were presented with a series of questions requesting specific, detailed information about the stimulus interaction. Alongside each question appeared a four-point confidence scale on which subjects rated their confidence in the accuracy of their answer (from 'guessing' to 'certain'). Subjects in group recall conditions were instructed to produce one agreed answer to each question and one agreed rating of confidence. As cued-recall measures are far more readily quantifiable than free-recall measures, we have been able to investigate several additional aspects of the relationship between individual and social remembering using a variety of experimental designs. Stephenson, Clark, and Wade's (1986) findings for cued-recall accuracy (see Table 5.1) had a pattern similar to their findings for reproductive free-recall: student four-person groups produced significantly more accurate answers than did individuals and dyads, and dyads produced significantly more accurate answers than did individuals.

Being sure that you are right—confidence and accuracy.   The relationship between accurate recall and a subject's own confidence in the accuracy of what they recall has been an important focus of research for applied psychologists in the area of eyewitness testimony for many years. A major part of this research has examined the accuracy and confidence of eyewitness identifications, focusing on factors which influence whether a witness who accurately (or inaccurately) identifies a suspect will report that identification or mis-identification with confidence or with doubt, and the subsequent effects of confidently presented testimony on mock-jury decision making (cf. Stephenson, 1984). In an influential series of studies, Cutler and his associates (e.g., Cutler *et al.*, 1986; Cutler, Penrod, & Stuve, 1988) criticised studies which investigate the influence of witness variables (e.g., confidence) on mock-jury decisions as they have generally only manipulated one or two variables within their studies. They argue that studies which employ such simplistic experimental designs may over-estimate the influence of witness variables in the far more complex multivariate environment of a real trial (e.g., Lindsay, Wells, & Rumpel, 1981; Wells, Ferguson, & Lindsay, 1981). Cutler, Penrod, and Stuve (1988) examined mock-jury decisions when ten witness and identification factors were systematically manipulated. They found that only one variable, witness confidence, had reliable effects on various indices of mock-jurors' perceptions. The highly confident witness was viewed by mock jurors as strengthening the prosecution case, and enhancing the credibility of the victim and the police.

Surprisingly little research has examined the relationship between accuracy and confidence for discourse recalled by a witness, and only the few studies mentioned above have investigated the effects of social remembering on that relationship. Given Cutler *et al.*'s (1986, 1988) findings for the influence of witness confidence in identifications on juries' verdicts, it might be expected that jurors might also be influenced by a witness's confidence in other aspects of their testimony, particularly by what a suspect is alleged to have said. In summary, a witness' reported confidence in his or her testimony is likely to influence whether or not a jury believes that testimony to be accurate or otherwise.

Stephenson, Clark, and Wade (1986) required the individuals and groups in their study to rate their confidence in the accuracy of each cued-recall answer they gave, with groups providing one agreed rating for each answer. Overall confidence scores were calculated for accurate and inaccurate answers separately. The outcome of comparisons between individual and group conditions was fairly clear. Firstly, both individuals and groups were consistently able to distinguish between their accurate and inaccurate answers in terms of reported confidence—confidence in accurate answers was consistently higher than that for inaccurate answers (Table 5.1 and Figure 5.2). However, there was an interaction effect between confidence in accurate and inaccurate answers and recall condition. Individual subjects made the greatest discrimination in terms of confidence between accurate and inaccurate answers. This discrimination reduced in dyads, and reduced even further in four-person groups.

The Second Study (Clark, 1987; Clark, Stephenson, & Kniveton, 1990)

Our second study had two aims: (a) to replicate and extend the findings for individual and social remembering by student subjects in the first study, and

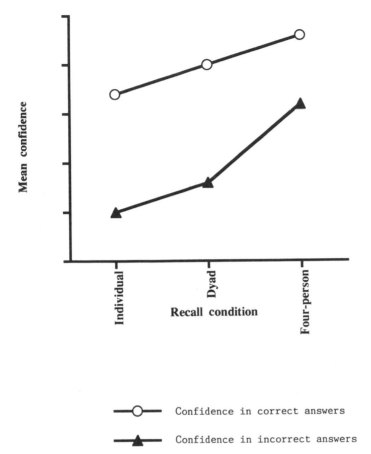

Figure 5.2 Social remembering and cued-recall confidence (Stephenson, Clark, & Wade, 1986)

(b) to compare the performance of student subjects with that of serving police officers.

Reproductive recall—quality.   Clark, Stephenson, and Kniveton (1990) compared individual and social remembering by student and police subjects. They found that although police four-person groups reproduced significantly more of the original than did individual police officers, four-person groups reproduced marginally *less* than did dyads (Table 5.3). In contrast, students in both group conditions only reproduced slightly more of the original than did individuals. Although student individuals produced significantly more reproductive recall than did police individuals, police groups outperformed student groups by a considerable margin. In terms of *correctly* identifying the speakers of particular utterances, police dyads and four-person groups significantly outperformed individuals, while for student subjects the number did not vary across conditions. The number of *incorrect* speaker identifications made did not vary across recall condition within subject samples, although police subjects identified more speakers, both correctly and incorrectly, than did students across all conditions. In line with Stephenson, Clark, and Wade's (1986) finding, the amount of the original reproduced in protocols was again generally low—although police dyads reproduced the greatest quantity of reproductive recall, this only represented approximately a quarter of the original.

Our finding that dyads reproduce significantly more of the original than individuals (student subjects in Stephenson, Clark, & Wade, 1986, and police subjects in Clark, Stephenson, & Kniveton, 1990) is consistent with the findings of earlier studies which employed less sophisticated methods of accuracy assessment (e.g., Warnick & Sanders, 1980). However, the finding that student reproductive recall did *not* increase in group conditions in Clark, Stephenson,

Table 5.3 Clark, Stephenson, and Kniveton (1990)—summary of free- and cued-recall measures: conditional means

		Individual	Dyad	Four-person group
Free-recall measures				
Total reproductive recall (including correctly identified speakers)	Student	75.5	78.5	77.0
	Police	65.7	114.0	105.8
Reconstructive (implicational) errors	Student	20.2	14.1	13.0
	Police	23.0	33.1	27.9
Confusional errors	Student	2.2	0.6	1.6
	Police	3.0	4.0	1.3
Metastatements	Student	40.8	27.5	17.9
	Police	20.2	2.7	3.8
Cued-recall measures				
Accurate answers	Student	9.1	10.8	12.4
	Police	10.7	13.1	14.0
Confidence (accurate answers)	Student	3.5	3.7	3.7
	Police	3.5	3.6	3.8
Confidence (inaccurate answers)	Student	2.8	3.0	3.3
	Police	2.3	3.0	3.0

Note: The data in this table is extracted from 'Social remembering: Quantitative aspects of individual and collaborative remembering by police officers and students' by N. K. Clark, G. M. Stephenson & B. H. Kniveton, 1990, *British Journal of Psychology*, **81**, 73–94.

and Kniveton's (1990) study is at odds with these findings, and we are still unable to offer an adequate explanation for this failure to replicate. As will be seen below, the lack of a difference between individual and group reproductive recall was not repeated in our analysis of cued-recall data from the same subjects. Interestingly, the quantity of four-person group reproductive recall (in comparison to dyads) only increased in our first study, and was slighly decreased for both police and student subjects in the second study.

Reproducing the gist of the original—quality.   Clark (1987) reported an additional qualitative analysis using data from our student and police samples. The predictive models tested were refined and revised versions of those used by Clark, Stephenson, and Rutter (1986). Most importantly, the identification of speakers and changes of speaker were now explicitly incorporated into the models. Interestingly, the revised model was marginally, but non-signficantly, more successful in predicting the dyadic and four-person reproductive recall than it was in predicting individual recall (see Table 5.2). An important general conclusion of both theoretical and applied significance that may be drawn from these analyses is that social remembering, in comparison to individual remembering, does not appear to either enhance or diminish the overall quality of reproductive recall. Quality, the ability to coherently recall the main points or gist of the discourse, appears to be mainly a function of the nature of the cognitive processes taking place within individuals during encoding and recall, rather than being dependent on the social context within which recall takes place.

A key assumption of the model of discourse comprehension employed in these studies is that in order to be generally comprehensible a discourse must contain a central 'core' of information—the main points of the discourse or the *gist*. One of the main purposes of such models is to make predictions regarding what is contained in the gist of particular discourses, and the analyses presented above tested the predictive value of these models for individual and social remembering. An alternative, pragmatic, method of investigating what constitutes the gist of a discourse is, or course, to examine what parts of the discourse are consistently recalled by subjects within particular recall conditions. Clark (1987) reported details of such an analysis, and found important differences between individual and group reproductive recall in terms of the *consistency* with which particular items of information were included in protocols. To examine consistency Clark calculated the number of items from the original interaction which appeared in 50% or more of protocols within each recall condition (Table 5.4). For both police and student subjects, those who recalled individually were the least consistent. Dyads consistently included more than twice as much accurate information, and there was a further marginal increase in consistency from dyads to four-

Table 5.4 Clark (1987)—consistency in recall: percentage of the original appearing in 50% or more of recall protocols with each recall condition

Recall condition	Police	Student
Individual	7.7%	2.8%
Dyad	16.2%	7.7%
Four-person group	17.7%	10.9%

Note: The data in this table is extracted from 'The analysis and prediction of individual and group remembering' by N. K. Clark, 1987, Unpublished doctoral thesis, University of Kent at Canterbury, UK.

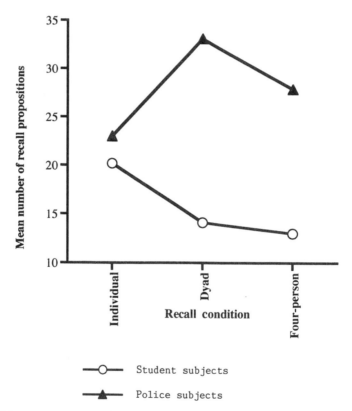

Figure 5.3 The effect of social remembering on reconstructive errors (Clark, Stephenson, & Kniveton, 1990)

person groups. Across all recall conditions police subjects were far more consistent in what reproductive information they included than were their student counterparts. To summarise, while social remembering does not appear to influence the general quality of what is recalled, it clearly influences the consistency with which particular items of information from the original are accurately reproduced in protocols. Social remembering, then, leads to *consistency in quality*.

Reconstructive errors.   Clark, Stephenson, and Kniveton (1990) found a pattern of results similar to that reported by Stephenson, Clark, and Wade (1986) for student subjects: individuals included a significantly greater number of reconstructions than did groups, while dyads and four-person groups did not differ in the number of reconstructions included (Table 5.3 and Figure 5.3). As in Stephenson, Clark, and Wade (1986), group recall led to the suppression of reconstructive errors. However, a reverse pattern of results was found for police subjects—group recall led to an increase in the number of reconstructions included, with police dyads and four-person groups producing significantly more reconstructions than individuals. Moreover, while individual police officers only produced marginally more reconstructions than did student individuals, police dyads and four-person groups included significantly more reconstructions than did their student counterparts.

A further, more detailed, comparison of both student and police protocols revealed an important stylistic difference between the two (Clark, Stephenson, & Kniveton, 1987). Regardless of recall condition, when students were asked to recall the interaction they consistently recalled it in one format—as a story. In contrast, while approximately half of the police individuals also recalled the interaction as a story, the remainder recalled it as a *script*. A protocol in script form appears similar to a script for a (short) play, with a speaker explicitly identified at the beginning of each utterance, and the content of each utterance reported in direct speech (i.e. as a quotation). Clark, Stephenson, and Kniveton (1987) compared the numbers of reconstructional errors made by police individual *scriptwriters* and *storytellers*. They found that the number of reconstructions made by individual scriptwriters was similar to that made by police subjects in the dyadic and four-person recall conditions (who were all scriptwriters). In comparison, the number of reconstructions by individual storytellers was far lower, and very similar to the number made by student individuals (who were all storytellers). To summarise, social remembering appears to exert a complex, dynamic influence on the inclusion of reconstructive error in free-recall. In the studies above the influence appears to be associated with recall strategy (script or story) employed by individuals and groups.

Clark (1995) has recently addressed this issue in more detail using student subjects, a different stimulus social interaction and an experimental manipulation of recall strategy. Subjects were exposed to the stimulus interaction, randomly assigned to either individual or dyadic recall conditions, and completed both free- and cued-recall measures. Within each recall condition, half

Table 5.5 Reconstructive errors—comparisons between script and story recall—individuals versus dyads. Conditional means (Clark, 1995)

Recall condition	Recall strategy	
	Script	Story
Individual	12.3	8.2
Dyadic	17.1	5.8

ANOVA: Recall strategy: $F = 47.5$; df 1,66; $p < 0.001$.
 Recall strategy × recall condition: $F = 10.5$; df 1,66; $p < 0.005$.
Note: The data in this table is extracted from 'Individual and social remembering: The consequences of different recall format strategies' by N. K. Clark, 1995, Submitted for publication.

the individuals or dyads were instructed to recall the interaction as a script, and half to recall the interaction as a story. The effects of recall condition and script/story instructions (and the interaction between the two) on the level of reconstructive error included in protocols were far more clearly illustrated than in the earlier studies. Individuals and groups who recalled the interaction as a script included significantly *greater* numbers of reconstructions than did those who recalled as a story (Table 5.5). In story conditions, dyadic protocols included significantly *fewer* reconstructions than did those of individuals, and the number of reconstructions was *negatively* correlated with the amount of reproductive recall in protocols (i.e., the more subjects were able to reproduce the original, the fewer reconstructions they made). In script conditions the reverse was true—dyadic protocols included significantly *more* reconstructions than did individual protocols, and the number of reconstructions was *positively* correlated with the amount of reproductive recall (i.e., the more subjects accurately reproduced of the original, the more reconstructions they introduced).

To summarise, recalling an interaction in story format as an individual leads to *lower* levels of reconstructive recall than does recalling the interaction as a script. When recalling as a story, social remembering *reduces* the level of reconstructive recall even further, while social remembering as a script *increases* the level of reconstructive recall. This interaction between a social process (individual/social remembering) and recall format (story/script) clearly indicates the importance of considering both the social and cognitive/discourse factors in gaining a fuller understanding of remembering.

Police and Students Answering Questions

Accuracy. Clark, Stephenson, and Kniveton's (1990) findings for both police and students as individuals and groups were consistent with those reported by Stephenson, Clark, and Wade (1986). In both police and student recall conditions four-person groups produced significantly more accurate answers than did either dyads or individuals. Interestingly, across all recall conditions police subjects consistently produced more accurate answers than did students. Social remembering in comparison to individual remembering clearly appears to *enhance* the quantity of accurate cued-recall produced, with the degree of enhancement being at least partially dependent on group size.

Confidence and accuracy. As in Stephenson, Clark, and Wade (1986), individuals and groups in Clark, Stephenson, and Kniveton's (1990) study rated their confidence in each answer they gave, with groups again providing one agreed rating for each answer. Comparisons between overall confidence scores for individual and group recall conditions revealed a consistent pattern in both police and students samples. Individuals and groups were again consistently able to distinguish between accurate and inaccurate answers— confidence in accurate answers was consistently higher than that for inaccurate answers (Table 5.3). Moreover, and consistent with Stephenson, Clark, and Wade's (1986) findings, there was an interaction effect between confidence and recall condition. Once again, individuals made the greatest discrimination between confidence in accurate and inaccurate answers, dyads discriminated less than individuals, and four-person groups were the least discriminatory. Although groups produced more accurate answers than individuals, and were more confident than individuals that their accurate answers were indeed accurate; when their answers were *inaccurate* they were significantly more confident than individuals that their answers were *accurate*.

To summarise, the findings for the effects of social remembering on cued-recall accuracy and confidence are highly consistent in both Stephenson, Clark, and Wade's (1986) and Clark, Stephenson, and Kniveton's (1990) studies: although the greater confidence of groups in their accurate answers may be viewed as a positive benefit of social over individual remembering, this advantage is achieved at a cost—the reduced ability of groups to distinguish appropriately between confidence for accurate and inaccurate answers.

Finally, it should be noted that it is possible that both Stephenson, Clark, and Wade (1986) and Clark, Stephenson, and Kniveton (1990) may have underestimated group performance. In both studies individuals, dyads and four-person groups were allowed the same lengths of time to produce their free- and cued-recall responses. It is arguable that performance in the group conditions may have been negatively affected by the delays inherent in discussing and reaching agreement on what responses to give while such delays would not have occurred in the individual recall conditions. In hindsight it might have been preferable to employ a yoked design, with individuals forced to experience similar delays to those experienced in the group conditions. However, given that all groups in both studies completed their recall tasks well within the time allocated and, indeed, some groups completed the recall tasks before some individuals did, the effect of this possible natural confound is likely to have been only marginal in these studies. However, it is worth noting that such a confound may have far greater impact on group performance when the discourse to be free-recalled is substantially longer, or when the number of cued-recall answers and confidence ratings is substantially greater.

The Consequences of Discussion

Recently, Yarmey (1992) has investigated the effects of group discussion on subsequent individual and dyadic free-recall using a between subjects design: recall condition (no discussion/individual recall vs. dyadic discussion/ individual recall vs. dyadic discussion/dyadic recall) × retention period (immediate vs. 48-hour delay). The stimulus discourses for the study were recordings of staged telephone calls by a kidnapper demanding a ransom, and subjects were blindfolded during the stimulus presentation. Subjects in both immediate and delayed discussion conditions were allowed ten minutes to discuss the discourse immediately after hearing the stimulus, while the experimenter engaged subjects in the no discussion/individual conditions in non-relevant conversation for ten minutes.

Using a propositional method of free-recall analysis similar to that used in Stephenson, Clark, and Wade (1986) and Clark, Stephenson, and Kniveton (1990), Yarmey found that although there was a significant overall decline in recall accuracy between the immediate and delayed recall conditions, there were no overall differences in accuracy between recall conditions. Yarmey also found that subjects in the discussion/individual recall condition produced significantly more errors than did those in the other two conditions. Although Yarmey reports no main effects of dyadic discussion on the accuracy of recall, an analysis of the degree to which dyads produced more conventionalised or consistent accounts than individuals revealed an interesting effect of delay. In the immediate conditions there was a relatively high level of consistency across all recall conditions regarding the particular items of accurate information included in protocols. In contrast, while consistency was maintained in the two discussion conditions, it declined significantly in the no discussion/ individual recall condition. Yarmey (1992) concluded that:

> group discussion prior to eyewitness and earwitness testimony in not an advantageous procedure. Police officers and the courts . . . should persist in being concerned with possible distortions in identification evidence without an independent basis in perception (p. 262).

Recalling both as an Individual and as a Group Member

Three additional studies that have examined the relationship between individual and social remembering have limited themselves to comparing individual and dyadic recall. These studies have addressed three major issues:

(a) The relationship between individual and dyadic remembering as a within-subjects factor, rather than as a between-subjects factor as was the case in the earlier studies.
(b) The origins of what is now known as the 'misplaced confidence' effect (Stephenson and Wagner, 1989) in social remembering.
(c) The cognitive, social and interpersonal factors which may influence accuracy and confidence in dyadic recall.

As noted earlier, one important applied example of social remembering is in the area of legal psychology. In the UK it is permissible in some circumstances for two or more police officers to present a joint statement rather than several individual statements as testimony in court. The studies reviewed above are analogous to situations where a police officer *either* recalls an event on their own, *or* recalls it in a group and agrees a joint statement. However, it is likely that in some circumstances police officers may either initially recall an incident on his/her own and then participate in a group recall/discussion of the incident, or vice versa, an officer may be initially involved in a group recall/discussion of an incident, and then recall it on their own.

Stephenson *et al.* (1986) investigated the effects of prior individual and dyadic recall on the accuracy and confidence of subsequent further individual and dyadic recall, within a single experimental design. Student subjects were first shown a video-recording of a real-life police interrogation of a woman who alleged she had been raped, and then assigned to one of two recall conditions: individual followed by dyadic recall (ID) or dyadic followed by individual recall (DI). All subjects were required to complete one individual free- and cued-recall, and one jointly agreed dyadic free- and cued-recall. Stephenson *et al.*'s (1986) cued-recall analysis revealed that there was no main effect of collaborative order (i.e., recalling before or after individual recall) on accuracy, or any difference between the two dyadic groups. In other words, prior individual recall did *not* enhance the accuracy of subsequent dyadic recall in comparison to initial dyadic recall. Individual recall was generally less accurate than dyadic recall, and initial individual recall (ID) was found to be less accurate than subsequent individual recall (DI).

In terms of confidence in *accurate* answers, subjects who initially recalled in a dyad (DI) were significantly more confident than those who initially completed their recall individually (ID)—a finding consistent with our earlier studies (Table 5.6). When subjects who had initially been in a dyad then recalled again individually (DI), their confidence only marginally decreased from that of their dyadic recall. In contrast, when subjects who had initially recalled individually then recalled in a dyad (ID), their confidence *increased*. However, this increased level of confidence was still well below that of subjects who initially recalled as a dyad (DI), and it was also below the level of confidence of DI subjects when they then completed the cued-recall individually subsequent to dyadic recall. Exactly the same pattern of results was found for confidence in accurate answers. Additionally, the difference in confidence levels between subjects who initially recalled in a dyad (DI) and those who recalled individually (ID) was far greater than was the case for accurate answers.

To summarize, dyadic cued-recall was again found to be more accurate than individual recall, even when individual recall was preceded by dyadic recall. In terms of confidence, subjects who recall in a dyad and then as individuals appear to retain their dyad's higher levels of confidence in both accurate and inaccurate answers in subsequent individual responses—a 'misplaced confidence' effect. In contrast, when subjects recalled first as individuals and then in dyads, the misplaced confidence effect in inaccurate answers, while present, appeared to be attenuated.

In a subsequent study, Stephenson and Wagner (1989) extended their investigation of the 'misplaced confidence' effect for inaccurate answers by comparing individual and dyadic recall in a 2 × 2 design: free-recall preparation (individual vs. dyad) × cued-recall (individual vs. dyad). This allowed comparisons between four experimental conditions: II (individual free-recall followed by individual cued-recall); ID (individual free-recall followed by dyadic cued-recall); DI (dyadic free-recall followed by individual cued-recall); and DD (dyadic free-recall followed by dyadic cued-recall). Once again, the focus of the analysis was on the individual and dyadic cued-recall responses.

Consistent with the earlier studies, Stephenson and Wagner found that the cued-recall accuracy of dyads was greater than that of individuals. Moreover, they also discovered that this was regardless of whether subjects had previously completed the free-recall task individually or in a dyad (Table 5.6). In addition, they found that, in comparison to prior individual free-recall, prior dyadic discussion during free-recall *increased* the accuracy of subsequent individual cued-recall. In terms of confidence, Stephenson and Wagner replicated earlier findings that (a) both individuals and dyads were able to distinguish between their accurate and inaccurate answers in terms of differential confidence ratings; and (b) that dyads generally reported greater confidence than did individuals in their answers, regardless of accuracy. They concluded that it was decision making rather than dyadic discussion *per se* which led to this effect—subjects who had earlier participated in dyadic free-recall did not display the misplaced confidence effect when they answered cued-recall questions individually, while those who free-recalled individually and then participated in dyadic cued-recall did display the effect. In a similar way, Hollin and Clifford's (1983) examination of the effects of discussion on recall accuracy and agreement reported that although discussion enhanced accuracy, people have beliefs about their own memory facilities (i.e., metamemories—Flavell & Wellman, 1977), and that the 'feeling of knowing' may well result in an over-confidence in their belief

Table 5.6 Comparisons of individual and dyadic cued-recall

Stephenson, Clark, and Wade (1986)—confidence for correct and incorrect cued-recall answers (higher scores = greater confidence in accuracy)

	Dyad → Individual	Individual → Dyad
Confidence—accurate answers		
First measure	2.89	2.64
Second measure	2.82	2.76
Confidence—inaccurate answers		
First measure	2.54	1.64
Second measure	2.40	2.29

Stephenson and Wagner (1989)—percentage of correctly answered questions (arcsine transformed) and mean confidence—individual versus dyadic answering

	Prior group discussion			
	No	No	Yes	Yes
	Individual (II)	Dyad (ID)	Individual (DI)	Dyad (DD)
Accurate answers	1.67	1.90	1.88	1.96
Confidence—accurate answers	3.57	3.83	3.55	3.84
Confidence—inaccurate answers	2.38	2.96	2.24	2.41

Note: The data in this table is extracted from 'Partners in recall: Collaborative order in the recall of police interrogation' by G. M. Stephenson, D. Abrams, W. Wagner and G. S. Wade, 1986, *British Journal of Social Psychology*, **25**, 341–3, and from 'Origins of the misplaced confidence effect in collaborative recall' by G. M. Stephenson and W. Wagner, 1989, *Applied Cognitive Psychology*, **3**, 227–36.

that they are recalling information accurately, which is then exaggerated by group discussion.

The investigation of the relationship between accuracy and confidence in individual and social remembering was further extended by Stephenson, Kniveton, and Wagner (1991), using both police and student subjects. Stephenson *et al.* were able to examine three factors which they hypothesised might influence recall confidence and accuracy: the combined cognitive resources of the dyad; the interpersonal acquaintance of dyad members; and professional salience. The stimulus discourse for the study was the transcript of the police interrogation first used by Stephenson, Clark, and Wade (1986), presented to subjects in slide form. The *cognitive resources* factor was examined by comparing individual and dyadic performance. The *interpersonal acquaintance* factor was examined by analysing the ratings of several independent judges of how well acquainted the subjects in each of six cued-recall conditions would have been with each other, given their earlier association during a free-recall task. Finally, the *professional salience* factor was examined by comparing the performance of police and student subjects across all conditions, as it was hypothesised that the stimulus discourse (a police interrogation) would have greater professional salience to police officers than to students.

In addition to taking simple measures of accuracy and confidence, Stephenson, Kniveton, and Wagner (1991) also undertook a far more detailed analysis of accuracy than had been made in the earlier studies. All of the cued-recall questions had a 'strictly correct' answer, and it was only when individuals or dyads gave this answer that an additional point was added to their accuracy total. However, in cases where an answer did not actually contradict the original but was not 'strictly correct', this would be counted as an *implicational* (or reconstructive) error. When an answer directly contradicted the original, it would be counted as a *confusional* error. This error classification system is very similar to that employed by Stephenson, Clark, and Wade (1986) for the classification of free-recall errors.

Stephenson, Kniveton, and Wagner (1991) found several significant relationships between their three factors and accuracy; error and confidence:

(a) the greater the cognitive resources available, the greater the number of accurate answers produced;
(b) the greater the interpersonal acquaintance of subjects, the greater the likelihood of higher confidence in the accuracy of implicational errors; and
(c) the more professionally salient the task, the greater the risk of implicational errors being included at the expense of accurate answers, and the greater the confidence in confusional errors.

On the basis of their findings, Stephenson, Kniveton, and Wagner (1991) propose a simple model of the social psychological influences at work during social remembering, and suggest that there are three 'group domains' within which the factors they examined operate:

> These are the intellectual, interpersonal, and intergroup. At the intellectual level, knowledge is shared and performance accordingly improved. At the interpersonal level, motivational processes lead to a greater confidence in generalization, and within the intergroup domain, the demands of social competition lead to illegitimate inference beyond the given evidence, with consequent impaired accuracy, and, in addition, a denial of error in the form of increased confidence in wrong information (1991, p. 473).

CONCLUSIONS

The research programme on social remembering of which the above studies comprise a part is far from complete. Our knowledge about the effects of group discussion on what is remembered, and how this may influence subsequent individual remembering still requires greater clarification. Many issues remain unresolved or uninvestigated. In particular, we have yet to investigate the nature and products of social remembering when each group member possesses both shared and unique information about an event. To date we have only examined cases where all subjects have been exposed to the same stimulus information. In addition, we have still to address several group interaction issues in order to identify relationships between the *nature* and *content* of group discussion and a group's memorial *products*.

As we discussed earlier, the study of social remembering is not only of theoretical social psychological interest, there are important applied psychological issues to be considered, particularly in the area of legal testimony. Despite the limited scope of social remembering research to date, it has already had some impact on police procedures in the UK. In June 1992 the Metropolitan Police in London ended the practice of allowing their officers to compile joint accounts of their arrest notes as a consequence of research on social remembering. Although officers are still permitted to 'confer', they are expected to prepare their own notes of incidents individually, in their own words, and from their own individual perspectives. They must only record what they themselves can individually recollect. Currently, the practice of compiling joint accounts continues, however, in the remainder of the UK.

In conclusion, Stephenson, Kniveton, and Wagner's (1991) emphasis on the importance of considering the influence of, and interactions between, cognitive, interpersonal and intergroup factors in understanding group (or social) cognition reinforces the views of Larson and Christensen (1993) in their general review of the group problem solving literature. Explanations at the level of group cognition are *not* intended as substitutes or replacements for explanations at the level of individual cognition—individual cognition is a precondition for group cognition. However, it is also clear now that explanations purely at the level of individual cognition are totally inadequate for the explanation of everyday cognition which takes place within, and is strongly influenced by, social interactional and group factors. Hopefully, the foolhardiness of simply considering social factors as 'context effects' which influence some form of 'pure' cognition will now be clear. If we are ever to gain a richer and deeper understanding of the relationship between human cognition and social behaviour we must begin to treat the cognitive and social as equal, mutually influencing and dynamically interacting factors.

REFERENCES

Allport, F. W. (1962). A structuronomic conception of behaviour: Individual and collective. *Journal of Abnormal and Social Psychology*, **64**, 3–30.

Alper, A., Buckhout, R., Chern, S., Harwood, R., & Slomovits, M. (1976). Eyewitness identification: Accuracy of individual vs. composite recollections of a crime. *Bulletin of the Psychonomic Society*, **8**, 147–9.

Baines, P. (1987). Insidious collaborators. *Police Review*, **95**, 1868–9.

Bartlett, F. C. (1932). *Remembering: A study in experimental and social psychology.* Cambridge. Cambridge University Press.

Bekhterev, W., & de Lange, M. (1924). *Die ergbnisse des experiments auf dem geiete der kolletiven reflexologie.* Reported in Hartwick, Sheppard, & Davis (1982).

Carraher, T. N., Diaz, S., Engestrom, Y., Hall, W., Hatano, G., Middleton, D., Moll, L. C., Wertsch, J., & Zinchenko, V. (Eds) (1987). Collective memory and remembering. *Quarterly Newsletter of the Laboratory of Comparative Human Cognition*, **9**, Number 1.

Clark, N. K. (1987). *The analysis and prediction of individual and group remembering.* Unpublished doctoral thesis, University of Kent at Canterbury.

Clark, N. K. (1995). Individual and social remembering: The consequences of different recall format strategies. Submitted.

Clark, N. K., & Stephenson, G. M. (1989). Group remembering. In P. B. Paulus (Ed.), *Psychology of Group Influence: New perspectives.* Hillsdale, NJ: Erlbaum.

Clark, N. K., Stephenson, G. M., & Kniveton, B. H. (1987). *Getting the gist: individual and collaborative recall by police officers and students.* Paper presented at Annual Conference of the British Psychological Society, Sheffield.

Clark, N. K., Stephenson, G. M., & Kniveton, B. H. (1990). Social remembering: Quantitative aspects of individual and collaborative remembering by police officers and students. *British Journal of Psychology*, **81**, 73–94.

Clark, N. K., Stephenson, G. M., & Rutter, D. R. (1986). Memory for a complex social discourse: The analysis and prediction of individual and group recall. *Journal of Memory and Language*, **25**, 295–313.

Cutler, B. L., Penrod, S. D., O'Rourke, T. E., & Mortens, T. K. (1986). Unconfounding the effects of contextual cues on eyewitness identification accuracy. *Social Behaviour*, **1**, 113–34.

Cutler, B. L., Penrod, S. D., & Stuve, T. E. (1988). Juror decision making in eyewitness identification cases. *Law and Human Behavior*, **12**, 41–55.

Dashiell, J. F. (1935). Experimental studies of the influence of social situations on the behavior of individual human adults. In C. Murchison (Ed.), *Handbook of Social Psychology* (pp. 1097–158). Worcester, MA: Clark University Press.

van Dijk, T. A., & Kintsch, W. (1983). *Strategies of Discourse Comprehension.* London: Academic Press.

Edwards, D., & Middleton, D. (1986). Joint remembering: Constructing an account of shared experience through conversational discourse. *Discourse Processes*, **9**, 423–59.

Edwards, D., & Middleton, D. (1977). Conversation and remembering: Bartlett revisited. *Applied Cognitive Psychology*, **1**, 77–92.

Fiske, S. T., & Taylor, S. E. (1991). *Social cognition* (2nd edn). Reading, MA: Addison-Wesley.

Flavell, J. H., & Wellman, H. M. (1987). Metamemory. In R. V. Kail & J. H. Hagen (Eds), *Perspectives on the Development of Memory and Cognition.* Hillsdale, NJ: Erlbaum.

Gergen, K. J. (1982). *Towards Transformation in Social Knowledge.* New York: Springer-Verlag.

Halbwachs, M. (1950). *La Memoire collective.* Paris: Presses Universitaires de France. Published in English (1950). *The Collective Memory.* Trans. F. J. Ditter, Jr., & V. Y. Ditter. New York: Harper & Row.

Hartwick, J., Sheppard, B. I., & Davis, J. H. (1982). Group remembering: Research and implications. In R. A. Guzzo (Ed.), *Improving Decision Making in Organizations* (pp. 41–72). London: Academic Press.

Heaton-Armstrong, A. (1987). Police officers' notebooks: Recent developments. *Criminal Law Review*, **34**, 470–2.

Hollin, C. R., & Clifford, B. R. (1983). Eyewitness testimony: The effects of discussion on recall accuracy and agreement. *Journal of Applied Social Psychology*, **13**, 234–44.

Hoppe, R. A. (1962). Memorizing by individuals and groups: A test of the pooling-of-ability model. *Journal of Abnormal and Social Psychology*, **65**, 64–7.

Kintsch, W. (1974). *The Representation of Meaning in Memory*. Hillsdale, NJ: Erlbaum.

Kintsch, W., & van Dijk, T. A. (1978). Towards a model of test comprehension and production. *Psychological Review*, **85**, 363–94.

Larson, J. R. Jr., & Christensen, C. (1993). Groups as problem-solving units: Towards a new meaning of social cognition. *British Journal of Social Psychology*, **32**, 5–30.

Latané, B., Williams, K., & Harkin, S. (1979). 'Many hands make light the work': The causes and consequences of social loafing. *Journal of Personality and Social Psychology*, **37**, 822–32.

Lindsay, R. C. L., Wells, G. L., & Rumpel, C. M. (1981). Can people detect eyewitness identification accuracy within and across situations? *Journal of Applied Psychology*, **66**, 79–89.

Lorge, I., & Solomon, H. (1955). Two models of group behaviour in the solution of eureka-type problems. *Psychometrika*, **20**, 139–48.

Lorge, I., & Solomon, H. (1962). Group and individual behavior in free recall verbal learning. In J. H. Criswell, H. Solomon, & P. Snappes (Eds), *Mathematical Models in Small Group Processes*. Stanford, CA: Stanford University Press.

Middleton, D., & Edwards, D. (Eds) (1990). *Collective Remembering*. London: Sage.

Morrissett, J. O., Crannell, C. W., & Switzer, S. A. (1964). Group performance under various conditions of workload and information redundancy. *Journal of General Psychology*, **71**, 37–347.

Neisser, U. (1976). *Cognition and Reality*. San Francisco: Freeman.

Neisser, U. (Ed.) (1982). *Memory Observed: Remembering in natural contexts*. San Francisco: Freeman.

Perlmutter, H. V. (1953). Group memory of meaningful material. *Journal of Psychology*, **35**, 361–70.

Perlmutter, H. V., & de Montmollin, G. (1952). Group learning of nonsense syllables. *Journal of Abnormal and Social Psychology*, **47**, 762–9.

R. v. Bass (1953). *All England Law reports*. V. 1. 1064–1068.

Rumelhart, D. E. (1978). Understanding and summarizing brief stories. In D. La-Berg & J. Samuels (Eds), *Basic Processes in Reading: Perception and comprehension*. Hillsdale, NJ: Erlbaum.

Rupp, A., Warmbrand, A., Karash, A., & Buckhout, R. (1976). *Effects of group interaction on eyewitness reports*. Paper presented at the meeting of the Eastern Psychological Association, New York City.

Ryak, B. L. (1965). A comparison of individual and group learning of nonsense syllables. *Journal of Personality and Social Psychology*, **2**, 296–99.

Shotter, J. (1984). *Social Accountability and Selfhood*. Oxford: Blackwell.

Shotter, J. (1987). Remembering and forgetting as social institutions. *Quarterly Newsletter of the Laboratory of Comparative Human Cognition*, **9**, 11–19.

Shotter, J. (1990). The social construction of remembering and forgetting. In D. Middleton & D. Edwards (Eds), *Collective Remembering*. London: Sage.

Steiner, I. D. (1972). *Group Processes and Productivity*. London: Academic Press.

Stephenson, G. M. (1984). Accuracy and confidence in testimony: A critical review and some fresh evidence. In D. J. Muller, D. E. Blackman, & A. J. Chapman (Eds), *Psychology and Law: Topics from an international conference*. Chichester: John Wiley.

Stephenson, G. M. (1990). Should collaborative testimony be permitted in courts of law? *Criminal Law Review*, **May**, 302–14.

Stephenson, G. M., Clark, N. K., & Kniveton, B. H. (1989). Collaborative testimony by police officers: A psycho-legal issue. In H. Wegener, F. Lossel, & J. Haisch (Eds), *Criminal Behaviour and the Justice System: Psychological Perspectives*. New York: Springer-Verlag.

Stephenson, G. M., Clark, N. K., & Wade, G. S. (1986). Meetings make evidence? An experimental study of collaborative and individual recall of a simulated police interrogation. *Journal of Personality and Social Psychology*, **50**, 6, 1113–22.

Stephenson, G. M., Kniveton, B., & Wagner, W. (1991). Social influences on remembering: Intellectual, inerpersonal and intergroup components. *European Journal of Social Psychology*, **12**, 463-75.

Stephenson, G. M., & Wagner, W. (1989). Origins of the misplaced confidence effect in collaborative recall. *Applied Cognitive Psychology*, **3**, 227–36.

Stephenson, G. M., Abrams, D., Wagner, W., & Wade, G. S. (1986). Partners in recall: Collaborative order in the recall of police interrogation. *British Journal of Social Psychology*, **25**, 341-3.

Stephenson, G.M., Clark, N. K., & Wade, G. S. (1986). Meetings make evidence? An experimental study of collaborative and individual recall of a simulated police interrogation. *Journal of Personality and Social Psychology*, **50**, 6, 1113–22.

Warnick, D. H., & Sanders, G. S. (1980). The effects of group discussion on eyewitness accuracy. *Journal of Applied Social Psychology*, **10**, 249–59.

Wegner, D. M. (1986). Transactive memory. In B. Mullen & G. Goethals (Eds), *Theories of Group Behavior*. New York: Springer-Verlag.

Wells, G. L., Ferguson, T. J., & Lindsay, R. C. L. (1981). The tractability of eyewitness confidence and its implications for triers of fact. *Journal of Applied Psychology*, **66**, 688–96.

Wells, G. L., & Loftus, E. R. (Eds). (1984). *Eyewitness Testimony*. Cambridge: Cambridge University Press.

Wittgenstein, L. (1953). *Philosophical Investigations*. Oxford: Blackwell & Mott.

Yarmey, D. A. (1992). The effects of dyadic discussion on earwitness recall. *Basic and Applied Social Psychology*, **13**, 251–63.

Yuker, H. E. (1955). Group atmosphere and memory. *Journal of Abnormal and Social Psychology*, **51**, 17–23.

Chapter 6

A Social Identity Model of Deindividuation Phenomena

S. D. Reicher
University of Exeter
R. Spears and T. Postmes
University of Amsterdam

ABSTRACT

This chapter challenges traditional models of deindividuation. These are based on the assumption that such factors as immersion in a group and anonymity lead to a loss of selfhood and hence of control over behaviour. We argue that such models depend upon an individualistic conception of the self, viewed as a unitary construct referring to that which makes individuals unique. This is rejected in favour of the idea that self can be defined at various different levels including the categorical self as well as the personal self. Hence a social identity model of deindividuation (SIDE) is outlined. Evidence is presented to show that deindividuation manipulations gain effect, firstly, through the ways in which they affect the salience of social identity (and hence conformity to categorical norms) and, secondly, through their effects upon strategic considerations relating to the expression of social identities. We conclude that the classic deindividuation paradigm of anonymity within a social group, far from leading to uncontrolled behaviour, maximizes the opportunity of group members to give full voice to their collective identities.

THE ROOTS OF DEINDIVIDUATION THEORY

If the term 'deindividuation' belongs to the era of modern experimental social psychology, the concept itself has a far longer history. Zimbardo traces it back

European Review of Social Psychology, Volume 6. Edited by Wolfgang Stroebe and Miles Hewstone.
© 1995 John Wiley & Sons Ltd.

to primal cultural concepts, claiming that: 'mythically, deindividuation is the ageless life force, the cycle of nature, the blood ties, the tribe, the female principle, the irrational, the impulsive, the anonymous chorus, the vengeful furies' (1969, p. 249). However, within the domain of psychology, it is possible to identify a more specific point of origin. As Cannavale, Scarr, and Pepitone (1970) acknowledge, the idea of deindividuation is taken straight from Le Bon's concept of submergence.

Gustave Le Bon's text on crowd psychology was first published in France in 1895. It was a period in which the French state appeared particularly vulnerable to mass agitation—in particular to a rising tide of syndicalist and socialist protests. Le Bon, in common with other theorists of the time, wrote not as a dispassionate observer but with the express aim of taming the challenge that crowd action represented to the social order. This is clearly apparent in the overwhelming negativism through which crowds and crowd members are characterized: according to Le Bon, crowds are only powerful for destruction and the individual who enters the crowd descends several rungs on the ladder of civilization. The perspective is also reflected, in more subtle terms, in the concepts through which he seeks to explain how crowds behave.

For Le Bon, becoming submerged in a throng leads individuals to lose both external and internal constraints upon their behaviour. The sense of power derived from strength in numbers leads individuals to express instincts that would otherwise be kept under restraint. Being indistinguishable from others in the crowd leads individuals to lose all sense of individuality and hence the sense of individual responsibility that normally controls behaviour. This loss of individuality has two consequences. Firstly, crowd members are unable to make conscious discriminations. Consequently they are liable to contagion—automatically echoing the emotions and actions of others. Secondly, the conscious personality is replaced by a collective unconscious which is the primitive racial substrate of the group. Consequently crowd members are liable to suggestion—uncritically following impulses emanating from their common unconscious. The atavistic characteristics which Le Bon ascribes to crowd behaviour—intellectual inferiority, fickleness, excessive emotionality and so on—are merely reflections of the atavism of the racial unconscious. By this account the crowd is, at best, incoherent and, at worst, generically destructive. It sits uneasily with successive ways of historical research showing not only that crowd action is patterned, but also that it is sensitive to structural, cultural and ideological aspects of the precise historical setting (e.g. Davis, 1978; Lefebvre, 1954; Reddy, 1977; Thompson, 1971, 1991).

As we have argued elsewhere (Reicher, 1987; Reicher & Potter, 1985) this inability to acknowledge the social form of action derives from the way in which crowd behaviour is abstracted from its social context. The events with which Le Bon was concerned were primarily encounters between groups, where crowds of strikers or of political factions clashed with the forces of 'law and order'.

However, in Le Bon's account, the crowd is lifted from this setting and analysed as if it were acting in isolation. The political consequence of this is that no responsibility for any violence can be ascribed to either the general social background or to the immediate actions of state forces. The crowd alone bears responsibility for violence and therefore repression rather than social change is the appropriate response. The intellectual consequence is that violence cannot be explained by reference to the dynamics of inter-group relations, but only by reference to the inherent characteristics of the crowd. This is underpinned by a particular conceptualization of the human subject. Rationality and the control of behaviour are seen as deriving solely from a unique and sovereign personal identity. Anything which obscures this identity undermines rationality and behavioural control. Thus only two states of being are possible: on the one hand there is the individuated subject who acts in a reasoned and discriminating manner, on the other there is the subject whose individuality is submerged and who acts without thought or restraint. The crowd serves as the gateway from one state to the other. Thus social setting, and social factors in general, may be of importance in determining the operation of individuality. However, what is excluded in this perspective is that social factors in general and the social group in particular may enter into the constitution of a person's identity and hence that there may be a social basis to behavioural control. Ultimately, then, the desocialized description which Le Bon gives of crowd events has its psychological concomitant a desocialized model of the self.

At one level, such issues may concern us a little more than objects of historical curiosity. After all, Le Bon's overt political bias, his journalistic style, his cavalier usage of evidence and his ideas of group mind and racial unconscious have all subsequently been largely discarded (Allport, 1924). Nonetheless, his broader conceptual legacy still influences even those who stand in traditions that overtly reject his ideas. Yet the clearest connection is with deindividuation theory which, as already stated, derives directly from Le Bon's ideas about submergence. As we shall see, however, the theory focuses predominantly on that aspect of submergence relating to the loss of internal constraints and largely ignores the effects of submergence on the perceived ability to ignore external constraints.

In the following section we shall review the successive waves of deindividuation research. We then argue that, for all the rigour and sophistication with which deindividuation researchers have pursued their enquiries, their research remains conceptually and empirically limited both by retaining Le Bon's desocialized conceptual constructs and also by ignoring his concern with the impact of crowd involvement upon perceived empowerment. Unless individualism is replaced by a socialized conception of the self, unless behaviour is analysed within its full social context and unless consideration is given to the impact of deindividuation procedures upon power relations between actors as well as the psychological state of actors, then deindividuation theory will continue to be incapable of accounting for the results of its own procedures, let alone proving a basis for explaining how crowds behave. Our aim, set out in the fourth and fifth sections of this chapter, is to show how deindividuation manipulations simultaneously affect both the social nature of selfhood and the strategic relations between self and other. By combining these two dimensions, we hope to unravel the complex consequences of such manipulations. In so doing, we also hope to contribute to the demise of a traditional and pathologizing conception of collective action.

MODERN THEORIES OF DEINDIVIDUATION

The term 'deindividuation' was introduced into the psychological lexicon by Festinger, Pepitone, and Newcomb (1952). They found that males in a group who remembered less individuating information were more likely to express hostility towards their parents. These results were explained as being due to the fact that 'under conditions where the member is not individuated in the group, there is likely to occur for the member a reduction of inner restraints against doing various things' (p. 382). The conceptual debt to Le Bon is quite apparent in this. As in all subsequent deindividuation research, it is assumed that individual identity is lost in the mass and that this results in a loss of behavioural control. Yet, in this first instance of the tradition, there is considerable vagueness as to antecedents of the deindividuated state, what constitutes it and what behaviours will result from it. What is more, insofar as the authors employ a correlational method, deindividuation is almost treated as an individual difference variable rather than arising as a general consequence of immersion in a group. This last issue was addressed by Singer, Brush, and Lublin (1965) who manipulated immersion by either getting a group of women to dress in old undistinguishing clothes or in a highly personalized and identifiable manner. In the former state, subjects were much freer in discussing the 'taboo' subject of pornography. It was Zimbardo, however, who provided the impetus for a flourishing of deindividuation research by providing a more exact conceptual specification.

It is important to note that Zimbardo's underlying concerns matched those of Le Bon. Writing in the late 1960s when the United States was witnessing an upsurge of urban disturbances and mass protests, Zimbardo felt that society was in the grip of 'Dionysiac forces' leading to 'motiveless murders, senseless destruction and uncontrolled mob violence' (1969, p. 248). Deindividuation was invoked as the explanation of these threatening phenomena. Moreover, deindividuation was equated with atavism much in the same way as Le Bon invoked the racial unconscious to explain crowds.

Within this general framework, Zimbardo (1969) proposed a model in which a series of antecedent variables lead to a state of deindividuation. Such variables include anonymity, arousal, sensory overload, novel or unstructured situations, involvement in the act, and the taking of consciousness-altering substances such as alcohol or drugs. Underlying this deindividuated state are minimization of self-observation and self-evaluation, and hence a lowered concern for social evaluation. The outcome of this is a weakening of controls based on guilt, shame, fear and commitment. This in turn leads to a lowered threshold for exhibiting inhibited behaviours. Thus, from a social perspective, deindividuated behaviour is characterized as being 'in violation of established norms of appropriateness' (1969, p. 251). From the actor's perspective, deindividuated behaviour is atypical and irrational. Moreover, insofar as contextual sensitivity is lost, the behaviours must be self-reinforcing and thus hard to terminate short of a dramatic change in conditions.

Two developments in this model are worth stressing. Firstly, although many of the antecedents of deindividuation are related to group membership, it is not exclusively a group phenomenon. Indeed, it may arise out of many factors from sensory overload to individual drug-taking. Similarly, it explains not only collective behaviour, but also individual acts such as suicide, murder and personal hostility. Secondly, while Zimbardo acknowledges that the deindividuated state need not necessarily lead to anti-social action, he does focus upon its negative aspects—both psychological and behavioural. Thus, on the one hand, deindividuation is associated with perceptual distortion, memory impairment, hyper-responsiveness to proximal others and unresponsiveness to distal others. On the other hand, deindividuation is equated with ritual destruction of traditional forms and structures. Not surprisingly, then, most of the supportive evidence comes in the form of showing how supposed antecedents of deindividuation are associated with anti-social acts.

Zimbardo (1969) himself asked subjects to deliver electric shocks to confederates allegedly in order to get 'actively involved' with them! Deindividuated subjects gave electric shocks of an average 0.90 seconds duration as opposed to 0.47 for individuated subjects. Zimbardo complemented this with a field study showing how a car was far more likely to be vandalized and stripped in more anonymous areas of a city (pp. 283–93). In similar vein, Donnerstein, Donnerstein, and Evans (1972) found that white subjects were willing to give higher levels of shock to a black victim who could neither see nor identify them, while Milgram (1974) found that—irrespective of race— level of shock rises as identifiability of victim to the subject falls. Watson (1973) complemented these findings with cross-cultural evidence that warriors who lower personal identifiability through such devices as war paint are far more likely to indulge in violent killings than those who do not.

The first cracks in this apparently consistent picture came with evidence that deindividuating circumstances can lead to lowered aggressivity (Diener, 1976; Zabrick & Miller, 1972) or even increased affection (Gergen, Gergen, & Barton, 1973). While the latter is not explicitly contrary to Zimbardo's model—he does, after all, claim only that behaviour is 'inappropriate', not necessarily negative—such findings do raise the question of what determines which of various possible behaviours will emerge when subjects are deindividuated. More problematic for Zimbardo was evidence showing that situational factors, far from being rendered irrelevant by deindividuation, are actually crucial to determining its behavioural consequences. Carver (1975), Diener and Wallbom (1976) and Scheier, Fenigstein, and Buss (1974) all showed that manipulating contextual features affects what subjects do when self-awareness is lowered. Thus Johnson and Downing (1979) argue that the reason for Zimbardo's classic association between deindividuation and aggressive behaviour is that subjects are typically rendered anonymous in costumes reminiscent of the Ku Klux Klan—a source of negative cues. Indeed using such a manipulation they replicated the findings. However, when subjects were made anonymous through wearing nurses' uniforms (a source of positive cues) aggression decreased.

According to Diener (1977, 1979, 1980) this failure to find a consistent relationship between manipulations and actions not only reflects a problem in conceptualizing the relationship between deindividuation and behaviour, there are two further problems. Firstly there is a lack of clarity concerning the psychological changes that constitute the state of deindividuation. Secondly, there is no evidence as to which factors bring this state about. As Diener puts it: 'no study has found that subjective experiences such as lack of self-awareness or feelings of group unity follow deindividuating conditions and covary together' (1979, p. 1161). Moreover, as he subsequently showed, supposed antecedents of deindividuation such as anonymity and diffusion of responsibility may alter levels of aggressive behaviour, without having any effect upon reported levels of self-consciousness (Diener, 1980).

In response to these conceptual and empirical difficulties, Diener (1979, 1980) reformulated deindividuation theory using the concept of objective self-awareness (Duval & Wicklund, 1972; Wicklund, 1975). High objective self-awareness is a state where individuals' attention is drawn inward towards the self such that active monitoring and self-regulation of behaviour takes place. Where objective self-awareness is low, attention is drawn outward, monitoring of behaviour comes to a halt, and behaviour falls under the control of external factors. For Diener, the factors which cause a lowering of objective self-awareness include perceptual immersion in a group, overloading of processing capacities, outward focus of attention, conceiving of the group as a united whole and relegating decision making to the group. Thus there are various causes of self-directed attention being blocked, not all of them to do with the group. However, immersion in a group has the particular consequence that not only do we cease self-monitoring, but also novel factors or situations do not restore self-monitoring. Thus Diener defines deindividuation as people in a group who are 'blocked from awareness of themselves as individuals and from monitoring their own behaviour' (1979, p. 210). The consequences of deindividuation include an inability to retrieve personal or social standards, a lack of planning and foresight and a lack of ego inhibitions concerning future punishments. However, in contrast to Zimbardo, this is not equivalent to a release of anti-social tendencies but rather an inability to respond selectively to stimuli.

For Prentice-Dunn and Rogers (1982, 1989), this reformulation still fails to account for the complex behavioural consequences of deindividuation measures. While behaviour may sometimes appear to be explicable in terms of the domination of environmental cues this does not explain all the findings in the literature. They therefore propose a two-factor model based on the distinction between public and private self-awareness (Carver & Scheier, 1981; Fenigstein, Scheier, & Buss, 1975). Public self-awareness has to do with the subject's concern with the evaluation of others. In the group, 'accountability cues' such as anonymity and diffusion of responsibility give subjects the feeling that they can safely ignore what others think. The result of lowered public self-awareness is therefore anti-normative behaviour akin to that predicted by Festinger and Zimbardo. On the other hand, the processes surrounding the dimension of private self-awareness are much the same as those suggested by Diener. In this case immersion in the group can draw attention away from the self and lead to an internal deindividuated state whereby loss of self-regulation leads to a decreased reliance upon internal standards and an increased responsiveness to environmental cues.

By specifying the precise antecedents and the intervening mechanisms that lead to the different effects found in the literature, such recent developments have given a new lease of life to deindividuation theory. It is certainly quoted in most introductory social psychology texts as one of the discipline's basic discoveries. It has also been accepted as fact in courtrooms and been used as grounds for extenuation (Colman, 1991). Certainly Prentice-Dunn himself considers that the theory, almost knocked from its apparently secure position in the early 1970s, has been firmly placed back on its pedestal. He asserts that 'two decades of research have now demonstrated the validity of the deindividuation construct. These results illustrate the potentially volatile effects of situations characterised by high degrees of group cohesiveness and physiological arousal' (1991, p. 16).

A CRITIQUE OF DEINDIVIDUATION THEORY

Conceptual Issues

For all the differences between the successive variants of deindividuation theory, there is common conceptual core. It has a number of key elements. The first has to do with the conceptualization of deindividuation as a loss, or else blocking, of the self. While authors may differ slightly in which antecedents and which consequences they stress, all concur in suggesting that the deindividuated individual is one who is acting in the absence of self-regulation. What is more, insofar as the self is the sole source of values, norms and standards, the implication is that deindividuated behaviour is out of the individual's control—or 'generically volatile' to use Prentice-Dunn's term. There are, however, two variants of this position. Those (such as Le Bon and Zimbardo) who tend towards a group-mind position, whereby some common atavistic substrate lies below conscious individuality, see individuation as the re-emergence of primitive urges normally kept hidden. The behaviour is not only wild but also characteristically destructive. Others (including Diener and Prentice-Dunn & Rogers) have no truck with group-mind concepts. They simply see internal control replaced by external control. Deindividuated behaviour may as easily be positive as negative. It simply blows with the wind.

This notion of deindividuation as loss of selfhood, and hence loss of control over one's own behaviour, depends upon a particular way of conceptualizing the construct. The self is regarded as unitary, and refers to the unique set of dispositions and characteristics that mark the person as distinct from all other individuals. It is also the sole source of rational action. To put it slightly differently, rational action is equated with the self and the self is equated with personal identity. The loss of personal identity is therefore equated with the loss of identity and the loss of rationality.

This equation is made quite explicit by Diener who states that 'people who are deindividuated have lost self-awareness and their personal identity in a group situation' (1979, p. 210). But the supposition is not only conceptual, it is also reflected in experimental manipulations and measures. For instance Diener and Srull (1979) seek to make individuals self-aware by portraying them on a television screen and playing a tape which says of the subject: 'My name is ————. I am from ————'. They then test for self-awareness by asking firstly, 'How self-conscious or embarrassed were you?', and then administering Fenigstein's self-consciousness scale (Fenigstein, Scheier, & Buss, 1975). This scale has three sub-scales referring to private self-consciousness, public self-consciousness and social anxiety. The following examples, one from each sub-scale in respective order, give a flavour of the items: 'I reflect about myself a lot'; 'I'm self-conscious about the way I look'; 'It takes me time to overcome my shyness in new situations'. They all clearly refer to idiosyncratic aspects of the self.

The second common feature is that all the variants of deindividuation theory regard the group as an antecedent of deindividuation. This is not to say that groups are the only route to a deindividuated state. Indeed, from Zimbardo onwards, a multiplicity of antecedents were invoked and this was reflected in the diverse manipulations of deindividuation employed in experimental studies—ranging from dimmed lighting to the use of mirrors. Nonetheless, no one went so far as to remove groups from the list and most saw it as more than simply one amongst equals. Thus, in Diener's formulation, not only are certain precursors collective by definition (such as perceptual immersion in the group) but even those that are not may be brought about by collective involvement (such as overloading of processing capacity).

The implication of deindividuation theory is that the group is uniquely subversive of selfhood, of intellect and of behavioural control. The picture of groups is of people who, literally, cannot help what they are doing. Certainly it is a vain enterprise to look for meaning or direction in group behaviour. In a phrase, the presence of others induces the absence of reason. Or else, to quote Gabriel Tarde, a crowd theorist and contemporary of Le Bon: 'La societe, c'est l'imitation, et l'imitation, c'est une espece de somnambulisme' (society is imitation and imitation is a sort of somnambulism; 1901, p. 95). The one exception to this, at least in part, might seem to be the position of Prentice-Dunn and Rogers. Their use of the concept of public self-awareness implies that the presence of others— or, to be more accurate, awareness of the presence of others—may lead people to adhere more closely to social norms. In this sense, they could be interpreted as arguing that co-presence increases behavioural control.

However, as Abrams (1990) notes, the concept of public self-awareness is not a matter of individuals being aware of themselves as members of a public and acting in terms of the associated ingroup standards. Rather, it means that individuals are aware of external public standards and will act so as to gain the approval of that public. Furthermore, the public as a generalized other is clearly differentiated from the actual presence of a group because Prentice-Dunn and Rogers explicitly argue that the latter excludes awareness of the former. It might be expected that, once anonymity within the group has removed accountability to the external audience it might increase accountability to fellow group members and hence to group standards. However, this possibility is not even considered. First of all it seems to be assumed that anonymity to the external audience is equated with total anonymity. Thus anonymity becomes a quality of the individual rather than being treated as a relational term: with respect to whom is one anonymous? This is a point we shall return to later. Secondly, it is presupposed that the group can only act to block standards. The apparent exception provided by Prentice-Dunn and Rogers is actually an extension of this principle from internal standards to external standards. They provide no departure from the vision of groups as necessarily anomic. We shall argue that this vision is unable to explain even the findings within deindividuation literature. It is certainly insufficient for an understanding of the wider phenomena of group and crowd action.

Empirical Issues: Accounting for the Deindividuation Literature

As a number of reviewers have noted (Diener, 1977; Lindskold & Propst, 1980), one of the most striking things about the deindividuation literature is its complexity. The success of the theory in accounting for diverse findings has, as we have seen in the previous section, come at the expense of constant refinement and respecification so that almost every contingency is covered (Spears, 1995).

Some Classic Studies Revisited

These problems are illustrated by reconsidering the three 'electric shock' studies reported by Zimbardo in his classic 1969 paper. The first study, using groups of four young women who were either identifiable to each other or else made anonymous by wearing baggy cloaks and hoods, found the latter to deliver higher levels of shock. As expected, anonymity increases 'transgression'. However the second study, which used identical manipulations of deindividuation but involved soldiers rather than young women, found exactly the opposite. This time the anonymous subjects delivered lower levels of shock. As Zimbardo puts it: 'the supposedly deindividuated subjects were behaving in a most individuated manner' (1969, p. 275). Indeed, he explains these apparently discrepant results by arguing that those alone in the cubicles, wearing hoods, without name tags, were actually more self-conscious, suspicious and anxious than those sitting together in their everyday uniforms. Zimbardo seeks to support this explanation through a further study, which reverts to employing young women but, instead of having them in groups, isolates subjects in individual booths and then either has them identifiable or anonymous. On the assumption that being the only person in an experimental setting who is wearing a hood will increase self-centred concern, it is hypothesized that those in the 'anonymous' conditions will be more individuated and hence deliver lower levels of shock than those wearing ordinary clothes. This prediction was upheld.

The problem with this line of reasoning is that it does not explain why, between the first and second studies, women subjects and soldiers should respond so differently to identical deindividuation manipulations (Zimbardo suggests that the soldiers, being in uniform, were already deindividuated in the identifiable conditions, but this does not explain why they should become less deindividuated when made anonymous). Nor is it fully explained why, between the first and third studies, women subjects should respond so differently to deindividuation manipulations as a function of whether they are alone or in groups. Both the groups to which people belong and the context in which they are made anonymous—or, to be precise, with respect to whom they are made anonymous—therefore seem to be crucial. Whereas Zimbardo's reaction is to cast around for post hoc explanations relating to the effects of these variables upon level of self-focus, there is a much simpler approach. It is reasonable to assume that young women and soldiers have very different norms regarding the acceptability of physical aggression: the former may be expected to be anti-aggression with the latter pro-aggression. It is further reasonable to assume that the experimenter is seen as regarding the administration of shocks as acceptable and indeed situationally appropriate, given his definition of the task. It is then plausible that procedures that isolate women from each other should increase levels of electric shock (acceptable to the observing experimenter) while isolating soldiers from their group should decrease shock levels. The sense of group and its respective norm is undermined in each case. Moreover, rendering the women anonymous in separate booths also isolates them from the observing experimenter (compared to the collective situation of the first study) allowing them more freedom to act in terms of their preferred group norm.

To adopt this line of reasoning, however, is to break with two fundamental tenets of deindividuation theory. In the first place it suggests that the group is a source of behavioural standards rather than their nemesis. These should be understood, not as general social standards with which people comply under duress, but rather in the sense of specific norms associated with the membership of specific groups. Secondly, it suggests that deindividuation manipulations should not be seen as inducing a unitary internal state but rather depend upon the ways in which they alter the relationship of subjects to others.

The normative basis of supposedly deindividuated behaviour is equally apparent in what is possibly Zimbardo's most famous study: the Stanford prison experiment. In line with traditional deindividuation theory, those allocated to both the positions of prisoner and of guard do exhibit extreme behaviour that is atypical of the ordinary student. However, the two groups also behave very differently—which is hard to explain if they are similarly deindividuated. These differences become more explicable if one considers that all the subjects are acting in ways that are consonant with the norms of the groups to which they have been allocated. In this regard, it is worth recalling Gergen, Gergen and Barton's (1973) finding that, when members of a liberal college are deindividuated as students as opposed to the groups invoked by Zimbardo, rather than acting aggressively or punitively they hugged and kissed each other—very reminiscent of the undergraduate ethos of the era!

It may be argued that such objections are only possible where the relationship between antecedents and deindividuation are loosely specified and hence it is impossible to know the psychological state of subjects in any given condition. However, the problems remain even where self-awareness is more directly addressed. Froming, Walker, and Lopyan (1982) showed that the effects of private and public self-awareness manipulations (a mirror and an evaluating audience) were moderated by subject's norms and expectations of other's norms. Thus subjects who were low in private self-awareness shocked more when they felt other people favoured it, and less when they felt others were against it. Similarly, the presence of an audience induced compliance to the perceived norm of the audience when the audience was present, whereas the individual norm was applied without an audience. Hence, direct manipulations of the mediating process once more point at the importance of the normative context, and undermine the idea that these deindividuating manipulations have uniform effects on individual functioning.

Meta-analytic Evidence

Thus far our empirical evidence has been somewhat piecemeal and anecdotal. In order to give this argument a more systematic grounding Postmes and Spears (1993) carried out a series of meta-analytic integrations on 59 deindividuation studies. For ease of interpretation, the terms were defined such that our prediction that deindividuating circumstances should produce an increase in normative behaviour would be reflected in a significant positive relation. Conversely, the prediction of classical deindividuation theory that deindividuating conditions should result in anti-normative behaviour would be reflected in a significant negative relation. Overall results give no clear support for the hypothesis that deindividuating manipulations of anonymity, group size and reduced self-awareness lead to an increase in anti-normative behaviour. There was a significant but weak negative overall effect size indicating a marginal support for deindividuation theory, but this effect is qualified by the extreme heterogeneity of results. The same near-zero effect sizes and great heterogeneity were obtained when this group of studies was split up into smaller meta-analyses investigating studies with similar manipulations. There appeared to be no clear effects for either manipulations of anonymity towards ingroup, or outgroup, or combined manipulations. Nor were large effects found for manipulations of group size, or private or public self-awareness.

In an attempt to explain this heterogeneity, a number of theoretically plausible moderators were tested. For instance, deindividuation theory would predict there to be an effect of group size such that larger groups lead to more deindividuation and consequently more anti-normative behaviour (Zimbardo, 1969). Also, more prolonged deindividuation manipulations should be more effective (Prentice-Dunn & Spivey, 1986). No support was found for either prediction.

Independent raters also judged to what extent the 'deindividuated' behaviour (the dependent variable) under observation was normative with regard to a general (pro)social norm. It appeared that, if anything, there is a reverse effect to the one predicted by deindividuation theory, namely a small positive correlation between effect size and the general social norm estimate. This indicates that, overall, deindividuated subjects behave more in line with the general social norm. However, the notion of general social norms is itself problematic given that, as we have been arguing, one must look at the norms and rules that apply to a specific group or situation (see also Lindskold & Propst, 1980; Singer, Brush, & Lublin, 1965). We therefore required raters to judge what they thought the specific situational norm or expectation was for each study. These ratings explain a large amount of the variance in results. Overall there is a strong positive relation between effect size and the situational-norm-rating indicating that people who display deindividuating behaviour conform more to group specific or situational norms.

In summary, both our analysis of individual studies and our meta-analyses of the general literature indicate that deindividuation manipulations (group immersion, group size, anonymity, lack of self-awareness) are not associated with an increase in anti-normative behaviour. In fact the precise opposite appears to be the case: deindividuation manipulations are associated with an increase in normative behaviour. Yet, if deindividuation theorists have difficulties in making sense of their own data, the problems become even more acute when one turns to the general group and crowd phenomena to which the theory claims to have relevance.

Accounting for Collective Phenomena

In a piece of considerable understatement, Rupert Brown begins his text on 'Group Processes' (1988) with the observation that 'For some years now, at least in the industrialized West, groups have received rather a bad press' (p. vii). He goes on to show that this attitude is not confined to the media but is also to be found in the psychological literature as exemplified in Buys' (1978) semi-ironic article entitled 'Humans would do better without groups'. Of particular note is the tendency for explanations of deviance to invoke group processes. Whether it be the psychology of delinquency, of drug-taking, of smoking or of drinking there is a continuous recourse to the logic of deindividuation theory; individuals, especially those with unformed or damaged selves, lose all sense of standards in the group and become liable to negative and dangerous influences (Hopkins, 1994; Reicher & Emler, 1987). The problem with such reasoning is that, while it is true that delinquency, say, is characteristically a group phenomenon, it is also true that non-delinquents have a rich collective life. Moreover, while being in some groups may increase the probability of delinquent action, being in other groups will decrease it. In other words, there is no generic group effect. The effect of groups on delinquency depends upon the normative structure of the groups in question (Emler & Reicher, 1995). More generally, a whole literature has grown up which shows how group behaviour observes clear norms and limits (Turner, 1991). In other words, the assumption that individuals are deindividuated in the group and hence become at best volatile and at worst anti-social is in opposition to most of what we know about group processes.

The deindividuation theorist could respond by arguing that there are groups and groups. Those employed in most psychological studies are relatively small, uncrowded and easily observable. Hence their lack of volatility simply reflects the fact that they are not deindividuated. On the other hand where the groups are large and dense such that individuals become anonymous in the mass, then deindividuated behaviour will be observed. The prototypical example of such groups, indeed the example from which deindividuation theory itself derives, is the crowd. The notion of the crowd as generically uncontrolled fits well with popular portrayals of collective phenomena. Thus Waddington (1992) talks of the way in which crowds tend to be represented in the press as: 'a rampaging mob, victim to primitive urges or the machinations of conspirators' (p. 177). Similarly, crowd members are described as roaring, maniacal and dangerous. Schickel (quoted in Jenson, 1992) equates deranged fans with serial killers and Jenson (1992) herself argues that the image of the frenzied fan predominates in discussions of music fans and sports fans.

One oft-cited example which seems to exemplify such frenzy occurred at a concert given in 1979 by The Who at Cincinnati's Riverfront Coliseum where 11 teenagers were crushed to death. Contemporary accounts described the crowd members as barbarians who were out of control and who, in the words of one columnist: 'stomped 11 persons to death (after) having numbed their brains on weeds, chemicals and Southern Comfort' (quoted in Jenson, 1992, p. 12). However, closer examination reveals a very different picture. The crush arose as too few doors to the arena were opened in order to accommodate those seeking to get in. Those pressing at the back had no idea of what was going on at the front and amongst those who were aware, most made strenuous attempts to save each other from the crush. This is far from the popular image of fans, hypnotized by the music, clambering over dead bodies in order to get closer to the stage (Johnson, 1987).

This tendency for images of the rampaging mob to disintegrate under closer scrutiny is not limited to fan culture. In recent years, one of the most startling images of disorder has been the urban riot. Indeed, deindividuation theory gained popularity partly in response to the wave of black protest that swept the United States in the 1960s and 70s. However, it is worth noting that studies of other riots show that the targets of crowd violence were largely restricted to the property of outsiders and in particular, of noted white racists (Berk & Aldrich, 1972; Brink & Harris, 1969; Caplan & Paige, 1968; Cohen, 1970; Marx, 1967; Tomlinson, 1970). Fogelson summed up the evidence by stating that: 'restraint and selectivity were among the most crucial features of the riots' (1971, p. 17).

But perhaps most disturbing of all is the revolutionary crowd. Le Bon originally formulated his concepts of submergence and crowd inferiority in response to the threats to his contemporary social order, but his illustrations mainly related to the French revolution of 1789 (Barrows, 1981; Nye, 1975).

However, after conducting a detailed study of the revolutionary crowds, Lefebvre (1954) argues that Le Bon had no direct knowledge of the social or political history of the revolution and hence that he completely misrepresents how the crowds behaved. Lefebvre himself concluded that only if one understands the collective ideologies associated with differing social groups will their mass action become comprehensible. He also argues that crowd leaders will only be listened to if what they say is in accord with the collective mentality. Finally, he asserts that perhaps only in the crowd will individuals, escaping from the petty concerns of daily life, become more sensitive to the ideas and emotions that stem from the larger collectivities to which they also belong.

What Lefebvre is arguing is that the tenets that became translated into deindividuation theory were only possible by obscuring the empirical reality of crowd phenomena and that these phenomena actually reveal the opposite to that implied by the theory. People immersed in crowds act in ways that are controlled and meaningful, even if the standards that guide them relate to social rather than idiosyncratic beliefs and values. However, in invoking revolutionary crowds there is one element of Le Bon's theory that does gain credibility. In revolutions, the powerless become powerful through combination and are able to act in unprecedented ways: attack their enemies, seize their goods, open the prisons. However, this collective power does not operate to the exclusion of reason, but rather its usage must—as Lefebvre insists—be linked to collective understanding.

If the accusation of volatility applies neither to the findings of deindividuation research, nor to the broader phenomena that is purports to explain, the validity of the deindividuation construct must at the very least be placed in doubt. If, on the other hand, one wishes to start from the empirical evidence—both experimental and historical—relating to the consequences of immersion in groups, then any theory must meet at least two criteria. It must explain the distinctive forms of behavioural control operating at the collective level and it must take account of the consequences of collective participation for empowerment in the face of a dominant outgroup or authority. We now turn to consider these issues from our own social identity perspective.

DEINDIVIDUATION MANIPULATIONS AND THE SALIENCE OF SOCIAL IDENTITIES

The Social Identity/Deindividuation (SIDE) Model: A Preliminary Outline and an Initial Study

Deindividuation theory depends upon the twin assumptions that a unique personal self is the basis of all rational action and that the group serves to impede the operation of such selfhood. European social psychology emerged largely in opposition to such individualistic and anti-collectivistic approaches (e.g. Israel & Tajfel, 1972). In particular the tradition of social identity theory (Tajfel, 1978, 1982) and, more recently, self-categorization theory (Turner *et al.*, 1987; Turner, 1991) is explicitly concerned with the social nature of self-hood and its relationship to group behaviour.

Social identity theory originates from research into inter-group relations. More specifically, it was developed in relation to a series of studies known as the 'minimal group experiments' (Tajfel, 1970; Tajfel *et al.*, 1971). In these studies, subjects are allocated to two groups according to trivial criteria or, later, even on a random basis (Billig & Tajfel, 1973). They are then asked to distribute points between another member of the ingroup and a member of the outgroup—in other words they stand to neither gain nor lose personally from their own distribution. In addition there is no interaction between groups either in the past, the present or the future, subjects do not even know who is in which group and therefore they do not know the identity of the individuals between whom points are allocated. This allocation is operationalized using specially designed points matrices which allow one to separate out the different distribution strategies used by subjects. The reliable finding is that subjects show a tendency to ensure that ingroup members are given more points than outgroup members even where this is at the cost of absolute reward to ingroup.

For social identity theory, these results are to be explained as follows. First of all, subjects define themselves in terms of the groups to which they are allocated: this is the act of social identification. Secondly, the group only has meaning in terms of how it relates to other groups. Hence, group definition depends upon social comparison between groups. If one assumes that people are motivated to achieve positive social identity through a positive definition of their group, this entails a third step. Group members will endeavour to make their group come out better on valued dimensions than the other group. In the minimal group paradigm such social differentiation can only be achieved by allocating more points to ingroup members than outgroup members.

For present purposes, the key aspect of this theory is the concept of *social identification*. To start with, the concept departs from a notion of self as a unitary construct. Rather it is conceived of as a complex system consisting of at least two major sub-systems. The first is personal identity which corresponds to the classic notion of those attributes that uniquely define the individual. The second is social identity which relates to the groups to which the individual belongs. Of course we may all belong to several social categories and therefore may have a series of social identifications which are salient at different times. Any specific social identification is defined as our knowledge of our membership of a social group along with the emotional significance that membership entails for us. In replacing a unitary with a multiple concept of selfhood, social identity theory also proposes that groups confer rather than destroy selfhood. Thus, in becoming part of a group, individuals do not *lose* all sense of self, rather they *shift* from the personal to the social level of identification. It follows that, in becoming a group member, individuals do not necessarily lose all bases for the control of behaviour. Rather, the criteria for action may shift from the personal to the social categorical level.

This last point is addressed more closely within self-categorization theory, which both develops the concepts of social identity theory and applies them beyond the limits of intergroup phenomena to a range of pivotal processes in social psychology, including group formation, social influence and stereotyping. To start with, instead of positing a simple dichotomy between personal and social identity, it is argued that selfhood can be conceptualized on a number of levels of inclusiveness: the subordinate or personal (I vs. you), the intermediate or categorical (we vs. they) and the superordinate whereby all people are conceptualized as a single whole. The level at which the self is defined therefore determines how one relates to others, but it also determines how one makes sense of the world. Conversely, whether one acts as an individual, as a group member or as representative of a common humanity will be a function of the level of cognitive self-definition.

To be a group member, then, is to define oneself as a member of the social category and for members of groups perception operates at the social categorical level. This is not only a matter of characterizing outgroup members in terms of an outgroup stereotype, it is also a matter of self-stereotyping such that individuals adopt the understandings and characteristics associated with the ingroup category. Thus the values and beliefs that underpin behavioural choice, the norms which are held as relevant, who will be influential and what messages will gain influence are all dependent upon the definition of the social category in question.

Turner (Turner *et al.*, 1987; Turner, 1991) refers to this shift from relating to others on an individual level to relating on a higher level of inclusiveness as a process of depersonalization. The difference between deindividuation and depersonalization is that once the self may be defined at more than the personal level then loss of the personal is not to be equated with loss of self. For self-categorization theory it results in enhanced salience of the social self. This means that behaviour in groups will be regulated by reference to social standards and hence will show social shape. According to the analysis presented above, these are precisely the characteristics of behaviour in deindividuation studies and of supposedly deindividuated groups. This approach promises to provide a theoretical basis for explaining the results of deindividuation manipulations. It remains to specify how.

Perhaps the prototypical deindividuation manipulation is to immerse individuals within a group and to reinforce this by anonymity as operationalized by dressing participants in masks and baggy overalls (cf. Diener, 1980; Zimbardo, 1969). From the perspective of self-categorization theory, such procedures migh be expected to have a range of effects depending on the salient self-category, and the details of the deindividuating manipulation. Firstly, immersion in the group should reinforce the salience of the corresponding social identity at the expense of personal identity, assuming of course that it is at least a potential membership group for the individuals concerned. Secondly, anonymity may either enhance or attenuate social identity as a function of the context in which it occurs. If the group level of identity is already emphasized, then anonymity is likely to enhance the salience of social identity still further by emphasizing the interchangeability of group members and obscuring interpersonal differences. However, anonymity is likely to have rather different effects if it is not accompanied by explicit group immersion. Where group salience is low and where group boundaries are indistinct, anonymity may undermine the process of depersonalization, by emphasizing one's isolation from the group or by further obscuring group boundaries. Hence the salience of social identity should decrease.

In sum, we are suggesting that deindividuation manipulations may work through their effects upon the level of self-categorization and the salience of particular social identities. These effects will be complex, depending both upon the manipulation that is used and the context in which it is used. What is more, in order to predict the behavioural consequences of these manipulations it is necessary to add a further factor. If deindividuation affects self-categorization and hence the level of adherence to categorical standards, the actual outcomes will depend upon the definition of the particular categories in question. For instance, to make identity as a soldier more or less salient will affect the expression of very different norms to those affected by altering the salience of a female college student identity.

These ideas were tested in our first formative study designed to examine the role of self-categorization in a classical deindividuation paradigm (Reicher, 1984). In contrast to classical deindividuation studies, however, this experiment was modelled on an intergroup context rather than focusing on a single group. This intergroup dimension reinforces the importance of social identity given that group identity only becomes meaningful through comparison with a relevant outgroup in the intergroup context (Turner et al., 1987). It is also more representative of the intergroup nature of crowd behaviour neglected by classical deindividuation research (Reicher, 1987; Spears, 1995). This study employed a group of science and a group of social science students and the design manipulated both group immersion (group versus individual) and anonymity (anonymous vs. identifiable). In the group conditions, the two groups were seated at separate tables in the same room, and subjects were told they were being tested as members of their group, not as individuals. They were referred to by group code numbers throughout. In the individual conditions the scientists and the social scientists were mixed together and sat in rows facing the front of the laboratory. Subjects in these conditions were informed that they were being tested as individuals and were referred to by individual code numbers. This manipulation of identity was crossed with an anonymity manipulation in which subjects were either dressed normally (identifiable) or in baggy overalls and masks, so that others were not identifiable to them (anonymous). However, in the group-anonymous condition one group wore red masks, whereas the group at the other table wore white, reinforcing the group distinction. In the individual-anonymous condition everyone wore white masks, so that any intergroup distinctions were further obscured.

The study was presented as a test of attitude–behaviour consistency. Subjects were presented with a videotape of arguments concerning vivisection where the scientists were depicted as consistently pro-vivisection, and social scientists consistently anti-vivisection. The main prediction was that subjects would show greater conformity to their own group norm when immersed in a group. It was further predicted, in line with the preceding analysis, that the effects of anonymity would depend on the social context and salient identity. Where group identity was salient and group boundaries were distinct, anonymity within the group should serve to further depersonalize perception by decreasing intragroup differences, increasing intergroup differences, and thereby increasing group salience and adherence to group norms. By contrast, anonymity amongst the two intermingled groups within individual conditions, should make it even less possible to distinguish intergroup and outgroup, undermining the group boundary and effectively isolating individuals from their group. In these circumstances, anonymity is predicted to decrease the salience of social identity and decrease adherence to group norms.

The results showed strong support for the predicted effects of group immersion. Scientists in a group were considerably more pro-vivisection than when isolated while social scientists were considerably more anti-vivisection in the group conditions. The effects of the anonymity manipulations were more mixed. The predicted three-way interaction between faculty and group immersion and deindividuation manipulations was only significant on the attitude measure and not on two behaviourals. Further inspection of the significant interaction revealed the predicted two-way interaction between the group immersion and deindividuation factors for the science students only. Figure 6.1 depicts this interaction and reveals the anticipated effect, namely that science students express significantly greater pro-vivisection attitudes (in line with their group norm) if deindividuated when group identity is salient than when individual identity is salient, whereas this difference disappears when subjects are individuated.

In overall terms this study supports our approach over traditional deindividuation accounts. In the first place the effects of the group immersion variable are inexplicable in terms of loss of constraints, submission to environmental cues or even public self-awareness, given that the two groups behaved in entirely different ways despite being within the same context. Secondly, the

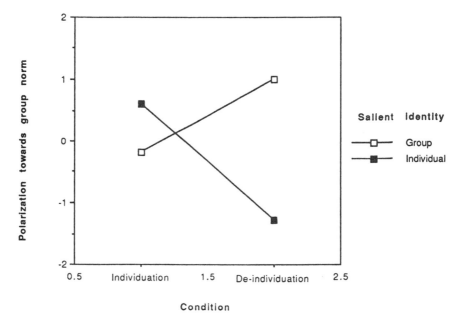

Figure 6.1 Pro-vivisection attitudes for science students as a function of salient identity and deindividuation

mixed effects of the anonymity variable can be accounted for from a social identity/deindividuation perspective by arguing that social identity was made so salient by the group manipulation that anonymity was unlikely to have any further effects upon salience at least in the group conditions (cf. Spears, Lea, & Lee, 1990). Conversely, the differing effects of anonymity for scientists in the group and individual conditions are very difficult to explain from a traditional perspective. This initial study can therefore be said at least to point to the potential fruitfulness of our approach.

Extending the Social Identity/Deindividuation Approach to New Domains: Computer-Mediated Communication and the Minimal Group Paradigm

In this section we extend our analysis of the enhanced role of social identity under 'deindividuating' conditions of anonymity in the group to other domains in which such conditions prevail. These are respectively the field of computer-mediated communication and the minimal group paradigm.

Computer-Mediated Communication

In recent years the concept of deindividuation has resurfaced in a line of research concerned with computer-mediated communication. It has been used to help explain evidence of uninhibited behaviour in this medium (so called 'flaming') and the fact that group discussion by means of computers can lead to more extreme or polarized decisions (cf. Kiesler, Siegel, & McGuire, 1984; Siegel *et al.*, 1986). These researchers have argued that certain features of computer-mediated communication, such as anonymity and immersion in the medium, produce the classic deindividuating conditions of reduced self-awareness and disinhibition, leading to the expression of more extreme arguments. They assume that polarization is a function of the extremity of novel arguments exchanged as predicted by the 'persuasive arguments' theory of Burnstein and Vinokur (1977).

An alternative interpretation of these findings can be offered, starting from a self-categorization perspective (Lea & Spears, 1991; Spears & Lea, 1992; Spears, Lea, & Lee, 1990) such that group polarization is conceptualized as a process of conformity to the 'prototypical' position of the group (Turner, 1987; 1991; Wetherell, 1987). However, this prototypical position is not simply defined as the group mean, but also takes into account the position of the relevant outgroup. Once again this is consistent with the self-categorization argument that group identity only becomes salient or meaningful through comparison with a relevant outgroup (Turner *et al.*, 1987). Polarization therefore reflects not simply conformity to the ingroup 'in a vacuum', but also contrast from an implicit outgroup. Because there is often no explicit outgroup in the group polarization paradigm, outgroup positions are implicitly represented by the scale positions avoided by the discussion group. Thus, where there is already a general preference for one or other scale pole, people will tend to contrast their own positions away from the opposite scale pole in the process of conforming to the group. Combining this element of intergroup contrast with ingroup conformity (the so-called metacontrast principle) results in a prototypical position which is more extreme than the ingroup mean in the favoured direction, producing polarization (Turner, 1987, 1991; Wetherell, 1987). Contrary to the persuasive arguments explanation, this explanation takes into account the information available in context but relates it to the normative positions of the group or groups involved. In so doing, it resolves the apparent contradiction between conformity and polarization (cf. Turner, 1987, 1991).

Our first computer-based study was designed to test this interpretation of the polarization phenomenon. It examined (a) whether the deindividuating conditions of computer-mediated communication (anonymity in the group) actually result in more polarization, and (b) whether this was due to the enhanced conformity to group norms rather than being due to deregulated and anti-normative behaviour as suggested by the earlier work. The study involved the use of computers for group discussion on a series of attitude issues (Lea & Spears, 1991; Spears, Lea, & Lee, 1990). The design was similar to the earlier study of Reicher (1984) described above, and involved manipulations of group salience and anonymity in a 2 × 2 design (group vs. individual; anonymous vs. identifiable). However, the operationalization differed in important ways. Firstly, instead of having two groups, this experiment employed only single discussion groups. This is more in line with both the classical group polarization paradigm and also the classical deindividuation studies. Secondly, the effects of psychological group salience and of anonymity within the group were more clearly separated out through the ways in which both variables were manipulated.

Group identity is conceptualized in self-categorization theory as involving a cognitive identification with a social category without being dependent upon interactions between individual group members (Hogg, 1992; Turner, 1982). We therefore manipulated group membership by simply referring either to subjects through individual code numbers or through group code numbers (as psychology students). For the deindividuation manipulation, instead of using overalls and hoods we took advantage of the facility under computer-mediated communication for allowing people to communicate even when physically separated. Thus subjects were isolated in different rooms (anonymous) or they were seated in the same room in full view of each other (identifiable). It is important to note that the critical factor here is the visibility of the other group members in highlighting the individual differences and undermining group salience, rather than the ability to match responses to individuals (response identifiability is, however, of critical importance for the strategic aspects of behaviour expression in the intergroup context that we consider in the following section).

All discussion took place by means of computer in three-person groups. Prior to discussing the issues, participants were presented with booklets containing graphs indicating the distribution of views among first-year psychology students, supposedly to help them get thinking about the discussion issue. The real aim of this information was to provide (genuine) normative feedback reinforcing the generally left-wing norm on the discussion topics and to ensure that subjects were aware of the general direction of this norm for their group. The main dependent measure was the degree of norm-directed polarization resulting from group discussion (cf. Lea & Spears, 1991; Spears, Lea, & Lee, 1990).

As in the earlier study by Reicher (1984), and following the same logic, it was predicted that there would be an interaction between group salience and deindividuation factors such that visual anonymity would produce greater polarization in the direction of the pre-established group norm under conditions of high group salience but, under conditions of low group salience, anonymity would decrease polarization. These predictions were fully upheld (see Figure 6.2). Norm-directed polarization was greatest in the deindividuated group identity condition and least in the deindividuated individual identity condition where, in fact, depolarization occurred. There was no difference between the two individuated conditions. These results provide further experimental support for our analysis of the effects of deindividuation manipulations upon the level of cognitive self-categorizations and replicate the pattern for the science students in the earlier study (Reicher, 1984). As with the earlier study, they directly contradict classical deindividuation theory by showing that the combination of psychological group membership and anonymity in the group result in enhanced conformity to group norms, rather than anti-normative behaviour. We have now also replicated these findings in an intergroup context, obtaining greater intergroup differentiation or bipolarization under conditions of anonymity compared to identifiability (Postmes *et al.*, in press).

The deindividuation explanation, as it refers specifically to the computer context is further undermined by the repeated finding that communication in this medium is not associated with a loss of self-awareness, but if anything an increase in (private) self-awareness (cf. Matheson, 1992; Matheson & Zanna, 1989; Siegel *et al.*, 1986). From our perspective, just as the self can no longer be viewed as a unitary construct, so it is insufficient to ask simply whether self-awareness is high or low. Rather, it becomes necessary to ask which level of self-categorization is operative and what are the norms associated with it? It thereby also becomes necessary to ask how differing computer contexts affect

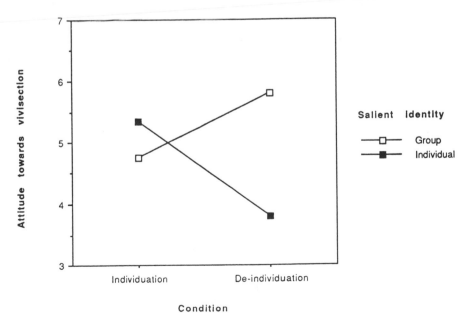

Figure 6.2 Polarization of attitudes as a function of salient identity and de-individuation

these several variables (Spears & Lea, 1992; Spears, Lea, & Lee, 1990). Indeed, by addressing these questions it is possible to make sense of a broad range of findings relating to social influence and group behaviour in various domains involving anonymity (see Spears & Lea, 1992, 1994, for reviews).

However, it is not just that self-categorization theory helps us understand deindividuation phenomena in general and computer-mediated communication in particular. Our results also serve to reinforce and extend self-categorization theory itself. Of special relevance is the seemingly paradoxical finding that isolation can actually serve to reinforce the salience of group identity and enhance conformity to group norms under appropriate conditions (Spears, 1994b; Spears & Lea, 1992). This provides perhaps the most compelling evidence yet for the definition of the group in cognitive rather than interactional terms (Hogg, 1992; Turner, 1982). In so doing it challenges all those models that either make the group dependent upon interactions between individuals (e.g. Asch, 1952; Homans, 1961; Shaw, 1976; Zander, 1979) or else argue that conformity to social norms depends upon the surveillance and co-presence of others (Deutsch & Gerard, 1955; Latané, 1980; Latané & Nida, 1980). None of this is to suggest that social interaction is irrelevant to group formation and group cohesion. Indeed there may be many situations in which such interactions increase the sense which members have of common fate and of being part of a common category. However, we propose that it is not co-presence and interaction *per se* but rather their effect upon category salience that is the key psychological mechanism underpinning group behaviour. This is demonstrated precisely by finding those limiting conditions where co-presence, as opposed to isolation, decreases category salience and hence attenuates conformity phenomena. In a phrase, physical isolation is not the same as psychological isolation. On the contrary, our analysis suggests that the social self can actually come to the fore when isolated (Spears, 1994a, 1994b).

The Minimal Group Paradigm

This observation takes us back to the minimal group experiments which lie behind the development of the whole social identity tradition. It will be recalled that the theoretical importance of these studies lay in the fact that they found strong and consistent evidence of intergroup differentiation without involving the forms of interdependence that were previously thought to be essential for such phenomena to occur. The groups are based on trivial or random criteria, they have no history and no future, there is no personal interest involved and members do not interact with fellow group members, who are unknown to them (Tajfel, 1970; Tajfel *et al.*, 1971). Yet, following our line of argument, these very features that supposedly render the context minimal actually provide its psychological power. By stripping the group of its history, of interaction and of personal interest, the social context is also stripped of all its interpersonal and individuating characteristics. Participants who do not know who is in their group or the outgroup can only treat them purely in terms of their social category membership. What is more, the response dimension of the reward matrices also forces subjects to respond in group terms if they are to make sense of an otherwise meaningless task. All in all, the features of anonymity and high social categorization are akin to the prototypical deindividuation study in which individuals are made anonymous within a social group. In the same way that we suggest that such conditions are designed to maximize the salience of social identity, so there seems to be a case for arguing that the minimal group is actually a 'maximal' group. Indeed, Tajfel himself makes this very point (1978, p. 42; see also Diehl, 1990).

In some unpublished work we have gleaned support for this idea (Spears & Oyen, 1992, reported in Spears, 1994b). In this study subjects were allocated either to an anonymous or 'deindividuated' condition or to an 'individuated' condition where group membership was publicly identified. Once again the purpose of the latter manipulation was to individuate subjects (cf. Wilder, 1978) rather than to manipulate *response* identifiability (cf. the following section). In line with predictions, subjects displayed greater ingroup bias in the deindividuated condition, and a similar difference between anonymous and identifiable conditions was also found when subjects received explicit feedback, supposedly from an earlier experimental session, suggesting the presence of a group norm to discriminate in favour of the ingroup. However, when subjects received feedback suggesting that people in both groups displayed a fairness or an equal reward allocation strategy, subjects in the deindividuated condition showed significantly less ingroup bias (they were actually fair) than in the comparable individuated condition. These results suggest that group behaviour is not necessarily generically selfish or biased towards the ingroup under the depersonalizing conditions of anonymity, but can also reflect conformity to more benign group norms under depersonalizing conditions. These results confirm our suggestion that differentiation occurs because of and not despite the lack of interaction in context. They also show that whether the process of differentiation reflects itself in discriminatory behaviour depends upon the norms operating in the situation.[1]

In terms of deindividuation theory, the results demonstrate in yet another domain that manipulations of group involvement and anonymity may gain their effects through the ways in which they alter the focus of cognitive self-definition. To the extent that such manipulations increase the salience of social identity, they can lead to more socially regulated behaviour that is

---

[1] This is important in terms of discouraging those interpretations of social identity theory that see it as implying that discrimination between groups is inevitable—an argument easily misused to racist ends (Barker, 1981).

sensitive to the content of group norms. If we assume, as is consonant with our own studies, that the classic deindividuation paradigm does indeed lead to enhanced group salience, then our social identity/deindividuation model provides an explanation not only for our own experimental results, but also for the finding of our meta-analysis that most deindividuation studies do in fact reveal an increase in normative behaviour (Postmes & Spears, 1993). What is more, this model also accounts for the socially meaningful shape of crowd action itself.

DEINDIVIDUATION MANIPULATIONS AND THE STRATEGIC EXPRESSION OF SOCIAL IDENTITIES

Identifiability and Power Relations betwen Groups

The whole thrust of the previous section was to argue that the increased impact of norms in deindividuating circumstances can be explained through the hypothesized effects of deindividuation manipulations upon the salience of social identity. However, it has been pointed out that the cognitive salience of category membership may be necessary but is not sufficient for the expression of group behaviour (Ng, 1980). In particular, if group members are to translate predispositions into actions they must be able to do so irrespective of the opposition of others: they must have the usable power to act. Thus it has been shown that ingroup favouritism is openly expressed towards other groups of equal or lesser power but not towards groups of greater power than the ingroup (Ng, 1982a; 1982b; Sachdev & Bourhis, 1985).

While this argument and the accompanying studies, have hitherto been directed towards the general process of differentiation between groups, it can be applied equally to all aspects of group behaviour—including, as is our interest, the expression of ingroup stereotypes associated with specific social categories. To be more explicit, we would propose that group members will express those behaviours that are consonant with their social identity but which are disapproved of by the outgroup, only to the extent that they have the power to overcome any anticipated or actual resistance and/or retaliation by that outgroup. Any variable that increases the power of the outgroup in relation to the ingroup will decrease the expression of such behaviours. Any variable which increases the power of the ingroup in relation to the outgroup will increase the expression of such behaviours.

This suggests a second level upon which individuation manipulations—particularly manipulations of anonymity—may be effective. We would argue that variations of identifiability will affect not only self-definition within the group but also power relations between groups. However, in order to understand how, it is necessary to examine the various ways in which identifiability is operationalized: who, precisely, is made identifiable in relationship to whom?

On the one hand, when ingroup members are made more identifiable with respect to the outgroup, the relative power of outgroup over ingroup will be increased by increasing their ability to hold ingroup members to account for their actions. On the other hand, when ingroup members are made more identifiable with respect to ingroup members, the relative power of outgroup over ingroup will be decreased by increasing the ability of ingroup members to support each other in resisting the outgroup.[2] Bearing in mind our outline of the consequences of power relations for the expression of social identity, and assuming that social identity is salient, this means that increasing identifiability to the outgroup should decrease the incidence of behaviours which are consonant with ingroup identity but disapproved of by the outgroup. Conversely, increasing identifiability to the ingroup should increase the incidence of behaviours which are consonant with ingroup identity but disapproved of by the outgroup.

At one level this argument marks a return to Le Bon. It reintroduces the dimension of power which was largely lost when the notion of submergence was translated into the concept of deindividuation. Like Le Bon, we complement an analysis of the effects of identifiability upon self-perception with an analysis of the effects of identifiability upon power. However, the way in which we do this differs from Le Bon's account in two crucial ways. Firstly, we do not treat identifiability as a singular attribute but rather as a relationship which may take differing forms. Secondly, we do not see power as being used indiscriminately. Rather, empowering the ingroup over the outgroup only affects the expression of ingroup identity in the face of potential or actual outgroup resistance. It will not lead group members to act in ways that are incompatible with their identity. It will not affect the expression of behaviours which would not invoke outgroup sanctions. In a nutshell, by suggesting that power be brought into the equation, we are proposing that the cognitive analysis of identity salience be complemented by a strategic analysis of the factors affecting identity expression. We are not suggesting that the strategic analysis should usurp the cognitive.

Studies on the Strategic Effects of Identifiability to the Outgroup

The seeds of our analysis were sown by a study (Reicher, 1987; Reicher & Levine, 1994a, study 1) in which subjects were divided into groups according

---

[2] It is possible to argue that greater co-presence of or identifiability to the ingroup may also enhance pressure within the ingroup to conform to ingroup norms. However, in line with self-categorization theory (Turner, 1991) we would argue that behaviour in line with group norms for genuine ingroup members (i.e. people who genuinely categorize themselves as members of the ingroup and identify strongly with it), does not reflect group pressure, but rather the willing and authentic expression of self. Nevertheless, it is quite possible that this may play an important role for group members who are less committed to the group. We are grateful to Bernd Simon for raising this issue.

to their support for or opposition to the British Campaign for Nuclear Disarmament (pro- or anti-CND), a unilateralist campaigning organization. Subjects watched a debate between pro- and anti-unilateralists and then were asked to allocate points between speakers on the two sides for the standard as opposed to the content of their debating. Subjects were also asked to fill in an 'orientation to nuclear disarmament' scale. According to the cover story, at the end of the study outgroup members would divide the total number of points allocated to the ingroup in the 'debate' task amongst the ingroup members. This was to ensure that the outgroup was perceived as having control over the fate of ingroup members. However, for half the subjects (anonymous condition) ingroup members compiled their responses internally before the aggregate was passed over to the outgroup. The other half (identifiable condition) read their scores to the outgroup who calculated the total themselves. Thus identifiability of responses to outgroup was manipulated (low or high) while identifiability of responses to the ingroup was kept uniformly high.

If it is assumed that power of sanction by the outgroup over the ingroup depends upon the identifiability of ingroup members to the outgroup, then those responses that are unacceptable to the outgroup should decrease under identifiable conditions. Given that the scale was scored by marking the number of points given to the pro-CND position, this means that pro-CND group scores should be high but lower in the identifiable conditions, whereas anti-CND group scores should be low, but higher in the identifiable conditions. As expected, ingroup bias in the points allocation task followed this pattern and was lower when subjects were identifiable to the outgroup (see Table 6.1).

The results on the 'orientation' scale were more complicated. Overall, the manipulation of identifiability had no effects. However, closer analysis showed the expected decrease in expression of the ingroup norm occurred for only one item. This addressed the willingness of subjects to participate in nonviolent civil disobedience to nuclear weapons. All the other items, which asked either for attitudes or willingness to express dissent (sign a petition, gather signatures for a petition etc.), lie within the consensus of acceptable political difference. The acceptability of civil disobedience, however, is a mat-

Table 6.1 Scale scores (point allocation) and overall impression scores on the 'debate evaluation' measure

	Scale score		Overall impression score	
	Unidentifiable	Identifiable	Unidentifiable	Identifiable
Pro-CND	174.84	142.75	22.24	19.00
Anti-CND	38.00	62.35	5.00	9.53

Note: Higher scores are more pro-CND.

ter of considerable controversy where some deem that it has no place in British political life while others strenuously contest attempts to outlaw such action. Hence the item addressing this issue is the only one where adherence to this norm is not only expressing difference from the outgroup but also expressing support for something the outgroup is likely to find unacceptable. It is therefore consonant with our predictions that this should be the one item where expression of the ingroup position is rendered less likely by identifiability to the outgroup.

Due, in large part, to the small scale of this study, we designed a second experiment (Reicher & Levine, 1994a, study 2) to address the issue. This time, instead of taking two groups and manipulating their identifiability to each other, we manipulated the identifiability of subjects to ourselves, academic psychology staff, as an outgroup. Moreover, we explicitly built in a distinction between items where difference would attract outgroup sanctions ('punishable' items) and items where the expression of difference is legitimate ('unpunishable' items) Students from the Science faculty who were studying psychology as an ancillary subject were defined either in terms of a 'scientist' identity or else a 'student' identity. They were then asked to complete a questionnaire about the psychology course which contained items where dissent would be either punishable or unpunishable by academic staff. Punishable items had to do with issues of academic commitment: willingness to plagiarize course work, willingness to cheat on experimental reports and so on. Unpunishable items had to do with moral attitudes towards psychology on issues such as animal experimentation. Subjects were either made identifiable to the experimenters, who were psychology staff members, by writing their name on the questionnaire, or else they wrote down a confidential code and were therefore unidentifiable.

On the basis of prior interviews, it was expected that the ingroup stereotype for 'scientists' would be compatible with that of staff members for the punishable items. However, the ingroup stereotype for 'students' would be incompatible with that of staff members. Consequently, it was hypothesized that, in the case of the punishable items, decreased identifiability to the staff outgroup should decrease the expression of academic commitment for 'student' subjects but have no effect upon 'science' subjects. Conversely, for the unpunishable items, it was hypothesized that the identifiability manipulations should have no effect for either group since, even if ingroup norms differ from those of staff, the expression of such norms will receive no sanction.

The pattern of results for the punishable items was exactly as predicted (see Table 6.2, top row). Insofar as a manipulation check showed that the identifiability variable had no effect on identity salience, the results cannot be explained in cognitive terms. They therefore confirm the argument that lowered identifiability to outgroup strategically enables ingroup members to express those aspects of their identity which would attract outgroup sanction.

Table 6.2   Item means for the 'punishable' and 'unpunishable' attitude questions

	Student identity		Scientist identity	
	Unidentifiable	Identifiable	Unidentifiable	Identifiable
Punishable	4.42	4.02	4.14	4.34
Unpunishable	4.20	5.12	4.58	3.64

Note: Higher scores = lower academic commitment and more anti-experimentation.

However, contrary to our prediction, the visibility manipulation also had a significant effect for the unpunishable items (Table 6.2, bottom row). Thus 'scientist' subjects became more pro-animal experimentation when visible and 'student' subjects became more anti-animal experimentation when visible.

One way of explaining these latter findings is to assume that the 'scientist' norm is more pro- and the 'student' norm is more anti-animal experimentation than that of psychology staff. If that is the case, then these results reflect a tendency for subjects to accentuate normative difference from the outgroup on unpunishable items when identifiable to them. This may be explained as a presentational phenomenon: where group members may do so without fear, they take advantage of identifiability in order publicly to express their difference from the outgroup and hence their adherence to the ingroup. One further study (Reicher & Levine, 1994b) was designed to investigate this possibility.

The study involved students who were training to be physical education teachers and defined them in terms of their 'PE student' identity. They were given a questionnaire which contained both 'punishable' items (relating to academic commitment) and 'unpunishable' items. For the latter, pilot interviews were used to determine how PE student norms differed from those of their lecturers on a number of different dimensions. The students were either made identifiable or unidentifiable to these lecturers as in the previous experiment. It was predicted that identifiability to outgroup should decrease expression of group identity for the punishable items and increase expression of group identity for the unpunishable items.

This predicted interaction between item type and visibility conditions was highly significant. What is more, on each of the various unpunishable dimensions, subjects significantly accentuated the difference between ingroup and outgroup norms—even though, on a behavioural level, this led to seemingly paradoxical results. For instance students had a more conservative educational philosophy than staff and this led them to be more disciplinarian under identifiable conditions. However, they also laid more stress on the social aspects of university life than staff and, in this domain, they were less disciplinarian under identifiable conditions.

Once again, the visibility manipulation had no effect on identity salience and therefore the results cannot be explained as deriving from differences in the nature of the relevant identity between conditions. Rather it lends credence to the argument that, instead of identifiability to the outgroup having strategic implications for the expression of social identity only in the case of punishable items, there are different strategic processes operative for punishable and unpunishable item types. Whereas enhanced identifiability to outgroup decreases the expression of punishable aspects of ingroup identity, it increases the presentation of unpunishable aspects of ingroup identity. Our unexpected findings for the unpunishable items therefore extend rather than undermine the strategic dimension of our analysis.

CONCLUSIONS

The aim of this chapter has been to challenge traditional deindividuation theory and with it the assumptions that such factors as lowered identifiability and immersion in the group lead to a loss of identity and hence to uncontrolled behaviour. We have sought to replace this approach with a social identity model of deindividuation (SIDE) which consists of two elements. On the one hand we argue that deindividuation manipulations affect the cognitive salience of social identity. In particular, immersion in the social group and lack of personalizing cues can enhance social identity and thus adherence to the standards associated with the relevant social category. On the other hand, we argue that the self-same deindividuation manipulations also have strategic effects upon the ability of group members to express their social identity in face of outgroup opposition. In particular, where subjects are non-identifiable to the outgroup but identifiable to the ingroup their ability to over-ride the outgroup will be maximized.

Three general points emerge from this analysis. Firstly, while it can be seen as a specific application of self-categorization theory, our position provides unprecedented support for the basic tenets of the approach. In particular it makes the point that social psychological processes in general and group processes in particular are not to be equated with the presence of others. Individuals may act as social subjects just as much if not more when isolated than when together. Indeed, we have repeatedly found that isolation may enhance the collective self (e.g., Spears, 1994b). To Allport's aphorism that 'the individual in the crowd behaves just as he would behave alone only more so' (1924, p. 295) we might retort that 'the crowd is in the individual just as much when alone, if not more so'.

However, it is not only that we provide support for self-categorization theory as it stands, it is also that our position marks an extension of the theory. This takes us to our second point. Self-categorization theory can be criticized for being overly cognitive. While it addresses the way in which self arises in particular social contexts (Turner et al., 1987; Oakes, Haslam, & Turner, 1994) it does not look at the way in which social identities are actively deployed and presented in specific sets of social relations. Conversely, models of self-presentation tend to beg the question of what self is being presented, what standards are underlying behaviour and so on: self-presentation is simply a matter of complying with others in order to maximize the rewards coming from them (Baumeister, 1982; Jones & Pittman, 1982; Leary & Kowalski, 1990). We suggest an integration of the two approaches whereby strategic considerations surrounding the presentation of self are combined with an analysis of which self is salient, the standards associated with that self and the implications for how subjects behave.

As it applies specifically to deindividuation, we have shown that the same manipulations of group involvement, and anonymity may simultaneously affect both which aspect of the self-concept is operative and the presentational concerns that govern its expression. However, such a finding was largely fortuitous. In order to isolate the cognitive and strategic elements of our analysis we largely attempted to control the one while manipulating the other. The obvious next step is to examine how they work together. Clearly this is essential if we are to understand the complex effects of seemingly simple manipulations such as identifiability as they operate in the social world.

Our final point takes us back to the roots of deindividuation theory. If the complexities of deindividuation manipulations remain to be fully unravelled, we have, nevertheless, some indications of which conditions maximize the salience and the expression of social identity: immersion in a group, lack of personalizing cues, identifiability to ingroup, lack of identifiability to out-group. In other words, precisely those conditions that result from being part of a large crowd. Crowds not only have the inclination but also the ability to act upon it. To the extent that this is so, crowd action should be the one place where groups can express their full understanding of the world without having to censor themselves for fear of others. As Reddy (1977) has concluded from his studies of mass action amongst French workers: 'the targets of these crowds thus glitter in the eye of history as signs of the labourers' conception of the nature of society' (p. 84). If a misrepresentation of crowds in history has propagated psychological theories that only see volatility in collective action, then time for change is long overdue. Such change promises not only to give us a better understanding of societal phenomena but also to resocialize the basic categories of the human psyche.

REFERENCES

Abrams, D. (1990). How do group members regulate their behaviour? An integration of social identity and self-awareness theories. In D. Abrams & M. A. Hogg (Eds), *Social Identity Theory: Constructive and critical advances.* Hemel Hempstead: Harvester.

Abrams, D., & Hogg, M. A. (1990). Social identification, self-categorization and social influence. In W. Stroebe and M. Hewstone (Eds), *European Review of Social Psychology* (Vol. 1, pp. 195–228), Chichester: John Wiley.

Allport, F. (1924). *Social Psychology*. New York: Houghton Mifflin.

Asch, S. (1952). *Social Psychology*. Englewood Cliffs, NJ: Prentice Hall.

Barker, M. (1981). *The New Racism*. London: Junction Books.

Barrows, S. (1981). *Distorting Mirrors*. New Haven, CT: Yale University Press.

Baumeister, R. F. (1982). A self-presentational view of social phenomena. *Psychological Bulletin*, **91**, 3–26.

Berk, R. A., & Aldrich, H. E. (1972). Patterns of vandalism during civil disorders as an indicator of selection of targets. *American Sociological Review*, **37**, 533–47.

Billig, M., & Tajfel, H. (1973). Social categorization and similarity in intergroup behaviour. *European Journal of Social Psychology*, **3**, 27–52.

Brink, W., & Harris, L. (1969). *Black and White*. New York: Simon & Schuster.

Brown, R. (1988). *Group Processes: Dynamics within and between groups*. Oxford: Blackwell.

Burnstein, E., & Vinokur, A. (1977). Persuasive argumentation and social comparison as determinants of attitude polarization. *Journal of Experimental Social Psychology*, **13**, 315–350.

Buys, C. J. (1978). Humans would do better without groups. *Personality and Social Psychology Bulletin*, **4**, 123–35.

Cannavale, F. J., Scarr, H. A., & Pepitone, A. (1970). Deindividuation in the small group: Further evidence. *Journal of Personality and Social Psychology*, **16**, 141–7.

Caplan, N. S., & Paige, J. M. (1968). A study of ghetto rioters. *Scientific American*, **219**, 14–21.

Carver, C. S. (1975). Physical aggression as a function of objective self awareness and attitudes towards punishment. *Journal of Experimental Social Psychology*, **11**, 510–19.

Carver, C. S., & Scheier, M. F. (1981). *Attention and Self-Regulation: A control theory approach to human behavior*. New York: Springer-Verlag.

Cohen, R. (1970). *The Los Angeles Riots: A socio-psychological study*. New York: Praeger.

Colman, A. (1991). Psychological evidence in South African murder trials. *The Psychologist*, **4**, 482–6.

Davis, N. Z. (1978). The rites of violence: Religious riot in sixteenth century France. *Past & Present*, **59**, 51–91.

Deutsch, M., & Gerard, H. B. (1955). A study of normative and informational influences upon individual judgement. *Journal of Abnormal and Social Psychology*, **51**, 629–36.

Diehl, M. (1990). The minimal group paradigm: Theoretical explanations and empirical findings. In W. Stroebe & M. Hewstone (Eds), *The European Review of Social Psychology* (Vol. 1, pp. 263–92), Chichester: John Wiley.

Diener, E. (1976). Effects of prior destructive behaviour, anonymity and group presence on deindividuation and aggression. *Journal of Personality and Social Psychology*, **33**, 497–507.

Diener, E. (1977). Deindividuation: causes and consequences. *Social Behaviour and Personality*, **5**, 143–55.

Diener, E. (1979). Deindividuation, self-awareness and disinhibition. *Journal of Personality and Social Psychology*, **37**, 1160–71.

Diener, E. (1980). Deindividuation: The absence of self-awareness and self-regulation in group members. In P. Paulus (Ed.), *The Psychology of Group Influence*. Hillsdale, NJ: Erlbaum.

Diener, E., & Srull, T. K. (1979). Self-awareness, psychological perspective and self-reinforcement in relation to personal and social standards. *Journal of Personality and Social Psychology*, **37**, 413–23.

Diener, E., & Wallbom, M. (1976). Effects of self-awareness on anti-normative behaviour. *Journal of Research in Personality*, **10**, 107–11.

Donnerstein, E., Donnerstein, M., & Evans, R. (1972). Variables in inter-racial aggression: anonymity expected retaliation and a riot. *Journal of Personality and Social Psychology*, **22**, 236–45.

Duval, S., & Wicklund, R. A. (1972). *A Theory of Objective Self-Awareness*. New York: Academic Press.

Emler, N., & Reicher, S. D. (1995). *Adolescence and Delinquency*. Oxford: Blackwell.

Fenigstein, A., Scheier, M. F., & Buss, A. H. (1975). Public and private self-consciousness: assessment and theory. *Journal of Consulting and Clinical Psychology*, **43**, 522–7.

Festinger, L., Pepitone, A., & Newcomb, T. (1952). Some consequences of deindividuation in a group. *Journal of Abnormal and Social Psychology*, **47**, 382–9.

Fogelson, R. M. (1971). *Violence in Protest*. New York: Doubleday.

Froming, W. J., Walker, G., & Lopyan, K. J. (1982). Public and private self-awareness: When personal attitudes conflict with societal expectations. *Journal of Experimental Social Psychology*, **18**, 476–87.

Gergen, K. J., Gergen, M. M., & Barton, W. H. (1973). Deviance in the dark. *Psychology Today*, **7**, 129–30.

Hogg, M. A. (1992). *The Social Psychology of Group Cohesiveness: From social attraction to social identity*. Hemel Hempstead: Harvester.

Hogg, M. A., & Abrams, D. (1988). *Social Identifications: A social psychology of intergroup relations and group processes*. London: Routledge.

Homans, G. C. (1961). *Social Behaviour: its elementary forms*. New York: Harcourt Brace Jovanovich.

Hopkins, N. (1994). Peer group pressure and adolescent health-related behaviour: questioning the assumptions. *Journal of Community and Applied Social Psychology*. In press.

Israel, J., & Tajfel, H. (1972). *The Context of Social Psychology*. London: Academic Press.

Jenson, J. (1992). Fandom as pathology: The consequences of characterization. In L. A. Lewis (Ed.), *The Adoring Audience: fan culture and popular media*. London: Routledge.

Johnson, N. R. (1987). Panic at 'The Who Stampede': an empirical assessment. *Social Problems*, **34**, 362.

Johnson, R. D., & Downing, L. L. (1979). Deindividuation and violence of cues: effects on pro-social and anti-social behaviour. *Journal of Personality and Social Psychology*, **37**, 1532–8.

Jones, E. E., & Pittman, T. S. (1982). Towards a general theory of strategic self-presentation. In J. Suls (Ed.), *Psychological Perspectives on the Self* (Vol. 1). Hillsdale, NJ: Erlbaum.

Kiesler, S., Siegel, J., & McGuire, T. (1984). Social psychological aspects of computer-mediated communication. *American Psychologist*, **39**, 1123–34.

Latané, B. (1980). The psychology of social impact. *American Psychologist*, **36**, 343–56.

Latané, B., & Nida, S. (1980). Social impact theory and group influence: A social engineering perspective. In P. B. Paulus (Ed.), *Psychology of Group Influence.* Hillsdale, NJ: Erlbaum.

Le Bon, G. (1895, trans. 1947). *The Crowd: a study of the popular mind.* London: Ernest Benn.

Lea, M., & Spears, R. (1991). Computer-mediated communication, de-individuation and group decision-making. *International Journal of Man-Machine Studies, Special Issue on CSCW and Groupware*, **39**, 283–301. Reprinted (1991) in S. Greenberg (Ed.), *Computer-Supported Co-operative Work and Groupware.* London: Academic Press.

Leary, M. R., & Kowalski, R. M. (1990). Impression management: A literature review and two-component model. *Psychological Bulletin*, **107**, 34–47.

Lefebvre, D. (1954). Foules revolutionnaires. In G. Lefebvre (Ed.), *Etudes sur la Revolution Française.* Paris: Presses Universitaires de France.

Lindskold, S., & Propst, L. R. (1980). Deindividuation, self-awareness and impression management. In J. T. Tedeschi (Ed.), *Impression Management Theory and Social Psychological Research.* New York: Academic Press.

Maas, A., & Clark, R. D. (1984). Hidden impact of minorities: Fifteen years of minority influence research. *Psychological Bulletin*, **95**, 89–104.

Marx, G. T. (1967). *Protest and Prejudice: a study of belief in the black community.* New York: Harper & Row.

Matheson, K. (1992). Women and computer technology: communicating for herself. In M. Lea (Ed.), *Contexts of Computer-mediated Communication.* Hemel Hempstead: Harvester-Wheatsheaf.

Matheson, K., & Zanna, M. P. (1989). Persuasion as a function of self-awareness in computer-mediated communication, *Social Behaviour*, **4**, 99–111.

Milgram, S. (1974). *Obedience to Authority.* New York: Harper & Row.

Moscovici, S. (1976). *Social Influence and Social Change.* London: Academic Press.

Mugny, G. (1982). *The Power of Minorities.* London: Academic Press.

Ng, S. H. (1980). *The Social Psychology of Power.* London, Academic Press.

Ng, S. H. (1982a). Power and appeasement in intergroup discrimination. *Australian Journal of Psychology*, **34**, 37–44.

Ng, S. H. (1982b). Power and intergroup discrimination. In H. Tajfel (Ed.), *Social Identity and Intergroup Relations.* Cambridge: Cambridge University Press, and Paris: Maison des Sciences de l'Homme.

Nye, R. A. (1975). *The Origins of Crowd Psychology: Gustave Le Bon and the crisis of mass democracy in the third republic.* London: Sage.

Oakes, P. J., Haslam,, A., & Turner, J. C. (1994). *Stereotyping and Social Reality.* Oxford: Blackwell.

Postmes, T., & Spears, R. (1993). *A meta-analysis of deindividuation research: how 'anti' is antinormative behaviour.* Xth General meeting of the European Association for Experimental Social Psychology, Lisbon, Portugal, September 1993.

Postmes, T., Lea, M., Spears, R., Croft, R., van Dijk, L., & van der Pligt, J. (in press). Bipolarisatie in intergroeps overleg: De invloed van groepsnormen op attitudes. *Fundamentele Sociale Psychologie*, Vol. 9.

Prentice-Dunn, S. (1991). Half-baked ideas: deindividuation and the non-reactive assessment of self-awareness. *Contemporary Social Psychology*, **14**, 16–17.

Prentice-Dunn, S., & Rogers, R. W. (1982). Effects of private and public-self awareness on deindividuation and aggression. *Journal of Personality and Social Psychology*, **403**, 503–13.

Prentice-Dunn, S., & Rogers, R. W. (1989). Deindividuation and the self-regulation of behaviour. In P. B. Paulus (Ed.), *Psychology of Group Influence* (2nd edn). Hillsdale, NJ: Erlbaum.

Prentice-Dunn, S., & Spivey, C. B. (1986). Extreme deindividuation in the laboratory. *Personality and Social Psychology Bulletin*, **12**, 206–15.

Reddy, W. M. (1977). The textile trade and the language of the crowd at Rouen 1752–1871. *Past and Present*, **74**, 62–89.

Reicher, S. D. (1984). Social influence in the crowd: Attitudinal and behavioural effects of deindividuation in conditions of high and low group salience. *British Journal of Social Psychology*, **23**, 341–50.

Reicher, S. D. (1987). Crowd behaviour as social action. In J. C. Turner, M. A. Hogg, P. J. Oakes, S. D. Reicher, & M. S. Wetherell (1987). *Rediscovering the Social Group: A self-categorization theory*. Oxford: Blackwell.

Reicher, S. D., & Emler, N. (1987). Managing reputations in adolescence: The pursuit of delinquent and non-delinquent identities. In H. Beloff (Ed.), *Young People in Society*. London: Methuen.

Reicher, S. D., & Levine, M. (1994a). On the consequences of deindividuation manipulations for the strategic communication of self: Identifiability and the self-presentation of social identity. *European Journal of Social Psychology*, **24**, 511–24.

Reicher, S. D., & Levine, M. (1994b). Deindividuation, power relations between groups and the expression of social identity 1: The effects of visibility to the outgroup. *British Journal of Social Psychology*, **33**, 145–63.

Reicher, S. D., & Potter, J. (1985). Psychological theory as intergroup perspective: A comparative analysis of 'scientific' and 'lay' accounts of crowd events. *Human Relations*, **38**, 167–89.

Sachdev, I., & Bourhis, R. (1985). Social categorization and power differentials in group relations. *European Journal of Social Psychology*, **15**, 415–34.

Scheier, M. F., Fenigstein, A., & Buss, A. H. (1974). Self-awareness and physical aggression. *Journal of Experimental Social Psychology*, **10**, 264–73.

Shaw, M. E. (1976). *Group Dynamics: the psychology of small group behaviour*. New Delhi: Tata McGraw-Hill.

Siegel, J., Dubrovsky, V., Kielser, S., & McGuire T. (1986). Group processes in computer-mediated communication. *Organizational Behaviour and Human Decision Processes*, **37**, 157–87.

Singer, J. E., Brush, C. A., & Lublin, S. C. (1965). Some aspects of deindividuation: identification and conformity. *Journal of Experimental Social Psychology*, **1**, 356–78.

Spears, R. (1994a). Isolating the collective self: The social context and content of identity, rationality and behaviour. NWO/Pionier research proposal, University of Amsterdam.

Spears, R. (1994b). Isolating the collective self. In A. Oosterwegel & R. A. Wicklund (Eds), *The self in European and North American Culture: Development and processes*. Amsterdam: Kluwer.

Spears, R. (1995). Deindividuation. In A. S. R. Manstead & M. Hewstone (Eds), *The Blackwell Encyclopedia of Social Psychology*. Oxford: Blackwell. In press.

Spears, R., & Lea, M. (1992). Social influence of the 'social' in computer-mediated communication. In M. Lea (Ed.), *Contexts of Computer-Mediated Communication* (pp. 30–65). Hemel Hempstead: Harvester-Wheatsheaf.

Spears, R., & Lea, M. (1994). Panacea or panopticon? The hidden power in computer-mediated communication. *Communication Research*, **21**, 427–59.

Spears, R., Lea, M., & Lee, S. (1990). De-individuation and group polarization in computer-mediated communication. *British Journal of Social Psychology*, **29**, 121–34.

Spears, R., & Oyen, M. (1992). *Is minimal really maximal? When group out of sight is group in mind.* Second European Small Group Meeting on Social Cognition, Bristol, UK, April.

Tafjel, H. (1970). Experiments in intergroup discrimination. *Scientific American*, **223**, 96–102.

Tajfel, H. (Ed.) (1978). *Differentiation between Social Groups.* London: Academic Press.

Tajfel, H. (Ed.) (1982). *Social Identity and Intergroup Relations.* Cambridge: Cambridge University Press.

Tajfel, H., Flament, C., Billig, M., & Bundy, R. (1971). Social categorization and intergroup behaviour. *European Journal of Social Psychology*, **1**, 149–78.

Tajfel, H., & Turner, J. C. (1986). The social identity theory of intergroup behaviour. In S. Worchel & W. G. Austin (Ed.), *Psychology of Intergroup Relations.* Chicago: Nelson-Hall.

Tarde, G. (1901). *L'Opinion et la Foule.* Paris: Alcan.

Thompson, E. P. (1971). The moral ceremony of the English crowd in the eighteenth century. *Past and Present*, **50**, 76–136.

Thompson, E. P. (1991). *Customs in Common.* London: Merlin.

Tomlinson, T. M. (1970). Ideological foundations for Negro action: A comparative analysis of militant and non-militant views of the Los Angeles riot. *Journal of Social Issues*, **25**, 93–119.

Turner, J. C. (1982). Towards a cognitive redefinition of the social group. In H. Tajfel (Ed.), *Social Identity and Intergroup Relations.* Cambridge: Cambridge University Press.

Turner, J. C. (1987). A self-categorization theory. In J. C. Turner, M. A. Hogg, P. J. Oakes, S. D. Reicher & M. S. Wetherell (1987). *Rediscovering the Social Group: A self-categorization theory.* Oxford: Blackwell.

Turner, J. C. (1991). *Social Influence.* Milton Keynes: Open University Press.

Turner, J. C., Hogg, M. A., Oakes, P. J., Reicher, S. D., & Wetherell, M. S. (1987). *Rediscovering the Social Group: A self-categorization theory.* Oxford: Blackwell.

Waddington, D. (1992). *Contemporary Issues in Public Disorder: A historical and comparative approach.* London: Routledge.

Watson, R. I. (1973). Investigation into deindividuation using a cross-cultural survey technique. *Journal of Personality and Social Psychology*, **25**, 342–5.

Wetherell, M. (1987). Social identity and group polarization. In J. C. Turner, M. A. Hogg, P. J. Oakes, S. D. Reicher, & M. S. Wetherell (1987). *Rediscovering the Social Group: A self-categorization theory.* Oxford: Blackwell.

Wicklund, R. A. (1975). Objective of self-awareness. In L. Berkowitz (Ed.), *Advances in Experimental Social Psychology*, Vol. 8. New York: Academic Press.

Wilder, D. A. (1978). Reduction of intergroup discrimination through individuation of the outgroup. *Journal of Personality and Social Psychology*, **36**, 1361–74.

Zabrick, M., & Miller, N. (1972). Group aggression: the effects of friendship ties and anonymity. *Proceedings of the 80th Annual Convention of the APA* (Vol. 7, pp. 211–12). Washington D.C.: American Psychological Association.

Zander, A. (1979). The psychology of group processes. *Annual Review of Psychology*, **30**, 417–51.

Zimbardo, P. G. (1969). The human choice: Individuation, reason, and order versus deindividuation, impulse and chaos. In W. J. Arnold & D. Levine (Eds), *Nebraska Symposium on Motivation*. Lincoln, NB: University of Nebraska Press.

Chapter 7

Intergroup Biases in Multiple Group Systems: The Perception of Ethnic Hierarchies

Louk Hagendoorn
Utrecht University

ABSTRACT

Results of social distance research suggest the existence of consensual ethnic hierarchies in social distance in Western societies. The phenomenon comprises an ingroup bias and a pattern of cumulative intergroup biases on which majority and minority groups appear to agree. In this chapter an explanation is sought for this phenomenon. Realistic conflict theory and social identity theory seem to be able to explain certain aspects of it, such as ingroup bias and the ethnic hierarchies of subordinate ethnic groups, but not the ethnic hierarchy of dominant ethnic groups and intergroup consensus. These aspects may be explained by a model about the different functionality of stereotypes for dominant and subordinate ethnic groups. In order to test these explanations, the generality of ingroup bias, the cumulative structure of intergroup bias and the existence of intergroup consensus on the ethnic hierarchy are investigated in different societies.

INTRODUCTION

The phenomenon to be examined in this chapter is that members of many ethnic groups seem to have specific preferences for contact with outgroups. Social distance and stereotype research in the United States, Canada, South Africa and The Netherlands indicates that outgroups are ranked as more or

European Review of Social Psychology, Volume 6. Edited by Wolfgang Stroebe and Miles Hewstone.
© 1995 John Wiley & Sons Ltd.

less attractive social partners and there is social consensus about the assigned rank. At the top of the hierarchy in social distance are positively stereotyped North Europeans, followed by South and East Europeans. Asians and finally Africans have a low place in the hierarchy (Berry and Kalin, 1979; Duckitt, 1992; Hagendoorn and Hraba, 1987; Pettigrew, 1960). This arrangement of outgroups suggests that intergroup bias has a cumulative pattern. Our aim is to present convincing evidence for this cumulative pattern and to offer some possible explanations for this phenomenon.

The structure of this intergroup bias towards multiple outgroups has not been reached extensively. Research on intergroup relations has focused on a simple ingroup–outgroup situation. In this situation several factors have been found to affect the tendency to discriminate outgroup members and favour the ingroup: the group members' need to perceptually differentiate between categories and groups (Doise, 1978; Tajfel, 1959), their need to feel positive about their identity (Tajfel, 1981a), the strength of their identification with the ingroup (Hinkle and Brown, 1990; Kelly, 1993), the salience of intergroup boundaries (Oakes, 1987; Van Knippenberg, Van Twuyver, & Pepels, 1994), tasks and roles converging with group boundaries (Marcus-Newhall *et al.*, 1993), group cohesiveness and adherence to ingroup norms (Dion, 1979; Wilder & Shapiro, 1984), and an emphasis on social comparison and collectivism (Hinkle, Brown, & Ely, 1990). Status affects intergroup bias as well: under laboratory conditions high-status groups exhibit stronger intergroup bias than low-status groups, but really high-status groups exhibit a (non-significant) weaker intergroup bias than low-status groups (Mullen, Brown, & Smith, 1992). Stable, legitimate and impermeable status barriers appear to diminish the intergroup bias of high- and low-status groups, although the results are contradictory (Duckitt, 1992).

It is less clear what happens in more complex intergroup situations, such as overlapping groups (crossed categorizations) and multiple groups on a single categorization dimension. The typical situation studied in crossed categorization research is a fourfold group system, constituted by the crossing of two dichotomous categorization dimensions (A/B and X/Y), in which group membership partially overlaps (for example, AX and AY have A in common). The central concern is to determine whether cross-cutting category membership reduces intergroup bias. The results are inconclusive. When measured in terms of allocation of rewards, outgroup discrimination seems to be reduced by overlapping group membership, but when measured in terms of negative intergroup evaluations intergroup bias persists (Vanbeselaere, 1987). Crossed categorization models have been extended to intergroup situations of more than four groups (Hewstone, Islam, & Judd, 1993) and models have been designed to capture variations in the salience of the categorization dimensions and to test competing explanations of the pattern of intergroup biases (Brewer *et al.*, 1987; Hewstone, Islam, & Judd, 1993).

In stratified and multi-ethnic, multi-religious or multi-linguistic societies, the real intergroup situation is a series of groups on each categorization dimension. It may be assumed that the perceived interrelations between the ingroup and the outgroups affect intergroup bias as well. Research in the field of ethnic and national groups suggests that there are remarkably stable evaluative (stereotype) and social distance hierarchies with respect to these groups, possibly reflecting aspects of their relative positions. Minority groups seem to accept these hierarchies, in spite of their often subordinate position, except that all groups always prefer the ingroup (Berry and Kalin, 1979; Duckitt, 1992; Pettigrew, 1960). Thus in multiple group systems there seems to be a hierarchy of biases as well as consensus on the rank of outgroups in this hierarchy.

A weak point in this social distance and stereotype research is that the hierarchies are indicated by differences in social distance means with respect to different outgroups or differences in the evaluations of these groups (Berry and Kalin, 1979; Owen, Eisner, & McFaul, 1981). Yet it has to be demonstrated that the pattern is actually cumulative, as in a Guttman scale. Therefore, we replicated these studies and tested the hierarchical structure of social distance towards outgroups by Guttman scalogram analysis. Scalogram analysis tests the number of violations of a common and nested evaluation of stimuli across respondents. In this case the evaluation is social distance and the stimuli are the ethnic target groups. Guttman's coefficient of reproducibility (CR in deterministic analysis, or Loevinger's H in probabilistic scalogram analysis) indicates how far the respondents' social distances follow a similar unidimensional pattern. Guttman's coefficient of scalability (CS, or Rho in probabilistic scalogram analysis) indicates the reliability of the scale (Sijtsma, Debets, & Molenaar, 1990). A scalogram of ethnic target groups indicates that respondents agree on the relative distances towards outgroups, in spite of individual differences in social distance (Jaspars & Fraser, 1984). Subsequently, the actual nature of consensus had to be specified. The next step in our research was to distinguish two possible forms of consensus on an ethnic hierarchy: consensus among ingroup members and consensus among ingroup and outgroup members. The first form of consensus may indicate that there is a social representation—in the sense of Moscovici (1984, 1988)—of an ethnic rank order in society. The second form of consensus is much broader and may indicate the existence of a collective representation of ethnic group positions (Durkheim, 1915/1976; Jaspars & Fraser, 1984).

In this chapter the following topics will be addressed. First, it will be argued that the phenomenon of an ethnic hierarchy in its various aspects—ingroup preference, ingroup consensus and intergroup consensus—cannot be explained by just one social psychological theory. Social identity theory may explain the ingroup bias and social representation theory offers a frame to understand ingroup consensus. However, the consensus among different ethnic groups escapes a simple explanation by either realistic conflict theory or social identity theory. It seems that the hierarchy results from different motives for different groups: justification of their position by dominant groups and intergroup differentiation by subordinate groups.

The next step is to present data on the hierarchical and consensual nature of intergroup bias. It will be shown that the ingroup is always preferred more than outgroups and that ingroup members of various groups agree on their version of an ethnic hierarchy. The ethnic hierarchy will be interpreted as a social representation of ethnic group positions and the consensual and non-consensual aspects of the hierarchy will be determined. The third step is to find out which are the correlates of the rank of ethnic groups in the hierarchy. Attention will be focused in particular on the perception of contact with outgroups as a threat to the status of the ingroup and on negative outgroup stereotypes. The fourth step is to determine the consensus between the hierarchies of minority groups and majority groups. Predictions following from the realistic conflict theory, from social identity theory and from assumptions about the different functionality of stereotypes for high- and low-placed groups with respect to the possibility of intergroup consensus will be tested. The effect of the majority–minority relations on intergroup consensus will be explored as well.

The last step is a test of the hypothesis that low-placed ethnic groups have a stronger need to differentiate the ingroup from outgroups in order to maintain a positive social identity and therefore show a stronger intergroup bias than high-placed groups. Finally the results of the research will be summarized and discussed.

WHY IS THERE AN ETHNIC HIERARCHY?

The ethnic hierarchies found in social distance and stereotype research have three different aspects: ingroup preference, ingroup consensus on the arrangement of ethnic outgroups in social distance, and intergroup consensus on the ethnic hierarchy. Ingroup members have, of course, many practical reasons to prefer contact with people of the same language, religion and culture (Hutnik, 1991). However, the ingroup preference may also indicate ingroup cohesion and the awareness of shared interests. These factors are central in the explanation given by ethnocentrism theory and realistic conflict theory of intergroup bias. Sumner (1906) explained the universality of intergroup bias (ethnocentrism) from the survival value of group cohesion; however, this does not explain why intergroup bias varies in different intergroup settings (Mullen, Brown, & Smith, 1992). An explanation from realistic conflict theory is equally unsatisfying because ingroup bias is more general than intergroup conflict. The most plausible explanation of ingroup preference and ingroup bias is offered by social identity theory: ingroup preference leads to the maintenance of a positive social identity and can be justified by intergroup comparisons on dimensions which are favourable for the ingroup (Tajfel, 1982).

In the evaluation of outgroups various considerations may play a role: differences in interests, cultural differences, and socio-economic status differences. However, ingroup members differ among themselves in interests and socio-economic status; therefore it is not plausible that these two factors lead to ingroup consensus on the ethnic hierarchy. However, if we consider the way in which intergroup bias is measured in social distance research there may be indirect status considerations involved. Social distance questions refer to the acceptance of outgroup members as marriage partners, neighbours, friends, classmates, colleagues and so on. In deciding about contact, ingroup members will consider the social position of the relevant outgroups. Contact with outgroups which are generally accepted will enhance the status and prestige of the ingroup member, while contact with outgroups which are rejected will damage their status and prestige. Hence, there are indirect status concerns operative in deciding about contact, possibly based on a social representation of which are the culturally dominant and subordinate outgroups in society. Paradoxically, the effect of indirect status considerations may run counter to the effects predicted by social identity theory of attempts to maintain a positive social identity. While contact with culturally subordinate groups may enhance a positive social identity by favourable comparisons, it may lead to a loss of status in the eyes of relevant others as well. Moreover, some types of contact with subordinate groups, such as the acceptance of outgroups living in the neighbourhood or at school, may be perceived to threaten the interests of the ingroup. In summary, ingroup consensus on the ethnic hierarchy cannot convincingly be explained by social identity theory and is at best only partially explained by realistic conflict theory. A more plausible explanation is that the ingroup has a social representation of the dominant and subordinate groups in society and accepts or rejects these outgroups on the basis of the indirect status effects evolving from contact with them. This means that possible contact with outgroups will be perceived more as a threat to the status and interests of the ingroup as the position of these outgroups in the ethnic hierarchy is lower.

We should be careful in the explanation of intergroup consensus on the ethnic hierarchy. The fact that intergroup consensus on an ethnic hierarchy has been found in stable Western societies with a socially dominant ethnic majority group does not imply that the same consensus will be found in societies with less stable or more complex ethnic relations. Moreover, intergroup consensus may be dependent on the perceived stability and legitimacy of the existing ethnic relations and on the permeability of ethnic and status group boundaries. Therefore an explanation of intergroup consensus should be restricted to the first set of conditions.

Can realistic conflict theory and social identity theory explain intergroup consensus on an ethnic hierarchy under these conditions? Let us first consider realistic conflict theory. It is clear that an ethnic hierarchy may refer to socio-economic differences between ethnic groups. However, socio-economic conflict is more likely between ethnic groups in more or less similar than in dissimilar socio-economic positions. Thus increased intergroup bias is more likely among ethnic groups with similarly high or similarly low positions in the ethnic hierarchy. This seems not to be the case, however. The prediction is correct for groups with a lower place in the hierarchy, but not for high-placed groups: high-placed groups differentiate themselves most from groups low in the hierarchy. Hence realistic conflict theory does not explain intergroup consensus, nor the ethnic hierarchy of groups with higher positions in it.

Social identity theory posits that groups seek positive distinctiveness from outgroups by negatively evaluating the differences of these outgroups. This would imply that intergroup bias increases towards outgroups which differ more from the ingroup. Social identity theory does not specify which types of differences are important; this depends on the circumstances. Hence socio-economic as well as cultural differences can be relevant. However, a more generally accepted interpretation of social identity theory is that the need for positive distinctiveness increases with respect to more similar groups, although the evidence for this effect is not very strong (Brown, 1988; Brown & Abrams, 1986; Duckitt, 1992). Thus, social identity theory is rather contradictory at this crucial point. However, neither of the two interpretations explains intergroup consensus on the ethnic hierarchy: if differences are used to accentuate positive distinctiveness, low-placed ethnic groups should reject culturally and economically different high-placed ethnic groups—which they do not— and if similarities are used to accentuate positive distinctiveness, high-placed ethnic groups should reject culturally and economically similar outgroups—and that is not the case either. The conclusion is that neither realistic conflict theory nor social identity theory predicts intergroup consensus on the ethnic hierarchy.

What then is the explanation of intergroup consensus on the ethnic hierarchy in Western societies? To explain the ethnic hierarchy of dominant ethnic groups, we have to assume that ethnicity is an indirect status criterion (Van Knippenberg, 1989). Research on the effect of status differences indicates that there is a pervasive tendency for the emergence of negative stereotypes against and evaluations of the low-status groups (Duckitt, 1992). Duckitt (1992) explains this by the tendency of those who benefit from social inequality to justify their advantages. These justifications may be based on a belief in a just world in which the victim's disadvantages appear as deserved, or on attribution biases in which the role of dispositional factors in other's behaviour is overestimated and groups considered inferior are attributed negative traits causing this inferiority. In this way negative stereotypes about low-status groups emerge. Applied to ethnic groups, this implies that dominant ethnic groups may use negative ethnic stereotypes to justify their high position in an ethnic hierarchy. However, subordinate ethnic groups may arrive at the same ethnic hierarchy by their need to distinguish themselves from ethnic groups in more or less similar positions, as is assumed by social identity theory. Hence, the same ethnic stereotypes may be used by dominant groups to justify their position and by subordinate groups to differentiate themselves from similar low-placed groups. Tajfel (1981b) explicitly referred to this possible multi-functionality of stereotypes in intergroup relations.

This explanation of intergroup consensus on the ethnic hierarchy has several implications. The first is that if contact with outgroups has indirect status implications for all ethnic groups in the hierarchy—for dominant groups because they lose status by contact with subordinate groups, and for subordinate groups because they are threatened in their social identity by similar subordinate groups—all groups should feel threatened by contact with outgroups which are placed low in the ethnic hierarchy. Second, if the arrangement of ethnic groups in the hierarchy is supported by negative stereotypes, more negative stereotypes should be found with respect to groups lower in the ethnic hierarchy than groups higher in the hierarchy. A third implication is that if the burden of social rejection falls disproportionally on the shoulders of the subordinate ethnic groups, these groups may react by accentuating ingroup solidarity and thus manifest a much stronger intergroup bias than dominant groups.

INGROUP BIAS AND THE ETHNIC HIERARCHY

We will now report the results of a number of surveys in which we tried to replicate the findings of a consensual ethnic hierarchy. The surveys were performed in The Netherlands and the former Soviet Union. The same format was used by others in France and the United States. The ethnic group preferences were measured by social distance questions referring to contact with outgroup members in different domains, for example neighbours, colleagues, classmates, and so forth. A prototypical question was 'It would not occur to me to become friends with a [member of outgroup Y]'. The questions were repeated for a number of ethnic/national groups and scored on a scale consisting of five or more response categories, ranging from 'agree' to 'disagree'. The existence of and consensus on an ethnic hierarchy was determined by Guttman scalogram analysis. If ingroup members have the same system of ethnic preferences, their social distance towards outgroups should follow a similar cumulative pattern. A scalogram indicates that this is the case. The test of a scalogram structure of ethnic preferences across respondents from different ethnic groups was used to determine intergroup consensus.

Ingroup Bias

Social distance towards the ethnic ingroup and outgroups was measured among 1,290 first- and fourth-year university students from six cities in the former Soviet Union in 1991 (Drogendijk, 1994; Hagendoorn *et al.*, 1995). The cities were situated in Byelorussia, the Ukraine, and Russia. In Russia students from two Russian cities (Moscow and Nizniy Novgorod) and from the capitals of two Autonomous Russian Republics (the Bashkir Republic in Central Russia and the Buryat Republic in Asian Russia) were surveyed. From each university, respondents from three or more different ethnic groups were interviewed; representatives of 27 ethnic groups participated in the research (see Table 7.3 further on). The respondents answered three questions about social distance (neighbours, classmates or colleagues, potential marriage partners), repeated for three, four or five important ethnic groups in their region and for the ingroup. It appeared that 23 of the ethnic groups preferred the ingroup more than any of the outgroups. There were four exceptions: Byelorussian respondents in Byelorussia, Ukrainians in Byelorussia and in Nizniy Novgorod (Russia) and Chuvashes in the Bashkir Republic preferred Russians more than the ingroup. This indicates that ethnic ingroup preference is a general, but not necessarily universal, phenomenon. The exceptions may signal that the ethnic identity of the groups concerned is rather weak. The results confirm the ingroup bias found in earlier social distance research and fit in with the prediction from social identity theory that there is a general ingroup bias under conditions of ingroup identification.

The Ethnic Hierarchy

To provide evidence of the hierarchical nature of ethnic outgroup preferences and to test consensus on these preferences within ethnic groups, a pilot study among 291 ethnic Dutch secondary school and university students was carried out in The Netherlands in 1984 (Hagendoorn & Hraba, 1987). The outgroup preferences were measured by eight social distance questions, referring to contact with outgroup members as neighbours, colleagues, superiors, classmates, friends, physician, potential marriage partners (of self and children). The questions were repeated for seven ethnic/national minority groups in The Netherlands: English, Jews, Moroccans, Spaniards, South Moluccans, Surinamese and Turks. To test the hierarchical nature of the outgroup preferences, scalogram analysis of the social distance across domains towards each ethnic target group was performed. It was found that the social distance scores scaled and cumulated from the English towards the Jews, Spaniards, Surinamese, Moluccans, Moroccans and Turks (see Figure 7.1).

The conclusion is that there is a hierarchical structure of outgroup preferences, which is shared by the majority of the respondents. Northern European

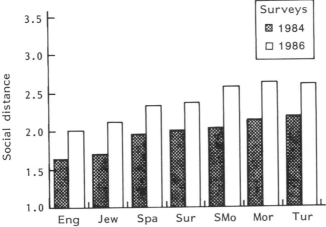

Figure 7.1   Dutch respondents' social distance on a scale from 1 to 5

groups and Jews are placed higher in this hierarchy than Southern Europeans and immigrants from former Dutch colonies. Islamic groups from Northern Africa and the Middle East have the lowest position. The results confirm the indications of earlier social distance research that there is an ethnic hierarchy in social distance among ethnic majority group members. The pattern has the form of a strong cumulative scale and the arrangement of ethnic groups is strikingly similar to the one reported for the United States (Duckitt, 1992) and Canada (Berry and Kalin, 1979). The hierarchy of the ethnic Dutch respondents indicates less social distance towards culturally and socio-economically more similar ethnic groups and more social distance towards culturally and socio-economically different ethnic groups. Realistic conflict theory and social identity theory would have predicted the reverse. The outcome is more in line with the expectation that ethnic outgroups are accepted or rejected according to the status they have in society at large and on the basis of the indirect status effects any association with them has.

The Ethnic Hierarchy as a Social Representation

The results of the 1984 Dutch survey may be interpreted as an indication that the ethnic hierarchy is a socially shared representation of the relative position of ethnic minorities in Dutch society (Hagendoorn & Hraba, 1987; Jaspars & Fraser, 1984; Moscovici, 1984, 1988). However, the shared aspect of the ethnic hierarchy concerns the rank of ethnic groups and not the number of discriminations among outgroups in social distance or their rejection. This raises the question of how such a shared cognitive representation works when it is applied in different contexts and with respect to different representatives of ethnic groups. To determine the stable and the variable aspects of the social representation of an ethnic hierarchy across respondents and contexts, two additional surveys (1986 Dutch survey of $n = 304$, and 1989 Dutch survey of $n = 1,116$ secondary school students) were carried out.

The purpose of the first study was to test the stability of the content and form of the ethnic hierarchy across domains of contact and with respect to different outgroup representatives (men, women, and the whole group; Hraba, Hagendoorn and Hagendoorn, 1989). The arrangement of ethnic groups in the hierarchy was considered as the content of the social representation and the number of discriminations in social distance between ethnic groups as its form. The idea was that the content is the stable aspect of the representation, while the form may be more or less different depending on the context (domains) and the specific representatives of the ethnic outgroups. In the research, different outgroup representatives were indicated by (a) a male, (b) female, or (c) unspecific group label, for example, 'Turkish men', 'Turkish women', and 'Turks'. The respondents were randomly assigned to one of these three labels and responded to five statements about social distance (about marriage, neighbours, work colleagues, classmates and friends) adapted to these labels. The social distance questions were repeated for seven ethnic minorities and the Dutch ingroup. The wording and response categories for the 5×8 items were the same as in the preliminary survey.

In the second study two other aspects of the ethnic hierarchy were tested (Kleinpenning, 1993, 1995). The first was whether the content of the ethnic hierarchy was shared across respondents who differ in their attitude towards ethnic minorities, namely racist versus non-racist respondents. This was a test of the thesis of Jaspars and Fraser (1984) that a social representation can be shared in spite of different attitudes towards the stimulus object. The second aspect was how far respondents think that their classmates agree with their idea of an ethnic hierarchy. This was done to test Moscovici's assumption that social representations circulate in social communication. If respondents are not aware of the ethnic preferences of their fellow classmates, or believe that these preferences are different from their own, then the ethnic hierarchy is not a social representation. Positive proof of a social representation is more difficult, however, because even if the preferences attributed to classmates do reflect the respondent's preferences, this might indicate that the respondents are simply attributing their own beliefs to other people. In this study, racism was measured by sixteen items, which clustered on four weakly correlated factors: (a) biological racism, indicated by items like 'Because The Netherlands is not their natural homeland, ethnic minorities in fact have no right to be here' and 'Ethnic groups are less intelligent than the Dutch', (b) symbolic racism, indicated by items like 'Meanwhile, ethnic minorities have more rights than they deserve' and 'All those different cultures in The Netherlands are a threat to our culture', (c) ethnocentrism, inidcated by items like 'Ethnic minorities living in The Netherlands have to adjust to our way of life' and 'The Dutch government is not authorized to exclude ethnic groups from our country on the basis of their behaviour' (negative answer) and (d) aversive racism, indicated by social distance items like 'To have a lot of ethnic group members as classmates seems annoying to me' (see, for a full report on the structure of these sub-scales, Kleinpenning & Hagendoorn, 1993). The ethnic hierarchy was measured with only one social distance item: 'To have [members of group X] as neighbours seems to me . . .', repeated for Spaniards, Surinamese, Jews, Moluccans and Turks as target groups. The ethnic hierarchy attributed to fellow classmates was measured by the item: 'When asked, your classmates will answer that having [members of group X] as neighbours is . . .'.

In both studies, the social distance responses towards ethnic groups formed highly consistent and reliable scalograms. The sequence of rejection of ethnic groups in the first study was: English least, then Jews, Spaniards, Surinamese, Moroccans, Turks and South Moluccans most (see Table 7.1 and Figure 7.1). Within each domain of contact, the ethnic hierarchy formed consistent scalograms as well. The sequence of the outgroups varied only marginally across domains (see Table 7.1). The main shift across representatives and domains was the position of the South Moluccans. In the second study, three years later, the sequence of ethnic groups was: Spaniards, Surinamese, Jews, Moluccans and Turks.

The form of the ethnic hierarchy was measured in the first study by the number of unequal social distance scores given to ethnic outgroups. It appeared that the number of unequal scores significantly differed across respondents, across outgroup representatives, and across domains of contact. Hence, respondents varied in the amount of differentiation among ethnic groups. These results indicate that the ethnic hierarchy is not a static representation, but a flexible cognitive scheme in which the ethnic differentiations vary depending on the type of respondent, the context, and the definition of the outgroups. In spite of this flexibility, however, the rank order in which outgroups are preferred or rejected remains largely the same.

In the second study, the social distance responses towards ethnic groups formed scalograms for each of the four types of racist and for the non-racist respondents (Kleinpenning, 1995; see Table 7.1). There was only one difference between the hierarchies of the racist and non-racist respondents, namely the position of the Jews. Apart from the rank assigned to Jews, the ethnic hierarchy was the same for respondents with completely different attitudes towards minorities in The Netherlands. The social distance scores ascribed to fellow classmates were analysed for each of the four types of racist and non-racist respondents (Kleinpenning, 1995). The perceived ethnic hierarchies of classmates appeared to mirror exactly those of the respondents themselves and formed strong scalograms (see Table 7.1). This indicates that

Table 7.1   Ethnic hierarchies of Dutch majority respondents

1986 Dutch survey: respondents' ethnic hierarchy

Outgroup representatives	Domain	Rank-position							H	Rho	N
		1	2	3	4	5	6	7			
People	all	Eng	Jew	Spa	Sur	Mor	Tur	SMo	0.85	0.95	139
Men	all	Eng	Jew	Spa	Sur	SMo	Mor	Tur	0.93	0.97	93
Women	all	Eng	Jew	Spa	Sur	SMo	Mor	Tur	0.94	0.97	85
People	marriage	Eng	Jew	Spa	Sur	SMo	Mor	Tur	0.82	0.94	140
People	neighbours	Eng	Jew	Sur	Spa	Tur	Mor	SMo	0.82	0.95	141
People	colleagues	Eng	Jew	Spa	Sur	Tur	Mor	SMo	0.90	0.97	142
People	classmates	Eng	Jew	Sur	Spa	SMo	Tur	Mor	0.95	0.98	139
People	friends	Eng	Jew	Sur	Spa	SMo	Mor	Tur	0.91	0.97	140

Eng = English; Jew = Jews; Spa = Spaniards; Sur = Surinamese; Mor = Moroccans; SMo = South Moluccans; Tur = Turks.

1989 Dutch survey: respondents' hierarchy

Types of racists	Rank-position					H	Rho	N
	1	2	3	4	5			
Non-racist	Spa	Sur	Jew	SMo	Tur	0.58	0.84	439
Aversive racists	Spa	Sur	Jew	SMo	Tur	0.34	0.63	166
Ethno/symbolic	Spa	Jew	Sur	SMo	Tur	0.32	0.63	284
Biological racists	Jew	Spa	Sur	SMo	Tur	0.40	0.77	57

Spa = Spaniards; Jew = Jews; Sur = Surinamese; SMo = South Moluccans; Tur = Turks.

1989 Dutch survey: ethnic hierarchy attributed to classmates

Types of racists	Rank-position					H	Rho	N
	1	2	3	4	5			
Non-racist	Spa	Sur	Jew	SMo	Tur	0.53	0.83	223
Aversive racists	Spa	Sur	Jew	SMo	Tur	0.56	0.76	73
Ethno/symbolic	Spa	Jew	Sur	SMo	Tur	0.57	0.84	154
Biological racists	Jew	Spa	Sur	SMo	Tur	0.63	0.89	33

Spa = Spaniards; Jew = Jews; Sur = Surinamese; SMo = South Moluccans; Tur = Turks.

respondents perceive that their classmates share their preferences with respect to ethnic minorities.

The conclusion from the surveys is that the shared and stable aspect of the ethnic hierarchy is the preference scheme it contains. The minor variations in the preference scheme of extreme racists, in some domains of contact and for the specification of outgroup members were outweighed by the similarities in the preferences across individuals with different attitudes, across domains of contact and across outgroup representatives. One important difference remains: Jews were rejected more and South Moluccans less in 1989 than in 1986, but that may be the effect of a different respondent group.

The evidence from the surveys suggests that the ethnic hierarchy found among Dutch youth is a social representation of the actual position of ethnic groups in The Netherlands. But the evidence is not completely convincing. An objection is that there is little evidence of public communication about the ethnic hierarchy in Dutch daily life, as should be the case with a social representation. Moreover, the reflection of the deviant position of the Jews in the hierarchy attributed by biological racists to their classmates suggests a simple projection of own beliefs on others. On the other hand, there is a lot of similarity between the ethnic prefer-ences of the Dutch respondents and there seems to be a general awareness of the position of ethnic groups in Dutch society.

Another objection against the results of the surveys might be that the ethnic hierarchy is an artefact of the method used. It could be argued that the response format forced the respondents to discriminate between ethnic groups. However, across all surveys the ethnic hierarchy was determined by the analysis of separate questions on the evaluation of a specific type of contact with a specific ethnic group. The number of questions varied with the number of domains and the number of ethnic target groups investigated. In the interviews, the questions referring to the same ethnic group were kept together to prevent an artificial differentiation in the reaction towards dif-ferent ethnic groups. Although the sequence of ethnic target groups was fixed in each survey, the starting point of the sequence varied across respondents in one survey (Hagendoorn & Hraba, 1987), and differed across surveys. The response categories differed across surveys as well, and item wording was marginally different. In spite of these variations comparable hierarchies were found. Therefore, the result does not seem to be an artefact.

The ethnic hierarchy may be a typical response pattern of just Dutch youth or Dutch people. Research on perceived ethnic hierarchies in other countries indicates, however, that the tendency to arrange ethnic groups in a hierarchy is a general phenomenon. De Vries (1994) found an ethnic hierarchy among French university students in Strasbourg, Pettigrew (1960) among South Afri-can students in Natal, Hraba and Mok (1991) among white students at a midwestern university in the United States, and Drogendijk (1994) among students in Byelorussia, the Ukraine, and Russia. In six of the seven countries surveyed the cumulative structure of the hierarchy was tested by scalogram analysis and the hierarchies formed strong scales in almost all cases.

CORRELATES OF THE ETHNIC HIERARCHY

The effect of contact with outgroups on ingroup status

A reason to accept contact with some ethnic outgroups more than others can be that the association with outgroups has indirect status effects. Contact with outgroups which are generally accepted will enhance the status and prestige of the ingroup members while contact with outgroups which are rejected may lead to negative reactions of other ingroup members.

The interpretation of the ethnic hierarchy as an indirect status hierarchy was tested in the 1991 Russian survey, in which 1,290 respondents from 27 ethnic groups in six regions across Russia, Byelorussia, and the Ukraine (see Table 7.3 for the groups involved) were interviewed (Drogendijk, 1994; Hagendoorn et al., 1995). How far contact with different ethnic outgroups was perceived as a threat to the position and the interests of the ingroup (member) was measured. This was done by a one-way polynomial ANOVA of each of the threat scores, in which the outgroups to which the threat was attributed were arranged in the sequence of the hierarchy in social distance in the region. The test was for a linear relation between the threat which contact with outgroups poses to the status of the ingroup and a lower position of the outgroup in the ethnic hierarchy. A significant linear component in the analysis indicates that the threat attributed to outgroups increases if their position in the ethnic hierarchy is lower. The respondents answered ten questions about the threat to ingroup status and interests posed by outgroups (Bobo, 1983). The items were constructed by Kleinpenning (1993). They referred to education, neighbourhood and marriage. There were five questions directly or indirectly referring to the status of the ingroup: (1) 'If [group X] were to live in your neighbourhood, you would lose the respect and esteem of your friends'; (2) 'If there were [group X] children at the local school, the education level would decrease'; (3) 'If you marry a [X], people will disdain you'; (4) Your chances for a good job decrease due to [group X] and (5) 'If [group X] are highly educated, they will use this to get more influence than your own ethnic group'. The five remaining items referred to threats to personal and group interests (for example: 'If there are more [group X] children at the local school, you will have more trouble raising your own children'). The items were scored on a 9-point scale from 'strongly disagree' to 'strongly agree'. Each respondent scored only one ethnic outgroup.

Factor analysis indicated that all items loaded high on one factor and that the scale formed by the items was reliable across all ethnic groups. A one-way polynomial ANOVA of the threat scores was carried out for the respondents in each of the six regions. The linear component appeared to be significant for the respondents in Moscow, Byelorussia, and the Ukraine, and close to significant in Nizniy Novgorod, the Bashkir Republic, and the Buryat Republic. Thus, outgroups were perceived as a greater threat to the status and interests of the ingroup the lower their position in the ethnic hierarchy. This indicates that the position of an outgroup in the ethnic hierarchy is related to indirect status considerations.

For the interpretation of this result two points have to be noted. First, the outgroups to which threat was attributed were always arranged in the rank order of the ethnic hierarchy shared by all the ethnic groups in the region. This makes the test stronger for regions with strong intergroup consensus on the hierarchy than in regions with weak intergroup consensus (such as Moscow, Nizniy Novgorod, and the Buryat Republic—see Table 7.3). Second, the ethnic hierarchies found in the Russian survey always reflected the generally acknowledged dominance structure of the ethnic groups surveyed (Karklins, 1986). That is to say that Russians were generally accepted most, followed by the culturally and economically similar Byelorussians and Ukrainians. Jews, Poles, and Armenians had lower positions in the ethnic hierarchies and the lowest positions were occupied by Tatars and Azeris (see Table 7.3). Of course, these hierarchies differed somewhat across the regions, but the differences reflected the local differences in ethnic dominance structure. Thus, for the interpretation of the results we can start from the assumption that the ethnic hierarchy against which the attributed threat scores were tested reflects the actual social dominance structure. This implies that the outcome that all ethnic groups perceive outgroups with low positions as a threat to their status and interests indicates that the hierarchy is not based on direct socio-economic competition or conflict. Realistic conflict theory would pose that dominant groups would have perceived similar groups as a threat and not low placed dissimilar groups. The ethnic hierarchy of the dominant groups does not follow from the need to differentiate the ingroup from similar outgroups either—the thesis of social identity theory. Instead, when it comes to contact with outgroups, dominant groups seem to consider the possible negative effects of this contact on their social standing and avoid ethnic groups with a low social status.

The Relation with Stereotypes

In his analysis of the function of stereotypes, Tajfel (1981b) argues that stereotypes fulfil several functions: they preserve ingroup values, justify group positions, and are used for intergroup differentiation. We have argued that dominant ethnic groups may justify their dominance in an ethnic hierarchy by negative stereotypes about subordinate groups while subordinate groups may use the same stereotypes to differentiate themselves from each other. On the basis of these negative stereotypes an ethnic hierarchy may evolve. If each ethnic group has stereotypes about a number of outgroups in which the negative differences of these groups are accentuated, outgroups will be arranged in an ethnic hierarchy according to these differences. Devine (1989) suggests that the tendency to act on the basis of activated stereotypes is rather automatic and that only explicit non-prejudiced attitudes can inhibit the response. However, Locke, McLeod, and Walker (1994) and Augoustinos, Ahrens, and Innes (1994) present evidence against the automatic activation model. Nonetheless, Devine's model may explain why racist as well as non-racist

respondents show evidence of an ethnic hierarchy: the activation of stereotypes leads automatically to a rank order of outgroups in social distance, but
the non-racists' egalitarian beliefs subsequently inhibit the rejection of these
outgroups.

Berry and Kalin (1979) provide empirical evidence for the effect of
stereotypes on ranking of ethnic groups. They measured the mutual evaluations of Anglo-Celts, French, Germans, Italians, and Ukrainian Canadians
in Canada. The subjects (n=1244) were selected from a national sample
covering 95% of the population of Canada. It appeared that each ethnic
group evaluated the ingroup most positively and rated the outgroups according to the same hierarchical scheme. The English were evaluated most
positively, followed by the French, Germans, Ukrainians, and finally the
Italians. Only the French respondents deviated from the shared scheme in
the placement of one group. These results indicate that stereotypes of multiple outgroups tend to lead to a (shared) hierarchical pattern of evaluations
of these outgroups.

The hypotheses that negative stereotypes are related to the position assigned to outgroups in the ethnic hierarchy was investigated in the 1986 Dutch
survey and in a study carried out among 200 French university students in
Strasbourg in 1993 (De Vries, 1994). Preceding the 1986 Dutch survey a pilot
study was carried out among 280 students of secondary schools in two cities in
The Netherlands (Hagendoorn & Hraba, 1989). The students were asked to
list all the stereotypes they had ever heard with respect to ethnic minorities. A
pool of 151 characteristics was obtained. The 48 characteristics listed by more
than 15% of the students for any one group, and by 10% across groups, were
selected for the 1986 Dutch survey. The characteristics were then phrased as
short statements about ethnic groups, for example: 'Turks have different food
habits than most people in Holland'. The 48 statements had to be scored on a
six-point scale indicating how many members of an ethnic group have the
characteristic ('all' to 'none'). This had to be done for seven ethnic target
groups.

To determine clusters of characteristics differentiating between target
groups, discriminant analysis was performed. Six discriminant dimensions
were found: stereotypes referring to (a) patriarchal and authoritarian family
relations, (b) foreign appearance, (c) differences in religion and culture, (d)
deviant and criminal behaviour, (e) the openness of the outgroup, and (f)
working class attitudes and behaviour (see Table 7.2). Characteristics with a
high loading on the respective discriminant function were subsequently
analysed for each separate target group on scale homogeneity by Rasch analysis, a method comparable to scalogram analysis (Rasch, 1966). The six dimensions scaled for all target groups and thus appeared to be dimensions on which
Dutch respondents evaluate all ethnic minorities. Therefore sumscores could
be computed indicating the attribution of each stereotype dimension to each

Table 7.2 Stereotypes attributed to seven ethnic groups in The Netherlands in percentages[a]

Stereotype dimension	Ethnic groups						
	Dutch	English	Jews	Span-iards	Surinam	Molucc	Turks
Patriarchal and macho	8	9	→27	→42	47	→53	→67
Foreign appearance	4	→18	→22	→30←	26	→34	→56
Different culture	18	15	→28←	23	23	→35	→49
Deviant	25←	15←	8	→24	19	21	21
Seclusive	58←	53←	45	45	→57	61	→69
Working class	25←	19	→23	→35	32	40	→51

[a]Significant differences (t-test, $p < 0.05$) between adjacent values are indicated by → or ←.

ethnic outgroup and the Dutch ingroup. These percentage sumscores are indicated in Table 7.2.

The relation between the stereotypes and the ethnic hierarchy of the Dutch respondents was analysed by determining which stereotypes were attributed in an increasing degree to groups from high to low in the ethnic hierarchy. This was done for each separate stereotype dimension by a test of the linear component in a polynomial ANOVA of the stereotype attributions to the seven ethnic (out)groups. In the analysis the ethnic target groups were arranged in the sequence of the ethnic hierarchy. A significant linear component indicates that the stereotype is attributed increasingly more when the position of a target group in the hierarchy is lower.

It appeared that the linear component was significant for four of the six stereotype dimensions: patriarchal family relations, foreign appearance, different culture, and working class (see Table 7.2). The conclusion is that not all stereotypes are related to the rank position of outgroups in the ethnic hierarchy: attributed social deviancy and seclusiveness are not attributed increasingly to outgroups in lower positions. The negative stereotypes that are related to the position of outgroups are: attributed patriarchal family relations, foreign appearance in dress and behaviour, different habits, religion and language, and deferential and working class attitudes. These stereotypes refer more to stable cultural or social characteristics than to behavioural traits. Thus the negative evaluation of cultural and social characteristics seems more suitable to justify differences in the social positions of ethnic groups than behavioural traits.

The hypothesis that stereotypes are related to the ethnic hierarchy was also tested by De Vries (1994) in the 1993 French survey in which the social distance towards Moroccans, Italians, Algerians, Jews, and Portuguese living in France was measured. De Vries tested four alternative hypotheses as well, namely that the sequence in the ethnic hierarchy reflects (a) the numerical size of outgroups, (b) their occupational status, (c) their cultural differences, or (d) their perceived adaptation to the host society. The respondents had to indicate the estimated numerical size of each outgroup, its educational level in terms of the percentage of university education and its income in terms of the percentage earning more than the average Frenchman, the difference in culture between each outgroup and the French, and each groups' degree of adaptation to French society (on a nine-point scale from 'none' to 'very much'). The stereotypes were measured by six trait adjectives. The respondents had to indicate on an 11-point scale (0% to 100%) how many of the representatives of five ethnic groups (Italians, Portuguese, Jews, Moroccans, and Algerians) had the trait.

The relation between each of the variables and the assigned ethnic rank was analysed by one-way polynomial ANOVAs for each variable. In the ANOVAs the outgroups were arranged in the sequence of the shared hierarchy of the respondents. A significant linear component indicates that the value of the variable increases or decreases over the sequence in the ethnic hierarchy. It appeared that the linear component was significant for four variables: three negative stereotypes—attributed aggressiveness, dishonesty, and laziness—and for the perceived degree of adaptation of the outgroup to the French society. Hence, groups were placed lower in the ethnic hierarchy as they were seen as more aggressive, dishonest, and lazy and as less adjusted to the French society. No significant linear component was found for perceived level of income and education or any of the other variables.

In contrast to the results of the 1986 Dutch survey, the French data indicate that in France behavioural traits attributed to outgroups are related to the position of outgroups in the ethnic hierarchy, next to the negative evaluation of perceived lack of adjustment to the society of the dominant ethnic group. The Dutch and the French data taken together indicate that a wide array of stereotypes is related to the ethnic hierarchy. A lower position of outgroups in the hierarchy is associated with negatively evaluated behavioural, social, and cultural characteristics. These evaluations may be used to justify the differential rejection of contact with outgroups in the hierarchy.

INTERGROUP CONSENSUS ON THE ETHNIC HIERARCHY

In the available social distance and stereotype research, intergroup consensus on the ethnic hierarchy has not been explicitly tested. We carry out the test in The Netherlands and in some successor states of the former Soviet Union. It was argued above that realistic conflict theory and social identity theory do not predict intergroup consensus on the ethnic hierarchy in society. Only if dominant ethnic groups use the same ethnic stereotypes to justify their dominant position as subordinate ethnic groups do to differentiate themselves from similar groups, is intergroup consensus to be expected. Another point was that intergroup consensus is not a hard and fast rule. It may be found in stable Western societies with one dominant ethnic majority group, but not in unstable societies or in societies with a more complex ethnic composition.

Our first aim is to explore intergroup consensus on the ethnic hierarchy and answer the question whether it is there or not. On the basis of realistic conflict theory and social identity theory the existence of intergroup consensus is not plausible and thus should be found nowhere. If it is found, however, the next question is whether it is found everywhere, or only in stable societies with a dominant ethnic group. To answer the second question we will first investigate possible intergroup consensus in The Netherlands with its dominant group of ethnic Dutch constituting 95% of the population. The third step is to investigate intergroup consensus on the ethnic hierarchy in the former Soviet Union.

The regions surveyed in this area can be provisionally ordered from rather stable and ethnically homogeneous to less stable and ethnically heterogeneous or complex. It may be assumed that ethnic heterogeneity and complexity reduce the possibility of intergroup consensus. Two cities in the Russian federation can be placed on the homogeneous/stable side of the line: Moscow and Nizniy Novgorod. These are typical Russian cities and have a majority of ethnic Russians of 90%, resp. 95% (Götz & Halbach, 1994). Two other regions are former Soviet Union Republics which recently have become autonomous states: Byelorussia and the Ukraine. The transformation from Soviet Republic to autonomous state has changed the ethnic dominance structure of these societies: the former dominant Russians have become minorities and the ethnic majority population has become the ruling ethnic group. Both states are ethnically fairly homogeneous, but less so than The Netherlands or the two Russian cities mentioned above. Byelorussia has an ethnic majority of Byelorussians of 78%. The Russian minority is 13%. In the Ukraine 73% of the population belongs to the ethnic majority of the Ukrainians, while 22% is Russian (McAuley, 1991). Byelorussia and the Ukraine can be placed in between the stable homogeneous versus unstable heterogeneous areas.

On the unstable and heterogeneous end of the line are the Bashkir Republic (Central Russia) and the Buryat Republic (Asian Russia). These are autonomous republics in the Russian Federation. Officially the so-called titular ethnic groups of the Bashkirs and Buryats have cultural autonomy in these republics, but in fact they are ruled by the Russians. Bashkirs constitute 22% of the population of the Bashkir Republic, 39% is Russian and 28% Tatar. In the Buryat Republic 24% of the population is Buryat and 70% Russian. Hence, Bashkirs and Buryats are ethnic minorities in their own titular republics, while Russians are a minority in the Bashkir Republic and a majority in the Buryat Republic. The Baskirs are Muslims and the Buryats are

Buddhists, so there is a clear cultural difference between these groups and the Russians.

Intergroup Consensus in Stable and More Homogeneous Societies

The study in The Netherlands was performed in 1993 among 800 students of vocational schools in Rotterdam (Verkuyten, Hagendoorn, & Masson, 1994). More than half of the respondents were members of one of the major ethnic minorities in The Netherlands. The respondents answered 3 × 5 social distance questions (classmates, neighbours, and marriage for Dutch, Surinamese, Moroccans, Turks, and Cape Verdeans) in the standard format. It appeared that the general social distance scores for the ethnic minority respondents, as well as for the Dutch respondents, formed average to strong scalograms (see Table 7.3: The Netherlands, Rotterdam). Hence, there was consensus within each ethnic group on an ethnic hierarchy. The hierarchy of the Turkish minority was, from high to low: Turks, Dutch, Spaniards, Moroccans and Surinamese. The hierarchy of the Surinamese was: Surinamese, Dutch, Spaniards, Moroccans and Turks. The hierarchy of the Moroccans was: Moroccans, Dutch, Spaniards, Turks and Surinamese. Cape Verdeans had the sequence: Cape Verdeans, Spaniards, Surinamese, Moroccans, Dutch and Turks (see Table 7.3).

The results indicate that there is a lot of similarity between the ethnic hierarchies of the five ethnic groups. The major difference between the hierarchies is that each ethnic group put itself first, which is the ingroup bias shown before. There are, however, minor differences as well. Turks and Moroccans elevate each others' position, and the hierarchy of the Cape Verdeans deviates from the general pattern. The general pattern is: Northern Europeans first, then Southern Europeans, next ex-colonial groups and finally Islamic groups, which reproduces the ethnic hierarchy of the Dutch majority.

In the 1991 Russian survey the respondents answered three questions about social distance (neighbours, classmates or colleagues, and potential marriage partners), repeated for the ingroup and for three, four, or five important ethnic minorities in their region (Drogendijk, 1994; Hagendoorn *et al.*, 1995). Scalogram analysis indicated that the social distance scores of 14 of the 15 ethnic minority groups formed Guttman scales; the only exception was the Tatars in the Buryat Republic. In most cases the ethnic hierarchies formed strong scales (see Table 7.3). To determine the degree of intergroup consensus on the ethnic hierarchy, two criteria were considered. The first was whether the sequence in the hierarchy of the minority groups was the same as the sequence in the ethnic hierarchy of the majority. The second criterion was that scalogram analysis across all the ethnic groups in the region ('overall' scalogram analysis) yields the sequence of the ethnic hierarchy of the majority group. Acceptable scale values of the overall scalogram would indicate that there is intergroup consensus among all ethnic groups on the ethnic hierarchy.

Inspection of Table 7.3 indicates that all minority groups in Moscow and Nizniy Novgorod copied the ethnic hierarchy of the Russians, except the Kazakhs and Azeris in Moscow who reversed some adjacent positions. Overall scalogram analysis in both Moscow and Nizniy Novgorod reproduced the hierarchy of the ethnic majority of the Russians. However, in both cases the scale was not reliable, which may be an effect of the ingroup preference manifested by almost all the ethnic groups.

The results are not conclusive. In The Netherlands there seems to be fair degree of intergroup consensus on the ethnic hierarchy, but the consensus is not perfect and one group clearly deviates. In the two Russian cities the degree of intergroup consensus is rather low. We can draw two conclusions from these results. The first is that stable and ethnically rather homogeneous societies do not necessarily produce intergroup consensus on an ethnic hierarchy. The second is that the results do not confirm the stereotype model used to predict intergroup consensus. However, the predictions following from realistic conflict theory and social identity theory are not confirmed either: the hierarchies of dominant and subordinate ethnic groups should be reversals of each other (similar groups should be rejected most), which is not the case.

Intergroup Consensus in Unstable and More Heterogeneous Societies

The 1991 Russian interviews were held in the period in which the Soviet Union was collapsing. For Byelorussia, the Ukraine, and the Autonomous Republics in the Russian Federation this was a period of instability. In spite of this instability, there was a general tendency among the ethnic minorities interviewed in Byelorussia and the Ukraine to copy the hierarchy of the ethnic majority, although there were also deviations from this pattern (see Table 7.3). In Byelorussia, the Russian, Polish, Lithuanian, and Jewish respondents reversed adjacent positions of outgroups in the hierarchy and the same was true for the Jewish respondents in the Ukraine. Scalogram analysis across the respondents from all ethnic groups in each of the countries indicated, however, that in spite of these reversals there was a high degree of intergroup consensus on the ethnic hierarchy (see Table 7.3, 'all groups' under each country). The overall scalograms were strong scales.

In the Buryat Republic, the overall scalogram analysis indicated low intergroup consensus on the ethnic hierarchy. The sequence of this hierarchy was a copy of the hierarchy of the Russians. In the Bashkir Republic, the ethnic hierarchy of the Russian minority differed from the ethnic hierarchy of the Bashkirs. The other two minority groups copied the ethnic hierarchy of the Russians and not the ethnic hierarchy of the Bashkirs. Overall scalogram analysis indicated high intergroup consensus on an ethnic hierarchy in the

Table 7.3 Ethnic hierarchies of majority and minority groups in The Netherlands, Russia (Moscow and Nizniy Novgorod), Byelorussia, the Ukraine, Bashkir Republic, and Buryat Republic

The Netherlands, Rotterdam

Respondent group	Rank-position 1	2	3	4	5	6	H	Rho	N
Dutch*	Dut	Spa	Sur	Mor	Tur	—	0.70	0.83	356
Turks	Tur	Dut	Spa	Mor	Sur	—	0.46	0.65	127
Moroccans	Mor	Dut	Spa	Tur	Sur	—	0.56	0.79	78
Surinamese	Sur	Dut	Spa	Mor	Tur	—	0.65	0.79	98
Cape Verdeans	Cap	Spa	Sur	Mor	Dut	Tur	0.44	0.64	43

Russia, Moscow

Respondent group	Rank-position 1	2	3	4	5	6	H	Rho	N
Russians*	Rus	Ukr	Jew	Arm	Kaz	Aze	0.72	0.82	61
Ukrainians	Ukr	Rus	Jew	Arm	Kaz	Aze	0.31	0.59	39
Jews	Jew	Rus	Ukr	Arm	Kaz	Aze	0.72	0.83	44
Armenians	Arm	Rus	Ukr	Jew	Kaz	Aze	0.67	0.81	50
Kazakhs	Kaz	Rus	Jew	Ukr	Aze	Arm	0.72	0.81	46
Azeris	Aze	Rus	Ukr	Jew	Kaz	Arm	0.33	0.60	49
All groups	Rus	Ukr	Jew	Arm	Kaz	Aze	0.25	0.63	298

Russia, Nizniy Novgorod

Respondent group	Rank-position 1	2	3	4	H	Rho	N
Russians*	Rus	Ukr	Jew	Tat	0.39	0.50	60
Ukrainians	Rus	Ukr	Jew	Tat	0.68	0.61	21
Jews	Jew	Rus	Ukr	Tat	0.66	0.80	36
Tatars	Tat	Rus	Ukr	Jew	0.69	0.73	50
All groups	Rus	Ukr	Jew	Tat	0.21	0.45	177

Byelorussia

Respondent group	Rank-position 1	2	3	4	5	6	H	Rho	N
Byelorussians*	Rus	Bye	Ukr	Pol	Lit	Jew	0.66	0.77	54
Russians	Rus	Bye	Ukr	Lit	Jew	Pol	0.55	0.73	34
Ukrainians	Bye	Rus	Ukr	Pol	Lit	Jew	0.34	0.64	40
Poles	Pol	Bye	Ukr	Rus	Lit	Jew	0.66	0.83	53
Lithuanians	Lit	Bye	Pol	Rus	Jew	Ukr	0.80	0.89	50
Jews	Jew	Bye	Rus	Ukr	Lit	Pol	0.96	0.92	19
All groups	Bye	Rus	Ukr	Pol	Lit	Jew	0.46	0.78	250

Table 7.3   (*cont.*)

Ukraine

Respondent group	Rank-position						*H*	*Rho*	*N*
	1	2	3	4					
Ukrainians*	Ukr	Rus	Jew	Arm			0.68	0.76	57
Russians	Rus	Ukr	Jew	Arm			0.64	0.74	64
Jews	Jew	Rus	Ukr	Arm			0.50	0.72	43
Armenians	Arm	Ukr	Rus	Jew			0.67	0.79	30
All groups	Ukr	Rus	Jew	Arm			0.46	0.69	184

Bashkir Republic

Respondent group	Rank-position						*H*	*Rho*	*N*
	1	2	3	4	5	6			
Russians*	Rus	Ukr	Tat	Bas	Jew	Chu	0.70	0.82	45
Tatars	Tat	Rus	Ukr	Bas	Jew	Chu	0.63	0.83	59
Bashkirs	Bas	Tat	Rus	Ukr	Chu	Jew	0.65	0.81	44
Chuvashes	Rus	Chu	Ukr	Tat	Jew	Bas	0.45	0.74	25
All groups	Rus	Tat	Ukr	Bas	Jew	Chu	0.53	0.78	173

Buryat Republic

Respondent group	Rank-position				*H*	*Rho*	*N*
	1	2	3	4			
Russians*	Rus	Bur	Tat	Jew	0.50	0.68	52
Buryats	Bur	Rus	Tat	Jew	0.42	0.58	52
Tatars	Tat	Rus	Jew	Bur	0.22	0.36	37
All groups	Rus	Bur	Tat	Jew	0.24	0.47	141

Dut = Dutch; Spa = Spaniards; Sur = Surinamese; Tur = Turks; Mor = Moroccans; Cap = Cape
Verdeans; Rus = Russians; Ukr = Ukrainians; Jew = Jews; Arm = Armenians; Kaz = Kazakhs;
Aze = Azeris; Bye = Byelorussians; Pol = Poles; Lit = Lithuanians; Tat = Tatars; Bas = Bashkirs;
Chu = Chuvashes; Bur = Buryats.
*Denotes ethnic majority group.

Bashkir Republic. This hierarchy was closer to the Russian than to the
Bashkir hierarchy (see Table 7.3, 'all groups' under Bashkir and Buryat
Republics).

CONCLUSION

In three regions there was a considerable amount of intergroup consensus on
the ethnic hierarchy. In three other regions this consensus was much weaker.
The results do not indicate a clear relation between stability or ethnic

homogeneity and intergroup consensus on an ethnic hierarchy. The results do indicate, however, that intergroup consensus on an ethnic hierarchy occurs. This is in contradiction to what might be expected on the basis of realistic conflict theory and social identity theory.

The fact that no intergroup consensus was found in some regions of the former Soviet Union may also have a methodological reason. The outcome of an overall scalogram analysis is sensitive to the number of target groups in the ethnic hierarchy. When the number of target groups is small, as for Nizniy Novgorod and the Buryat Republic, the weight of the ingroup preferences becomes higher and thus lower scalogram values are found. A small number of target groups nonetheless may reflect the actual intergroup situation and thus the actual weight of the ingroup preference in the pattern of intergroup preferences of the region. The effect of the ingroup preference cannot explain the low intergroup consensus found in Moscow.

A general characteristic of the ethnic hierarchies of the ethnic groups surveyed in the former Soviet Union was that northern Slavic groups were preferred more than southern Islamic and Asian groups. Kazlas (1977), who measured social distance towards different Soviet nationalities among German and Lithuanian emigrants from the Soviet Union, and Gitelman (1991), who did the same among Jewish emigrants, found similar results. This pattern of preferences reflects the contrast between the centre and the periphery in the former Soviet Union. But it is also similar to the high position assigned to Caucasians and the low position assigned to Islamic and Asian ethnic groups in the ethnic hierarchies of Western Europeans and North Americans.

POSITION IN THE ETHNIC HIERARCHY AND INTERGROUP BIAS

The results of the studies reported above indicate that ethnic groups at the bottom of the ethnic hierarchy are rejected by dominant ethnic groups as well as by other ethnic minorities. This will have a disproportional negative effect on the self-esteem of these groups. The consequences of this effect on the intergroup bias were explored in the 1991 Russian survey (Drogendijk, 1994; Hagendoorn et al., 1995). The expectation was that ethnic groups with a low position in the ethnic hierarchy manifest a stronger intergroup bias than groups with a high position in the hierarchy.

The intergroup bias was computed for each ethnic (respondent) group as the difference between the ingroup preference and the averaged social distance towards outgroups. The intergroup bias scores are presented in Table 7.4. The hypothesis that low-placed groups show a higher intergroup bias was tested by arranging the ethnic (respondent) groups in the sequence of the

Table 7.4 Intergroup bias[a] of ethnic majority and minority groups in the former Soviet Union

Russia (Moscow)		Byelorussia		Ukraine		Russia (N. Novgorod)		Bashkir R.		Buryat R.	
Rus	3.02	Bye	1.57	Ukr	1.85	Rus	2.88	Rus	3.11	Rus	3.55
Ukr	2.57	Rus	2.43	Rus	1.75	Ukr	2.43	Tat	2.12	Bur	2.64
Jew	3.29	Ukr	1.22	Jew	1.79	Jew	1.66	Bas	1.88	Tat	1.57
Arm	2.85	Pol	2.43	Arm	1.28	Tat	3.48	Chu	1.92		
Kaz	3.53	Lit	2.43								
Aze	3.84	Jew	2.67								

[a]Measured as the difference between social distance towards the ingroup and the average social distance towards all outgroups. Thus higher scores indicate more bias.
Rus = Russians; Ukr = Ukrainians; Jew = Jews; Arm = Armenians; Kaz = Kazakhs; Aze = Azeris; Bye = Byelorussians; Pol = Poles; Lit = Lithuanians; Tat = Tatars; Bas = Bashkirs; Chu = Chuvashes; Bur = Buryats.

ethnic hierarchy in the region and analysing the trend in the computed intergroup biases by polynomial ANOVA. The test was for a significant linear component in the intergroup bias scores. Note that the intergroup consensus on the ethnic hierarchy varied over the regions and that the test thus was stronger for the Ukraine, Byelorussia, and the Bashkir Republic.

It appeared that the linear component was significant in Byelorussia and Moscow, indicating a higher intergroup bias of low-placed groups. Table 7.4 indicates that the linear trend does not capture the higher intergroup bias of Jews and Russians in Moscow, and of Russians and Byelorussians in Byelorussia. These non-linear components were not significant, however. In Nizniy Novgorod the lowest-placed Tatars had the highest intergroup bias, but the linear component was not significant. In the Ukraine there were no significant differences between the ethnic groups, but the trend was not towards the expected direction. In the Buryat Republic and the Bashkir Republic not the low-placed groups, but the highest-placed Russians had the highest intergroup bias, and this was significant for the Buryat Republic.

Thus the results indicate two patterns in the relation between the position in the ethnic hierarchy and intergroup bias. The first pattern was that the lowest-placed groups have the highest intergroup bias, as was the case in Byelorussia, Moscow, and Nizniy Novgorod. This confirms the hypothesis, but occurred in two of the regions with low consensus on the ethnic hierarchy. The second pattern was the opposite, namely that high-placed groups have the highest intergroup bias. This was the case for the Russians in the Bashkir and Buryat Republics. This pattern is understandable if the position of the Russians in these republics is taken into account. Russians form a majority of 70% in the Buryat Republic and a minority of 39% in the Bashkir Republic.

Their intergroup bias may be an expression of their uncertain position in a region where native non-Russian groups may claim political and cultural dominance. The conclusion is that not only a low position but also an uncertain position in the ethnic hierarchy intensifies intergroup bias. The intergroup bias of groups in uncertain positions confirms a basic assumption of social identity theory.

CONCLUSIONS

Some important conclusions can be drawn from the reported research. A first result was that almost all ethnic groups preferred contact with the ingroup more than with outgroups. This may seem logical if one considers the type of social distance questions used to measure the ethnic preferences. Moreover, ingroup preference is part of an almost universal ethnocentrism (LeVine & Campbell, 1972). But there were exceptions to this rule as well. In the Russian survey, the Byelorussians and Ukrainians in Byelorussia, the Ukrainian minority in Nizniy Novgorod, and the Chuvashes in the Bashkir Republic preferred the Russians more than the ingroup. A positive evaluation of high-status groups compared to the ingroup has been reported for low-status groups by others as well (Sachdev & Bourhis, 1987), and the preference of the low-placed Chuvashes for the Russians may fall in this category. The outgroup preference of the higher-placed Byelorussians and Ukrainians, however, more likely indicates that the ethnic consciousness of Byelorussians and Ukrainian minorities is not very articulate. It is known that identification with the ingroup is a precondition of intergroup bias (Hinkle & Brown, 1990). This interpretation could have been tested if respondents' ethnic self-identification had been measured. A general interpretation of the ingroup bias found is that a preference for contact with ingroup members satisfies several needs: a need for the safety of a culturally understandable context (Hutnik, 1991), the need for a supportive and cohesive social environment (Sumner, 1906), and the need for a positive social identity resulting from evaluating outgroups more negatively than the ingroup (Tajfel, 1982).

Second, it appeared that respondents belonging to the same ethnic or national group agreed on their preferences of ethnic outgroups. This was found in The Netherlands, France, USA, and the former Soviet Union. Although ingroup members differed in their acceptance or rejection of outgroups, or in the number of discriminations in social distance made among ethnic groups, and in racism, they agreed on the group sequence in the ethnic hierarchy. This sequence is the non-variable aspect of the ethnic hierarchy. Of the 37 Dutch, French, American, and ex-Soviet ethnic groups surveyed, just one group did not show this type of consensus. This shared scheme of inter-ethnic preferences can be considered as a social representation of the ingroup's view on the relative positions of ethnic groups in society. The available shades of inter-ethnic discrimination contained in the representation appeared to be tuned to fit in with the type of contact and outgroup representatives. However, respondents with extreme, biological racist views differed in their ethnic hierarchy from other respondents and incorrectly assumed that their social environment shared their ethnic preferences. This suggests that the ethnic hierarchy is not a social representation which is actively communicated and that the implicit understanding on which it may be based may lead to 'false' consensus as well. This aspect of the ethnic hierarchy deserves further research.

Third, the structure of the preference scheme was hierarchical. It formed a cumulative Guttman-type scale in almost all cases. This confirms the global indications of an ethnic hierarchy from prior social distance and stereotype research (Berry and Kalin, 1979; Duckitt, 1992) and specifies the nature of the phenomenon. Not only ethnic majorities agreed on a perceived ethnic hierarchy, but also minority groups. The fact that as a rule the socially dominant majority was the most preferred outgroup, and that contact with low-placed groups was perceived as a threat to the status of the ingroup, confirms that the shared scheme of ethnic preferences reflects a perceived status hierarchy of ethnic groups. Dominant ethnic groups seem to justify their unequal social position by negative stereotypes about subordinate ethnic groups, while subordinate groups seem to differentiate themselves primarily from similar groups in order to maintain a positive social identity. The relation between negative stereotypes and the place assigned to outgroups in the ethnic hierarchy by majority groups suggests that stereotypes offer the arguments for at least the first and maybe also the second process.

A fourth finding was that there was intergroup consensus on the ethnic hierarchy in The Netherlands and in three regions of the former Soviet Union. Even in the remaining three regions of the former Soviet Union there was some agreement among ethnic groups on the sequence of the ethnic hierarchy, in spite of low scalogram values. The lack of consensus in two of the three regions of the former Soviet Union was mainly dissensus between Islamic and non-Islamic groups. A high degree of consensus indicates that the ethnic rank system is accepted and acknowledged by all ethnic groups. This may be the result of the acceptance of a common standard of citizenship, or of the acceptance of the values and lifestyle of the dominant group as a criterion to evaluate outgroups (Hagendoorn, 1993).

Fifth, there were two patterns in the relation between the intergroup bias of ethnic groups and their position in the ethnic hierarchy. The first pattern was that the intergroup bias increased as the position of a group in the ethnic hierarchy was lower, which indicates that ingroup favouritism and outgroup rejection are functionally related to maintaining a positive social identity. The second pattern was that high-placed groups showed a larger intergroup bias.

This was only the case among Russians in the two Autonomous Republics in the Russian Federation, which indicates that an increased intergroup bias can be a reaction to an uncertain group position as well, as is predicted by social identity theory.

REFERENCES

Augoustinos, M., Ahrens, C., & Innes, J. (1994). Stereotypes and prejudice: The Australian case. *British Journal of Social Psychology*, **33**, 125–41.
Berry, J., & Kalin, R. (1979). Reciprocity of inter-ethnic attitudes in a multicultural society. *International Journal of Intercultural Relations*, **3**, 99–112.
Bobo, L. (1983). Whites opposition to busing: Symbolic racism or realistic group conflict. *Journal of Personality and Social Psychology*, **45**, 1196–210.
Bogardus, E. (1925). Measuring social distance. *Journal of Applied Sociology*, **9**, 299–308.
Brewer, M., Ho, H., Lee, J., & Miller, N. (1987). Social identity and social distance among Hong Kong schoolchildren. *Personality and Social Psychology Bulletin*, **13**, 156–65.
Brown, R. (1988). *Group Processes, Dynamics within and between Groups.* Oxford: Basil Blackwell.
Brown, R., & Abrams, D. (1986). The effects of intergroup similarity and goal interdependence on intergroup attitudes and task performance. *Journal of Experimental Social Psychology*, **22**, 78–92.
Devine, P. (1989). Stereotypes and prejudice: their automatic and controlled components. *Journal of Personality and Social Psychology*, **56**, 5–18.
De Vries, E. (1994). *Een ethnische hierarchie in Frankrijk* [An ethnic hierarchy in France]. Unpublished doctoral thesis, Utrecht University, Department of General Social Sciences.
Dion, K. (1979). Intergroup conflict and intragroup cohesiveness. In W. Austin & S. Worchel (Eds), *The Social Psychology of Intergroup Relations* (pp. 211–25). Monterey, CA: Brooks/Cole.
Doise, W. (1978). *Groups and Individuals: Explanations in social psychology.* Cambridge: Cambridge University Press.
Drogendijk, R. (1994). *Ethnic hierarchies and inter-ethnic tension in post-communist Europe.* Unpublished doctoral thesis, Utrecht University, Department of General Social Sciences.
Duckitt, J. (1992). *The Social Psychology of Prejudice.* New York: Praeger.
Durkheim, E. (1915/1976). *The Elementary Forms of the Religious Life.* London: Allen.
Gitelman, Z. (1991). Ethnic identity and ethnic relations among the Jews of the non-European USSR. *Ethnic and Racial Studies*, **14**, 24–54.
Götz, R., & Halbach, U. (1994). *Politisches Lexikon Russland.* Munich: Beck.
Hagendoorn, L. (1993). Ethnic categorization and outgroup exclusion: the role of cultural values and social stereotypes in the construction of ethnic hierarchies. *Ethnic and Racial Studies*, **16**, 26–51.
Hagendoorn, L., & Hraba, J. (1987). Social distance toward Holland's minorities: Discrimination against and among ethnic outgroups. *Ethnic and Racial Studies*, **10**, 120–33.

Hagendoorn, L., & Hraba, J. (1989). Foreign, different, deviant, seclusive and working class: Anchors to an ethnic hierarchy in The Netherlands. *Ethnic and Racial Studies*, **12**, 441–68.

Hagendoorn, L., Drogendijk, R., Tumanov, S., & Hraba, J. (1995). *Perceived ethnic hierarchies in the former Soviet Union.* Unpublished manuscript, Utrecht University, Department of General Social Sciences.

Hewstone, M., Islam, M., & Judd, C. (1993). Models of crossed categorization and intergroup relations. *Journal of Personality and Social Psychology*, **64**, 779–93.

Hinkle, S., & Brown, R. (1990). Intergroup comparisons and social identity: Some links and lacunea. In D. Abrams and M. Hogg (Eds), *Social Identity Theory: Constructive and critical advances* (pp. 48–70). Hemel Hempstead: Harvester-Wheatsheaf.

Hinkle, S., Brown, R., & Ely, P. (1990). Individualism/collectivism, group-ideology and intergroup processes. Paper presented at British Psychological Society Annual Conference, London.

Hraba, J., Hagendoorn, L., & Hagendoorn, R. (1989). The ethnic hierarchy in The Netherlands: social distance and social representation. *British Journal of Social Psychology*, **28**, 57–69

Hraba, J., & Mok, W. (1991). *Ethnic hierarchies as social representations.* Unpublished paper, Iowa State University, Department of Sociology.

Hutnik, N. (1991). *Ethnic Minority Identity.* Oxford: Clarendon Press.

Jaspars, J., & Fraser, C. (1984). Attitudes and social representations. In R. Farr & S. Moscovici (Eds), *Social Representations* (pp. 137–66). Cambridge: Cambridge University Press.

Karklins, R. (1986). *Ethnic Relations in the USSR: the perspective from below.* Boston, MA: Unwin Hyman.

Kazlas, J. (1977). Social distance among ethnic groups. In E. Allworth (Ed.), *Nationality Group Survival in Multi-Ethnic States* (pp. 228–55). New York: Praeger.

Kelly, C. (1993). Group identification, intergroup perceptions and collective action. In W. Stroebe & M. Hewstone (Eds), *European Review of Social Psychology* (pp. 59–83). Chichester: John Wiley.

Kleinpenning, G. (1993), *Structure and content of racist beliefs: An empirical study of ethnic attitudes, stereotypes and the ethnic hierarchy.* Dissertation, Utrecht, ISOR.

Kleinpenning, G. (1995). The ethnic hierarchy as a social representation. *European Journal of Social Psychology* (forthcoming).

Kleinpenning, G., Hagendoorn, L. (1993). Forms of racism and the cumulative dimension of ethnic attitudes. *Social Psychology Quarterly*, **56**, 21–36.

LeVine, R., & Campbell, D. (1972). *Ethnocentrism.* New York: John Wiley.

Locke, V., MacLeod, C., & Walker, I. (1994). Automatic and controlled activation of stereotypes: Individual differences associated with prejudice. *British Journal of Social Psychology*, **33**, 29–45.

Marcus-Newhall, A., Miller, N., Holtz, R., & Brewer, M. (1993). Cross-cutting category membership with role assignment: A means of reducing intergroup bias. *British Journal of Social Psychology*, **32**, 125–46.

McAuley, A. (1991). *Soviet Federalism.* Leicester: Leicester University Press.

Moscovici, S. (1984). The phenomenon of social representations. In R. Farr and S. Moscovici (Eds), *Social Representations* (pp. 3–69). Cambridge, England: Cambridge University Press.

Moscovici, S. (1988). Notes towards a description of social representations. *European Journal of Social Psychology*, **18**, 211–50.

228   LOUK HAGENDOORN

Mullen, B., Brown, R., & Smith, C. (1992). Ingroup bias as a function of salience, relevance, and status: An integration. *European Journal of Social Psychology*, **22**, 103–22.

Oakes, P. (1987). The salience of social categories. In Turner, J. C. (Ed.), *Rediscovering the Social Group: A self-categorization theory* (pp. 117–41). Oxford: Basil Blackwell.

Owen, C., Eisner, H., & McFaul, T. (1981). A half-century of social distance research: National replication of the Bogardus studies. *Sociology and Social Research*, **66**, 80–98.

Pettigrew, Th. (1960). Social distance attitudes of South African students. *Social Forces*, **38**, 246–53.

Rasch, G. (1966). An item analysis that takes individual differences into account. *British Journal of Mathematical and Statistical Psychology*, **19**, 49–57.

Sachdev, I., & Bourhis, R. (1987). Status differentials and intergroup behaviour. *European Journal of Social Psychology*, **17**, 277–93.

Sijtsma, K., Debets, P., & Molenaar, I. (1990). Mokken scale analysis for polychotomous items: Theory, a computer program and an empirical application. *Quality and Quantity*, **24**, 173–88.

Sumner, G. (1906). *Folkways*. New York: Ginn.

Tajfel, H. (1959). Quantitative judgement in social perception. *British Journal of Psychology*, **50**, 16–29.

Tajfel, H. (1970). Experiments in intergroup discrimination. *Scientific American*, **223**, 96–102.

Tajfel, H. (1981a). Social categorization, social identity and social comparison. In Tajfel, H. (Ed.), *Human Groups and Social Categories* (pp. 254–67). Cambridge: Cambridge University Press.

Tajfel, H. (1981b). Social stereotypes and social groups. In J. Turner & H. Giles (Eds), *Intergroup Behaviour* (pp. 144–67). Oxford: Basil Blackwell.

Tajfel, H. (1982). *Social Identity and Intergroup Relations*. Cambridge: Cambridge University Press.

Vanbeselaere, N. (1987). The effects of dichotomous and crossed social categorizations upon intergroup discrimination. *European Journal of Social Psychology*, **17**, 143–56.

Van Knippenberg, A. (1989). Strategies of identity management. In J. Van Oudenhoven & T. Willemsen (Eds), *Ethnic Minorities* (pp. 59–76). Amsterdam: Swets & Zeitlinger.

Van Knippenberg, A., Van Twuyver, M., & Pepels, J. (1994). Factors affecting social categorization processes in memory. *British Journal of Social Psychology*, **33**, 419–31.

Verkuyten, M., Hagendoorn, L., & Masson, C. (1994). *The ethnic hierarchy among majority and minority youth in The Netherlands*. Unpublished paper, Utrecht University, Department of General Social Sciences.

Wilder, D., & Shapiro, P. (1984). The role of outgroup cues in determining social identity. *Journal of Personality and Social Psychology*, **47**, 342–8.

Author Index

Subject Index

accessible constructs, judgments based on, 38
accountability, as motivation, 39
accuracy motivation
  and directional/closure-seeking motivation, 17
  heightened by sad affect, 49
  impact on information processing, 49
accuracy of recall *see* recall, accuracy of
achievement, relation to plans and goals, 21
actor/observer differences
  and motivational determinants hypothesis, 17
  in prediction, 13–16, 22–7
additivity hypothesis, 42–3
affective evaluations of behaviour, 85
  and behavioural beliefs, 88–90
  extension of TPB, 92
affective states, co-occurrence of heuristic and systematic processing, 44–9
aggression, associated with deindividuation, 166
anchoring procedure, and optimistic/pessimistic predictions, 18–20
animal experimentation, minority influence study, 52
anonymity
  accountability cue, 167
  and deindividuation, 166
  enhancing/attenuating social identity, 178

and increased transgression, 170
manipulation of, in study of self-categorisation, 178
as quality of individual, 169
anticipated regret
  included in personal norms, 92
  related to moral norms, 86, 87
  underestimation of affective factors in determining behaviour/intentions, 88
aspiration level, 99–100
asymmetry, loss-gain, 101–2
atavism, equated with deindividuation, 164
attenuation, 43–4, 46
attitude accessibility
  determinant of strength of attitude–behaviour relationship, 81
  reason for low correlation between direct and belief-based measures, 82
attitude to behaviour
  determinants, 70, 92
  importance of attitude accessibility, 81
  measurement of, 76
    affective and cognitive measures, 89
    in driving violations, 73
  and theory of planned behaviour, 70
attribution perspective, 56
attribution process, 35
attribution theory, 62
attributional mechanisms, 22

Indexes compiled by A.C. Purton

European Review of Social Psychology

Contents of Previous Volumes